GLOBALIZATION AND SPORT

Playing the World

Toby Miller, Geoffrey Lawrence,
Jim McKay, and David Rowe

SAGE Publications
London • Thousand Oaks • New Delhi

SAGE Publications Ltd
6 Bonhill Street
London EC2A 4PU

SAGE Publications Inc
2455 Teller Road
Thousand Oaks, California 91320

SAGE Publications India Pvt Ltd
32, M-Block Market
Greater Kailash - I
New Delhi 110 048

British Library Cataloguing in Publication data

A catalogue record for this book
is available from the British Library

ISBN 0-7619-5968-8
    0-7619-5969-6 (pb)

Library of Congress catalog record available

Typeset by Siva Math Setters, Chennai, India
Printed in Great Britain by Athenaeum Press, Gateshead

Contents

Acknowledgements

Many thanks to those who have been involved along the way: Ian Antcliff, Rebecca Barden, Tony Bennett, Sarah Berry, David Birch, Hugh Campbell, C.L. Cole, David Denham, Jane Evans, Faye Ginsburg, Richard Giulianotti, Steve Hardy, Natalie Hirniak, Mariana Johnson, Suzanne Laberge, Dimity Lawrence, Marie Leger, Monica Marcickiewicz, Paul Martin, Randy Martin, John Nauright, Chris Rojek, Phil Smith, Deborah Stevenson, Alan Tomlinson, Dave Whitson, Federico Windhausen, and the University of Newcastle's Outside Study Programme.

Introduction – Why This Book?

> What is it that compels these men to attack? Why are men so disturbed by this spectacle? Why do they get involved so entirely? Why this needless fighting? What is sport? (Roland Barthes, 1997: 75)

Sport is probably the most universal aspect of popular culture. It crosses languages and countries to captivate spectators and participants, as both a professional business and a pastime. Unlike other aspects of audiovisual entertainment, we play sport as much as we watch it. And when we watch it, passions are invoked that go beyond most other experiences. Sporting culture is at once intensely local (we support 'our' team and we go to the nearby gym) and very distanced (we watch that local side on a TV network owned by a foreign company, or do a workout because our employer expects its labour force to appear fit). Sport has long been a crucial component of the government of everyday life, whether through the formalization of sporting holidays by the state across Europe in the eighteenth and nineteenth centuries, the nineteenth- and early twentieth-century rational-recreation movements in public education, or the uptake of physical education by state-socialist and capitalist countries throughout the latter part of the twentieth century and today.

This book assumes that sport is so central to our contemporary moment's blend of transnational cultural industrialization and textualization that it does more than reflect the global – sport is big enough in its effects to modify our very use of the term, 'globalization'. As sports professionalize and internationalize, their commodification and bureaucratization become fundamental if we are to understand profound changes in national culture. In keeping with this set of issues, the book applies concepts from critical political economy, sociology, and media and cultural studies to investigate globalization, addressing the activities of national and transnational organizations, the tensions emerging between the bureaucratic and the commercial, and how gender, class, sexual practice, race, and age affect both performance and spectatorship.

Throughout, we are implicitly and explicitly posing one question: where is the cultural nation, the nation we experience through feelings, policies, and practices? Is it an empirical group of people arrayed before the TV or radio, as when Australia 'stood still' to watch the America's Cup in 1983, the English abroad listened to the 1966 World Cup Final, 60% of Dutch citizens came out on to the street to celebrate a 1988 defeat of Germany in the European Cup of soccer (the biggest public gathering since the Liberation), Canadians erupted 'spontaneously' after their hockey team's dramatic defeat of the Soviet Union in 1972, the US rejoiced as *its* hockey team did the same in 1980, or Russians watched the USSR beat the Americans and go on to claim basketball gold at the 1972 Olympics, ending a 63-game winning streak for the US team?

Binding together the people of a country through culture is usually discussed via social and political theory and public policy. But popular culture – notably televised sport – is a crucial site where populations are targeted by different forms of governmental and commercial knowledge/power. Try to imagine a major international sporting event, such as the Olympic Games or World Cup, with no comprehensive media coverage, no national flags flying, no playing of national anthems, no politicians involved in the ceremonies, no military displays, no tables comparing national standings, and athletes competing in whatever clothing they desired instead of national uniforms.

Consider again the America's Cup. We might juxtapose two quotations here that illustrate the point. The first comes from Bruno Trouble, owner of a French marketing and advertising agency: 'With Australia's success in '83 many thought the America's Cup was going to die; it was as if the America's Cup was a virgin, untouched for 132 years – then when the Aussies took her, well she sort of lost her virginity, so they thought, "this girl is of no more interest".' Here we can see an intensely patriarchal metaphorization at work that twins the sexist delineation of boat as female with nation as female: their protection and control became a matter of national and international pride among men. When the 1992 Cup race was over, Bill Koch, skipper of the winner, called it 'a triumph for America, for American technology, for American teamwork'. In this instance, gender is over-determined by a scientific rationality and human collaboration that testify to the implied power of men to stand for the nation.

Women certainly have an iconic role in national fitness: like men, they are targets of state-directed campaigns designed to improve health, gender reproduction, and labour productivity across the nation. And their achievements as individual athletes may become sources of great media significance (say, the success of Chris Evert). But at the level of team sports, where the source of pride is collectivized, women are generally denied the status of nation-bearers that the media and the state conventionally accord to men (contrast coverage and fanfare for the Davis Cup versus the Wightman Cup in tennis, or the fact that the 'World Cup of Soccer' is unmarked by gender – it is the province of men on national duty – whereas the 'Women's World Cup of Soccer' is gendered and hence not universal). Heroines may enunciate desirable qualities of femininity, but that significatory power seldom extends into the domain of the team, the group of like-minded and like-bodied representatives of national pride. Women can represent the nation in static iconographic forms, but as bodies in motion they will not do.

Between 1948 and 1996, women won 40% of Australia's gold medals at the Olympic Games despite comprising just 24% of Australia's representatives. Similarly, between 1911 and 1990 women won 35% of Australia's gold medals at the Commonwealth Games in a period when they were allowed to participate in only 31% of the sports available and constituted 27% of all Australian athletes. Yet despite this astonishing performance, women's sport generally receives about 2% of Australian media sports coverage, and much of it is stereotypical, trivializing, and sexually objectifying. Two vivid reminders of the tenuous links among femininity, sport, and nationhood in Australia occurred in 1999. First, it was announced on the official Parliament House noticeboard that Prime Minister

John Howard and his wife would attend a reception in honour of Australia's world champion women's field hockey team, the Hockeyroos, who were identified as the Australian women's *cricket* team. Second, after the Australian netball team won its third consecutive world championship, Howard congratulated the team's captain for her squad's effort, but mistakenly referred to her charges as the women's *hockey* team. This error was portrayed as a minor gaffe in the media. However, it is inconceivable that a Prime Minister would be so easily forgiven for mistaking the national men's cricket and rugby union teams, especially when he has also claimed that the captaincy of Australian cricket is 'the absolute pinnacle of sporting achievement, and really the pinnacle of human achievement almost, in Australia'. Male soccer in Brazil, cricket in the West Indies, and rugby union in Wales and New Zealand/Aotearoa are examples of sports that are often said by the media to embody the character of a nation or region. Richard Gruneau and David Whitson (1993) remark that ice hockey has often been portrayed as having an 'enduring link to the idea of "Canadianness"'. But as they demonstrate, the idea of hockey representing a unified Canadian identity is mythical, in that it dissembles social divisions and US corporate control.

Myths are not total delusions or utter falsehoods, but partial truths that accentuate some versions of reality and marginalize or omit others. They embody fundamental cultural values and character-types and appeal to deep-seated emotions. Myths depoliticize social relations by ignoring the vested interests surrounding those stories that become ascendant in a given culture. And critically, myths disavow or deny their own conditions of existence: they are forms of speech that derive from specific sites and power relations, but are passed off as natural and eternal verities (Barthes, 1973).

National mythmaking through sport is common as a means of generating new habits amongst the citizenry. Myths encourage active participation at the physical as well as the ideological level. Many accounts of sport situate it as a central tenet of national culture, in either a welcoming or a critical way. This reifies the term 'sport,' denying the social fissures – of gender, class, race, ethnicity, age, sexuality, media coverage, public participation, and region – that it engages. Increasingly, though, these tensions find expression, and in ways that are not restricted to intra-national sites. During the 1994 (men's) World Cup, for example, Iranian TV viewers were reportedly given a special form of montage: whenever US cameras cut from the players in the scorching heat to shots of the crowd, programmers in Iran edited in footage of people in winter garb from other matches, to hide the decadence of Western women's attire from their fragile audience. Meanwhile, US marketers continued to advertise the sport as more truly international than the World Series, the Super Bowl, and so on, which look so intramurally North American by contrast.

And there are indications across the history of nation, sport, and media that powerful political issues can be put on the international public agenda. For example, Leni Riefenstahl's film of the 1936 Berlin Olympics, *Olympia*, became a major source of and site for public debate over the rise of Nazism. The entry of the Soviet Union into the Olympics in 1952 produced a medal-table rivalry along Cold War lines that was constantly nourished and analysed by the media. The salutes by Tommie Smith and John Carlos after the 200-metre sprint in the 1968 Mexico Games captured the world spotlight for African-American politics. Minute-by-minute coverage of the 1972 Olympic deaths in Munich, and subsequent boycotts of sporting competitions by African nations, the US, and the USSR, emphasized the deeply conflictual intersection of domestic and international politics. Much of that history is tragic. But again, it opens up a series of major ideological differences to the international public gaze, frequently via transnational protocols that go beyond the chauvinism of individual interests through the public–private straddling of international sports law. Less spectacularly, attempts to maintain and develop the British Commonwealth now centre on international sporting exchange, via the Working Party on Strengthening Commonwealth Sport. It has been active since 1989 in reforming the Commonwealth Games to increase representation of women and do more for underprivileged young people.

At the same time, the move towards a global sports complex is as much about commodification and alienation as it is to do with a utopian internationalism. We discern five simultaneous, uneven, interconnected processes which characterize the present moment in sport: Globalization, Governmentalization, Americanization, Televisualization, and Commodification (GGATaC). They are in turn governed by a New International Division of Cultural Labour (NICL). Hence the paradox animating this project, that the processes nominated by GGATaC operate in both complementary and contradictory ways. It is not appropriate to view globalization as always already a homogenizing force: we provide ample evidence throughout the book that it is not. Yet many components of globalization are common across sites, leading to the acceptance of certain governing rules, media norms, and economic tendencies.

We have divided this volume into four key sectors. Chapter 1 introduces theories of globalization as they affect sport, examining GGATaC through histories of trade, the professionalization of sports, the ownership of teams, the increased export of American codes, and commodity tie-ins. This is both an empirical and a theoretical/ exegetical chapter on the literature about economic globalization and its cultural significance, with a consideration of discourses of modernization, cultural imperialism, and the global market for labour and audiences/consumers. We look at the spread of sport across the world as it has followed governmental and commercial empires, matching an historical overview with consideration of how contemporary developments shape national identity, and what is happening with the NICL.

Chapter 2 brings the analysis down to the somatic level where sport begins and ends, at least mythically – the body and its part in the NICL. This chapter analyses the body images of élite athletes and their exemplary relationship to national, gender, and racial norms. It involves examining bodies as trained and commodified players and spectators, honed by the human sciences, the media, capital, and government to perform and to be interpreted. The focus is on the high level of professional sport, via case studies of soccer and hockey and their deterritorialization through the NICL.

Chapter 3 focuses on the work of television in altering sport. The media, especially television, are a key arena for the diversification and standardization of audience experience. They put sport at the centre of global culture and the neoliberal project of deregulation. We address the end of organic, locally driven spectator sport, as teams professionalize and the electronic media operate in an increasingly transnational mode. Particular reference is made to advertising, commodification, and the binding and unbinding of time and space across and beyond the nation-state, as we question the effect that these carriers of image and meaning have on local, regional, and national cultures by operating in a transnational mode.

Chapter 4 returns to where we began – the fundamental problematic of governance. In a globalizing cultural economy, who rules, and who benefits? How is the state involved in sport through nationalistic rhetoric and public-health policy, which seek to position the public as loyal and fit citizens ready to function in the NICL's world economy? Government is understood here as a series of internal and external forces of control and negotiation that both police a national populace and deal with international commerce and culture. We assess the significance of global sport for national identity and citizenship by looking at various levels of government: international organizations, like the International Olympic Committee (IOC) and the Fédération Internationale de Football Associations (FIFA), and national public institutions that assist élite sport and run public-fitness campaigns.

At this early point we offer a disclaimer – you have an argument before you, a book of tendency. It is the product of committed scholarship that uses a methodological blend of Marxist, feminist, queer, and postcolonial work. We reject what Pierre Bourdieu refers to as the '*escapism of Wertfreiheit* (value-free-ness)', of merely 'relaying the discourse which, in sport as elsewhere, the object produces about itself' (1999: 15). We stand not as fans or observers of globalization, but as critics. For while globalization may have begun its life as a universalist utopia of world governance and peace, it has quickly mutated into a battleground for the US, Japan, and Western Europe over state and business domination. The point of analysing such developments is both to understand *and* to change them, to remodel GGATaC and the NICL through democratic means. In the spirit of social justice, our abiding concern throughout will be to ask *cui bono* (who wins)?

1

The 'G-Word' Meets the 'S-Word'

NEW YORK & ATLANTA, June 9 – The National Basketball Association [NBA] and The Coca-Cola Company today announced the next four-year chapter in their unprecedented '100-year global marketing partnership'. This partnership reflects the expected limitless length of the relationship between the two organizations and their powerful brands worldwide. The arrangement includes increased global advertising and extensive promotional and grassroots activities for Sprite, as well as several new initiatives to encourage international growth and brand awareness. ('NBA', 1999)

Sprite showed the biggest growth of any soft drink in the world in the last five years of the 1990s, and the NBA led US sports franchises. Their interpenetrated strategies for sales, or 'joint brand-building', saw over 100 NBA–Sprite promotions in 47 countries during that period. Coke's CEO proudly announced that 'the two brands have already become almost synonymous – both hip and cool' (quoted in 'NBA', 1999). The sporting spectacularization of a carbonated sugary drink, and the liquid branding of a pick-up asphalt sport, mark an extraordinary moment in cross-validation of worlds that once were quite separate. We address such changes in this chapter, following an engagement with one foundational question: what is globalization?

Montréal hosted the 14th quadrennial World Congress of Sociology in the late Northern summer of 1998. The conference marked the end of postmodernity – in a sense. The postmodern is often taken to include: an aesthetic style, in architecture or novels for example, that tropes or quotes other forms in a *mélange* of cultural features; an historical template, designating an economic turn by industrialized states towards internationalism and away from manufacturing in favour of trade in services; a philosophical discourse that deconstructs existing forms of knowledge by using their own precepts to undermine them; a specific form of identity politics, transcending constitutional and class bases for defining political agency; the decline of the major forms of social reasoning of the past century (liberalism, Marxism, psychoanalysis, and Christianity); and cultural theories derived from and informing the above.

This trope, ever present four years earlier at the 13th Congress, was gone by 1998, erased (or at least rendered palimpsestic) by globalization: 'and the postmodern/the postmodern and' saw their status as suffix and prefix written all over. So polysemous was globalization that it included sameness, difference, unity, and disunity – in short, globalization, like postmodernity before it, had come to stand for nothing less than *life itself*. As such, it risked being of dubious analytic utility. Still, globalization had arisen from 1960s origins in French and US discussions of the future to a position of great prominence. How?

What the *Financial Times* calls 'the G-word' (1997) is not the exclusive property of sociologists, of course. The concept has great currency in the logics of businesses, unions, and governments – *Forbes* magazine launched *Forbes Global* in 1998 via a full-page social-realist-style advertisement, complete with red flags (which included currency signs), Castro- and Mao-garbed workers, and the slogan 'Capitalists of the World Unite!' The avowed intent was to acknowledge and sell 'the final victory of capitalism' as embodied in the new 'zine. The 'G-word' is also expressed in the international commodity plans of the sports industry. Just a month after the Montréal Congress, Washington, DC hosted a 'Travel, Events, and Management in Sports' conference, which agreed that globalization was the keyword for that business sector ('Sports is Global', 1998).

Capital certainly makes the connection, in both textual and commercial terms. For example, from the late 1980s, massive resources were dedicated to staging the 1994 Winter Olympics in Lillehammer on the basis that they would place Norwegian culture and commerce at a 'Ski-Jump Take-Off Point' for global renown and rewards. Construction of the downhill *piste* was represented as a leap into modernity, as the nation was readied for total commodification through tourism. Exchange value came to be *the* manifestation of use value (Klausen, 1999a: 1–2; Berkaak, 1999a: 164–67; Saint-Germain and Harvey, 1998). Similarly, one of the key priorities of the Sydney 2000 Olympics was tourism. The State Minister for Tourism repeatedly stressed: 'While we were delivering a near-perfect Games my overriding priority was to gain long-term tourism benefits' (Tourism New South Wales, 2000). The federal Minister for Financial Services and Regulation boasted that there were no 'beggars' in Sydney which made it a desirable tax haven (Phillips, 2000). Businesses that want to be seen as 'homeless' for the purposes of commercialism, of course, push a different, deterritorialized, message: Reebok advertises itself as a 'planet' with 'no boundaries,' and Delta Air promoted its international service during the 1996 Olympics with images of Nigel Havers (who starred in *Chariots of Fire* [Hugh Hudson, 1981] as an aristocratic runner) making his merry way from airport to airport as the fortnight progressed, symbolizing the cosmopolitan sports consumer. The year 1999 saw the announcement of three events that cut across ideological and economic boundaries. They emphasize the point. A fourth-division German soccer team in Bonn bought the entire Cuban national squad, with the approval of the government in Havana. And China, where horse racing had been banned since the Revolution fifty years earlier, announced that Australians would build a US$256 million racecourse complex and provide officials, veterinarians, and managers for what was described locally as 'horse racing intelligence competition', a semantic ruse to get around the law. Finally, a major American trade press published a best-seller entitled *Michael Jordan and the New Global Capitalism* ('German Team Takes on a Cuban Flavor', 1999; 'Australians Plan Track in China', 1999; LaFeber, 1999).

When Jordan announced his second retirement from basketball that year, a Chinese newspaper reported the news with the headline 'Flying Man Michael Jordan Coming Back to Earth', and children of the People's Republic of China (PRC) rated him alongside Zhou Enlai as one of the two most important figures of the century – hardly surprising, given that for some years children in parts of the world with neither running water nor electricity could be found wearing number 23 on their backs. For over a decade, Japanese schoolchildren had rated a pair of Air Jordan sneakers and Coca-Cola as their most desirable commodities (Berkow, 1999; LaFeber, 1999: 27, 66). Jordan was soon in business with recently retired football and hockey stars John Elway and Wayne Gretzky (and CBS) to sell sporting goods on line via mvp.com, a challenge to the imposingly named Global Sports, Inc. (Anders, 1999; 'Global Sports', 1999). Meanwhile, plans were under way to transform professional golf, concentrating tournaments into a World Championship of the top 50 players that would squeeze out thousands of pros and venues in favour of a new élite. This was announced as 'the sport's globalization' (Townsend, 1997). On the business end of things, the millennial craze was for IBM and similar corporations to dispatch young executive-types to three-hour, US$3,500 per person business-golf seminars. The links had displaced the martini lunch as a key site for doing deals (Weinbach, 1999). And the *Wall Street Journal* advertised a Master's in Business Administration with a shot of people playing soccer and a written offer of 'success in any global business environment' (Fordham University, 1999). If the 'G-word' has a signified, it includes the 'S-word': sport. What does it mean?

Accounts of globalization veer between three tendencies: celebration or lamentation in the face of the supposed universal triumph of the market and decline of the state; scepticism about the degree of change and the reality of a non-state system; and caution that the fallout from transformations in the relation of private and public is not yet clear. Globalization is a knowledge effect with definite impacts on intellectual, economic, social, and governmental practice. But the notion that it represents a major epistemological break – an accurate *description* of change, rather than its *symptom* – is problematic.

In this chapter, we track the relationship of sport to globalization, arguing via GGATaC and the NICL *against* a singular phenomenon of globalization as the truly worldwide operation of multinational capital, and claiming that the sport experience must be a weighty one in wider deliberations on globalization, because it intricates nationalism, public policy, the media, and contemporary cultural industrialization. Just as sport manages to be a global phenomenon when it stands for the nation, so the nation, as embodied in sovereign politics, continues to be the critical unit of international commerce. And just as most of the money in so-called 'global' sport circulates between Western Europe, Japan, and the United States, so they are the real centres of international capital as sites of both investment and disinvestment. Of course, these processes were not birthed by gaggles of sociologists or *Financial Times* employees suddenly pronouncing on them – they have a past in the binding and unbinding of space and time through the NICL's circulation of capital and labour.

Global Economies

The notion that space and time are routinely compressed under globalization draws on two key events: the Treaty of Tordesillas in 1494 and the Washington Conference of 1884. The first of these acknowledged the emergence of empire, as the Pope mediated rivalries between Portugal and Spain through a bifurcation of the world – the first recorded conceptualization of the globe as a site of conquest and exploitation. The second event, taking place the same year as the imperial division of Africa at the Conference of Berlin, standardized Greenwich as the axis of world time and cartography. This development effectively marked the globe as a site of interconnected government and commerce (Schaeffer, 1997: 2, 7, 10–11). The phenomenology of sporting experience is very much about this notion of dominion over space and time, whether at the human or the cybernetic level (Barthes, 1997: 76) – and of course spectator sport, as an international phenomenon, relies on spanning the dual coordinates of work and leisure.

Capitalism's uneven and unequal development paralleled the trends of Tordesillas and Washington, as mercantilist accumulation and imperialism between 1500 and 1800 were followed by the classical era of capital and its Industrial Revolution, founded on large amounts of land and key natural resources for manufacturing, such as copper, iron, and coal. A period of Northern industrial development and agrarian change was partnered by European emigration to the Americas to deal with population overflow, while colonial possessions offered raw materials (Amin, 1997: 1, x; Reich, 1999). The key shift occurred between 1870 and 1914 (not surprisingly, Bahá'u'lláh, the founder of the Bahá'i faith, coined the phrase 'New World Order' in 1873: quoted in Calkins and Vézina, 1996: 311). During this period, global output and exchange increased by upwards of 3% annually – an unprecedented figure (Hirst, 1997: 411).

In response to capital relocation, socialists, syndicalists, and anarchists formed large international associations of working people (Herod, 1997: 167). Up to the Second World War, trade focused on national capitals, controlled by nation-states. The period from 1945 to 1973 represented an 'interregnum between the age of competing imperial powers and the coming of the global economy' (Teeple, 1995: 57), while the international régime following the Second World War was based on US hegemony and the expansionary needs of its corporations. With the growth of other economies came a growing interdependence of nations, and of companies within nations. After 1950, world trade was dominated by the triad of Europe, Japan, and the US, 'each with their immense hinterland of satellite states' (Jameson, 1996: 2). Between 1950 and 1973, total trade grew by almost 10% annually, and output by more than 5%, most of it between the triad (Hirst, 1997: 411). Whereas modern manufacturing techniques were restricted in the nineteenth century to Europe and the north-eastern US, they proliferated across the world, as applied intellect and science became easy to deterritorialize (Hindley, 1999; Reich, 1999). The Cold War constructed a polarized world of two totalizing ideologies, struggling just as empires had done in the previous century. This totality, which obscured other differences, encouraged the view that the future would see the triumph of one pole (Bauman, 1998: 58) – hence today's mavens of *laissez-faire* and the supposed demise of the state.

But certain critics argue that the promiscuous nature of capital has been overstated, that the nation-state, far from being a series of 'glorified local authorities' (Hirst, 1997: 409) is in fact crucial to the regulation of multinational corporations (MNCs), with regional blocs strengthening, rather than weakening, the ability of the state to govern. Most people continue to look to it for both economic sanction and return (Smith, 1996: 580). The argument here is that the US, Western Europe, and Japan are the only key sites of MNC activity, housing more than two-thirds of MNC sales and assets. Direct foreign investment elsewhere is distinctly limited (Hirst, 1997: 418; Kozul-Wright and Rowthorn, 1998). Perhaps one in 20 MNCs actually invests globally (Gibson-Graham, 1996–97: 7–8). Multinationals look around for marginal utility and then retreat to what is known and controllable – so the explosion of foreign investment in the three years from 1994 saw an increase of 40% in MNC money poured into the US, while investment the other way was primarily in Britain, the Netherlands, Canada, France, and Australia ('Trade Barriers', 1997). Public institutions, many of them international but many also domestic, still provide the framework and in fact much of the investment for the world economy (Atkinson, 1997; Gibson-Graham, 1996–97: 8).

Sport

The high point of trade for imperial Europe was also its high point for setting in place the global governance of sport. The inaugural Test Match between English and Australian cricket teams took place in 1877, the new Olympic movement was proclaimed in 1894 and held its first Games two years later, soccer gained its world governing body in 1904, and equivalents were established for cricket (1909), athletics (1912), and tennis (1913) (Horne et al., 1999: 277). Not surprisingly, this codification saw local élites adopt British pastimes and methods of governance to assist in their own social reproduction, with racial, class, and gender divisions replicated in access to sport (for the Brazilian case, see Lopes, 1997: 53). Today, the US–Western Europe–Japan triad's continuing significance is clear in sporting terms, too – they are responsible for well over 90% of the money expended on the right to telecast the 2000 Sydney Olympics (White, 1998). These investments centre on the division of labour. What began as a cultural exchange based on empire has turned into one based on capital.

The urge that animated thousands of sociologists to displace 'pomo' (postmodern) with 'globo' (globalization) in a summery Québec derived from contemporary debates about the direction and penetration of multinational capital and its sign value (Pieterse, 1997). Sport appears to be an obvious instance of this. For example, hockey gear is financed by Canada, designed in Sweden, manufactured in Denmark, Japan, and the US, and distributed across North America and Northern Europe (Donnelly, 1996: 240), while Canada's sporting goods industry has internationalized. Between 1960 and 1992, local manufacturers' market share dropped from 66% to 47%, even as exports grew from 9% of total business to 33%

(Saint-Germain and Harvey, 1998). Of course, somewhat further south, Nike has transformed itself several times in search of global profit (see Chapter 2).

Emergent world-economic sites of the post-war era gained international visibility with the Tokyo Olympics (1964) and the Mexico City Olympics (1968) and men's soccer World Cup (1970). Such events marked and promoted global integration. At the same time, of course, the 1980 and 1984 Olympics were dominated by superpower assertiveness, with Moscow an advertisement for state socialism, and Los Angeles for private enterprise (Whitson and Macintosh, 1996: 279). Following the emphasis on Catalonian cultural and economic resurgence at Barcelona in 1992 and the reassertion of American corporate capitalism at Atlanta 1996, the main 'pitch' for Sydney was that Sydney should be regarded by US and European capital as an ideal regional location for 'jumping on' into south-east Asia. The Peace Corps was once close to being renamed the 'Sports Corps,' and emergent states routinely utilize sport to demonstrate the benefits of nation-building (Monnington, 1993: 128). To many critics, sport's manifest nationalism has masked dependency, with indigenous pastimes displaced by those of the colonizers (Kang, 1988) – the process of competition, ranking, and nationalism inscribes a deep structure of Western culture (Galtung, 1984).

The sporting corollary of the general trend towards MNC economic domination is the preeminence of privately owned teams rather than nationally representative ones. It has been argued from the Left that '[f]or all the horrors of globalism, one more nail is driven into the coffin of cultural nationalism with every step towards a sporting circus' (Blake, 1995: 48). The same expectation is evident on the Right. In 1992, Silvio Berlusconi, owner of the AC Milan football club and later both the Italian Prime Minister and a convicted criminal, announced that 'the concept of the national team will, gradually, become less important. It is the clubs with which the fans associate' (quoted in Maguire, 1994: 460). Given that Nike 'owns' the Italian, Brazilian, and Nigerian national sides (Blount, 1997: 37), his prediction was conservative – the nation *became* a club. From another angle, some analysts suggest that vast city-states will displace nations in the coming century, with urban radials the new trade routes (Kaplan, 1999). This would suit the city–club nexus.

It is certainly the case that economic, political, technological, and cultural changes have forged new relations of TV, sport, and nation. What constitutes a national game or a contest between representatives of local, regional, and national identities is subject to constant reformulation. In 1970s cricket and 1990s rugby league, corporate media takeovers of the very sports themselves produced brief but tumultuous schisms, new discourses of tradition and modernity, and a vigorous contest over the right to claim national representative status. The immediate cause of these dramatic events was a contest over free-to-air TV rights between public and private networks (in the case of cricket) and competing media proprietors (in the instance of league, for which see Chapter 2) (Miller, 1989; Rowe and McKay, 1999). Each time, governments stood about and flailed their arms, as per the Clinton Administration during the 1994 baseball strike over revenue distribution. But this does not mean the state has become obsolete.

With the spread of sport around the world has come an intense codification, both formally and informally, to the point where quite rigid laws now cross borders under the sign of state and intergovernmental agencies that deal with 'political boycotts, nonrecognition of national teams and individuals by host governments, eligibility of athletes, substance abuse, and commercialization and jurisdictional squabbles between competing sports organizations' (Nafziger, 1992: 490).

There is both civil- and state-based global governance at work in sport. For good or ill, neither is fully corporate or nationalistic. For instance, the IOC and FIFA are immensely powerful civil associations of cultural élites from across the world that frequently dictate terms to governments and businesses through a complex relationship of interdependency with nationalism and corporate funding. When he was FIFA's President, João Havelange decreed that the real triad of world power was the IOC, FIFA, and the United States (Giulianotti and Armstrong, 1997: 4). FIFA and the IOC are even granted 'international personality' in legal discourse. Since 1984 the IOC has gone so far as to operate an international Court of Arbitration for Sport (Confederation of Australian Sport) to which many sovereign legal systems and sports federations of the world have deferred, although there has been strong Third World opposition to its undemocratic ways (Nafziger, 1992: 491 n. 9, 506–7, 510; Jarvis and Coleman, 1999: 314; Houlihan, 1994: 86). This is not to deny a strong corporatizing tendency. The US Olympic Committee sued the Gay Games over ownership of the Olympic name in the Supreme Court in 1987 and placed the home of founder Tom Waddell, a decathlete from the 1968 Mexico Olympics, under lien, even as he was dying. It did not take such actions against the Police, Diaper, or Dog Olympics (Villarosa, 1994: 18; Clark, 1994). From the earliest days, the Olympics were commodified – Kodak has been a sponsor since 1896 and the Tokyo Games of 1964 featured a special Olympic cigarette – but the Los Angeles Olympiad of 1984 saw a careful niche move that offered corporations exclusive naming rights within their industry in return for vast sums (Clarey, 1998; Echikson, 1998).

All this occurred under the guidance of a leading remnant of twentieth-century totalitarianism. On the joyous 1977 day of Fascism's death in Spain, 100,000 Catalans gathered in the Placa St Jaume to call for the removal from office of Juan Antonio Samaranch, a Falangist politician/functionary: 'Samaranch, get out!' was their repeated cry (quoted in Copetas et al., 1999: A1). Two decades on, as President of the IOC, he likes to be addressed as 'Your Excellency', and tells the *New York Times* that 'Franco did good things for my country' (quoted in Cohen and Longman, 1999: 26). Samaranch even announced in 1998: 'We function as a state.' That year, the IOC's 114 members (12 were women) included four African generals (one who served under Idi Amin), three European princes and one princess, assorted businessmen and lawyers, a few former athletes, Boris Yeltsin's old tennis coach, a recruit from the South Korean Central Intelligence Agency, and the disgraced previous head of Italy's fraudulent drug-testing centre. As the IOC aims to take over all international sport, the countervailing pressure of individual federations is strong, but frequently mounted by similarly unrepresentative figures (Clarey, 1998; Echikson, 1998). For all that, this is no picture of a commodified, corporate, or nation-driven organization – it operates a multimillion Olympic Solidarity programme in support of African sports development via coaching clinics, equipment, and scholarships for training

(Longman, 1999a). We shall read more of the IOC later in this chapter. For its part, FIFA entered 2000 stating that annual expenditure on soccer amounted to US$250 billion, providing jobs for 450 million people, while its own assets as an organization included £2.5 billion. FIFA had 204 affiliated nations, leaving the UN some distance behind numerically (Hare, 1999: 124). Later chapters discuss soccer in further detail.

Sport is commonly characterized as the global culture industry *par excellence.* Cultural commentators find evidence of this new phenomenon in international sports media spectacles (such as the Olympic Games and the soccer World Cup), geographically mobile sports (such as tennis and golf), and US-originated advertising, promotion, marketing, and packaging practices (such as celebrity endorsements and the high-pressure sale of sports paraphernalia). While the global diffusion of much sport cannot be denied, arguments to this effect usually present a highly mechanistic and theoretically dubious scenario. It is as if the dust storm of globalization is blowing over every nation, depositing upon each the same brown particles. In the end, none can escape, and each has the same (dirty!) look.

The nomenclature of culture industries calls up a remotely conceived but locally delivered sense of culture. For all the loss of organic unity when religion was replaced by the economy as a dominant organizing principle in modern capitalist society, this culture is far from chaotic. Rather, it is frequently logical and coherent. The idea that culture industries 'impress ... the same stamp on everything' derives from the work of Theodor Adorno and Max Horkheimer (1977). Their theory of production-line culture says that because demand is dispersed and supply centred, management must operate via an administrative logic. This is socially acceptable because it is said to reflect the already established and revealed preferences of consumers, a reaction to their tastes and desires. But for Adorno and Horkheimer, such an account denies a cycle of power. They see consumers as manipulated through the mobilization of cultural technology by those at the economic apex of production. Culture becomes one more industrial process subordinated to dominant economic forces within society seeking standardization. The one element that might stand against this levelling sameness is 'individual consciousness'. But that consciousness has itself been customized to the requirements of the economy.

Dwight Macdonald equates the culture industries with standardization and dissemination. Once parasitic on high-cultural innovation, by the 1950s they could draw on their own archive as a source of dross material to produce a 'political domination' that was guaranteed by a predigested ordering of audience response that was democratic in its constituency but anti-democratic in its effects (1978: 167–69, 171). For such critics, in place of the 'rigorous training' that enables an appreciation of high culture, the popular is regarded as a 'domain of simple, bodily pleasure' (Rowe, 1995b: 3). As Ross Gibson says, this discourse elevates 'true art' by contrasting the virtues of courage, innovation, and energy with the popular's 'lazy and craven ... "contentment" ... with prefabricated signs and materials' (1992: 201).

Whilst much of this Enlightenment disappointment was shared by conservatives, for some 1960s theorists, such as Edward Shils, mass society represented the apex of modernity. Far from being supremely alienating, it signified an expanded civil society, the first moment of history when central political organs and agendas were receptive to and part of the broader community. The population was now part of the social, rather than excluded from the means of political calculation. Centralized authority lessened, individual rights were promoted, and interpersonal, large-scale human interaction was necessitated by industrialization and aided by communication systems, while advertising broke down barriers between high and low culture (Shils, 1966: 505–6, 511).

Cultural industrialization has clear material costs as well as benefits. Benjamin Barber's account of a world divided 'between global commerce and parochial ethnicity', bereft of 'civic virtues', could be said to find full expression in sport, where intense regional, ethnic, and national rivalries are still powerful, and even utilized as marketing tools, while commodification gathers pace. Far from being part of a civil society that sees multiple checks on centralized economic or governmental power, as per his vision for 'the sovereignty of the democratic state' (1996: 7, 296), contemporary sport amounts, in such a view, to a continuing spiral into ultra-market, ultra-chauvinist, ultra-American forms of life. This association of the culture industries with the US is crucial.

Americanization

We live during what has been described as 'the global triumph of the United States and its way of life' (Hobsbawm, 1998: 1). The *Wall Street Journal* trumpets this loudly: 'the U.S. enters the 21st century in a position of unrivaled dominance that surpasses anything it experienced in the 20th.... America's free-market ideology is now the world's ideology; and the nation's Internet and biotechnology businesses are pioneering the technologies of tomorrow' (Murray, 1999). For all the misery internal to that country, viewed from outside, or from the heights of its commanding bourgeoisie and hopeful small investors, the US has influence of a kind only imagined during the earlier part of the century (Bell and Bell, 1996). Consider a mundane but problematic aspect of sovereignty – that the modern state makes its own stamps, featuring national images. Today, 70 countries, mostly in the Third World, have their stamps produced by the New-York-based Inter-Governmental Philatelic Corporation. The dominant images are recyclable icons from US popular culture (Mingo, 1997).

Adherents of the Americanization thesis, much debated in sports sociology, regard it as a counter to a more polycentric notion of global flow, pointing to the power of such MNCs as Disney, McDonald's, and Coca-Cola to dominate taste formation across the world, in a one-way cultural transfer that exploits sport to vend useless pleasures (Donnelly, 1996: 242; Kang, 1988). For such critics, the notion of customizing US culture to other languages and forms of life, and reciprocal influence, is merely 'fashionable'. For while US popular culture may 'take on the colors of the cultures it swallows up', the mediated/synthesized outcome is imported and processed as a new, unitary phenomenon that blends cosmopolitan urban life to manufacture 'common behaviors' via 'common markets' and standardization. Shopping becomes today's 'common signature' (Barber, 1998: 29–30).

How did this happen, and what does it signify? One plausible way of dividing global sport history is between the British and American empires. The first empire, a profoundly immigrant phenomenon, sought to reside in and govern sites. The British had a 'great triad of consideration: economic necessity, strategic calculation, and civilising zeal'. Sport embodied the latter via the promise of 'egalitarian and apolitical agency' (Stoddart, 1988: 649, 651). This zeal saw the successful spread of association football (soccer) virtually worldwide and the export of cricket to those colonies which Britain controlled through the twentieth century. On the US end, Allen Guttmann (1994) sees American football as a lightning-rod of expansionary development from within. Its essence is modernization: English rugby's 'relatively continuous play' was transformed into a system of downs, with the capacity for routine, often tiny, incremental advance fetishized into value. US football is utterly Tayloristic in its division of labour – think of the umpires with their huge measuring sticks, for all the world the pompous time-and-motion experts of the 1950s – in a structural homology with industrialization and Fordism (Guttmann, 1994: 113–14).

This second empire, a profoundly corporate phenomenon, sought to visit and influence sites – baseball came from the US to Mexico courtesy of railway engineers, to Panama thanks to canal construction workers, to Japan via missionaries, and to Nicaragua through the US consulate (Rosenberg, 1999). Since 1970s deindustrialization at home, the US has been interested in selling services, notably cinema, television, and sport, both domestically and overseas. US TV sports have stagnated in ratings terms (Pursell, 1998: 27), so like nineteenth-century empires before them, they are turning overseas to generate demand. Homegrown MNCs have developed basketball, American football, and baseball as international commercial interests, repatriating profits apart from those designated to seed new players and spectators from the rest of the world.

The National Basketball Association (NBA) has 11 offices outside North America, drawing up to 15% of its merchandising revenue internationally and sponsoring youth leagues in Latin America as sources of labour. NBA teams played games in Mexico thoughout the 1990s, and are now venturing to Israel and Japan (Bloomberg News, 1997; Blount, 1997: 33; 'Global Basketball', 1999). A survey of Western European youth across 44 nations in 1997 found 93% recognition of the Chicago Bulls' logo (Tagliabue, 1997: D4), while Magic Johnson was the most featured person in worldwide TV coverage of the 1992 Olympics (de Moragas Spà et al., 1995: 3). <NBA.com> draws 35% of its hits from outside the US and features programming in Italian, French, and Spanish (Gunther, 1997). This expansion is relatively recent: sales of US sporting goods to the Caribbean and Latin America increased by 61% in the four years from 1991 (745% in Brazil) to US$209 million and overall expenditure on sporting merchandise in these regions went up by between 10% and 50% between 1995 and 1996 (Blount, 1997: 31, 36), while Footlocker has 234 European stores today compared to just one in 1987 (Tagliabue, 1997: D4).

What was the biggest ever crowd for a National Football League (NFL) game? Mexico City's 112,000 for a 1994 fixture (Blount, 1997: 32). Guttmann sees the spread of US football as a case of 'ludic diffusion impelled by American power'.

He cites orchestrated media campaigns in the UK and elsewhere and some displacement of soccer and rugby (1994: 112). In 1982, Britain's Channel 4 premiered 75 TV minutes a week of the NFL. Coverage was dominated by rock music, video inserts, and a general impression of *Américanité*. Attendance at local games grew to several million in just a few years, and the Super Bowl telecast drew six million viewers by 1990. That support was skewed towards the desirable advertising demographic of the young white male (Guttmann, 1994: 115). Financial support for the game came from a bastion of high-Tory conservatism, *The Daily Telegraph*, which produced a football magazine and underwrote broadcast costs. The commodification process then emerged from elsewhere, via Anheuser-Busch, eager to confirm its expansion into the UK as a brewer by endowing a semi-pro league. Teams quickly became associated with multinational corporate sponsors, many from the US. In 1986, the Chicago Bears and Dallas Cowboys played a pre-season Bowl game at Wembley, sponsored by US companies. NFL Productions was now interested in merchandising possibilities (not, of course, directed at the development of the game as an amateur sport) (Guttmann, 1994: 116–17).

American football leagues were formed in all the major Western European nations between 1978 and 1988, with particular strength in Germany, the UK, and Italy. In 1991, the NFL set up franchises in Montréal, London, Barcelona, and Frankfurt via its World League of American Football, but ran into financial difficulties and suspended play in 1992 until Fox bought half of it (Herman and McChesney, 1997: 77). The League continues to lose US$100 million annually and is underwritten by NFL teams, with no profits anticipated before 2002 (Gunther, 1997; Andrews, 1998). Expansionary plans are still under way, however, in Western Europe, to be followed by Latin America (Mexico's NFL Tochito kicked off in 1998) and what the league, in a splendidly nineteenth-century way, insists on referring to as 'the Far East' (Guttmann, 1994: 117) – Japan has professional leagues and has hosted an NFL exhibition fixture, as has Australia, while Japan and Mexico now contest a World Cup of American Football (Sheats, 1998: A2; 'NFL International', 1999). Faced with a stagnant domestic audience – *Monday Night Football* produced its lowest-ever ratings in 1998–99 and 1999–2000 – the League must expand elsewhere (Adalian, 1998). Its strategies are to educate people to play the game, via football leagues established in Japan, Canada, Mexico, and Western Europe, to provide scholarships for promising young players to attend US colleges, to televise games globally, and to seek more and more local sponsors (Buckley, 1999).

Ethnographic studies of the spread of baseball in the Caribbean, specifically the Dominican Republic, suggest a process of Americanization, albeit with strong customizing trends as well (Klein, 1991). The same could be said of baseball in Japan. What began as an object lesson of Americanization in the 1870s has seen the sport altered to local circumstances and the successful migration of stars in each direction (J. Cooper, 1998). Major League Baseball (MLB) has failed to expand into Europe, but increased its overseas TV revenues by 300% in the five years to 1998, and that year held 11 baseball festivals, in Caracas, San Juan, Winnipeg, London, Sydney, Nuremberg, and Monterrey, drawing over 700,000 participants. It also signed licensing agreements to sell merchandise in 109 countries from 1998, and projected a 200% increase in global sales by 2003. Ice hockey expanded into Asia in the late 1990s, with a National Hockey League (NHL) fixture played in Japan in 1997 and immediately successful merchandising (Gunther, 1997; Pursell, 1998; Marcano and Fidder, 1999: 518; 'Market Development', 1999).

Against this claim for a causal link between modernization and US practice, consider the Americanization thesis applied to Australia. Some (mostly working-class) Australians refer to Americans via rhyming slang as 'septic tanks' – Yanks. That hardly suggests naïve endearment or total domination. But when you look at a long history of mimesis in music, fashion, food, and media trends, it becomes an ambivalent flattery. Differentiation and imitation go hand in hand. Joan Nelson Algren, a creator of *Sesame Street*, gleefully proclaimed that 'Australians absorb American culture like blotting paper' (quoted in McKay et al., 1996: 215–16). Australians frequently deploy such terms as 'Californication', 'Coca-Colonization', and 'McDonaldization' to describe this predicament/pleasure. Until the 1970s, most sports in Australia were administered by 'old boys' of the British 'school', dilettantes who relied on grass-roots support. Now, professionalization has brought in experts from advertising, management, marketing, and public relations, plus a reliance on corporate underwriting. Australian TVnetworks cover the World Series, the Super Bowl, the Kentucky Derby, US Open Tennis, the Masters and PGA, and weekly NFL highlights on terrestrial television, plus live games on Fox's cable network. The most Americanized game is basketball – it now has weekly NBA telecasts, and the local professional competition mostly features Yankee starting fives. Many coaches are US citizens, and the Most Valuable Player is usually an import. Jordan was the most popular athlete with the Australian public in 1993 (and with teenagers in 45 countries) and Magic Johnson was in tenth place. Apart from the Barcelona Games, neither player at that time had been seen on Australian television other than in commercials (Waddingham and Stead, 1993). T-ball (the entry sport to baseball and softball for young players) has suddenly become the most popular school sport, and Coca-Cola's marketing department notes massive interest in basketball (Russell, 1993; Gunther, 1997). During the Gulf War, Australian broadcasters were criticized by the Right for occasionally presenting a non-Fascist, non-jingoistic, anti-imperialist point of view. So they were delighted to show Super Bowl XXV's repugnant militarism, glorifying US military aggression at half-time (McKay et al., 1996: 217–20). The Australian Baseball League's privately owned clubs are linked to Major League teams, with a quota of four imported players per roster and Pepsi a major sponsor, while Coca-Cola underwrites Australian soccer (which insists on Anglo, 'de-ethnicized' team names in order to localize the game for Anglo-Celtic spectators, but does not ask the same of its sponsor – see Chapter 4). At the 1994 Coca-Cola World Rugby League Sevens championship, the winning team, sponsored by Pepsi, was prevented by security guards from displaying Pepsi cans at the post-game ceremony. Organizers dropped the idea of a presentation by Coke's management so it would not have to look at Pepsi signs on the winners' shirts.

But Australian sport is equally global – there is certainly the Ford Australian Tennis Open, but at various times tennis has been supported by BP; Shell has sponsored women's cricket; Dunlop was involved with netball; basketball's principal sponsor was Mitsubishi; and Japan Air Lines underwrote the Gold Coast marathon. Telstra funds the women's national basketball team, as well as the now notorious Sydney-to-Hobart yacht race (interesting that a company which is half-owned by the government can simultaneously make huge profits, lay off thousands of workers, and finance billionaires to sail boats across Bass Strait). Sports grounds are forever swapping their signage as icons of public culture in favour of corporatization: Brisbane's QEII stadium (named after a monarch) has become ANZ (named after a bank). These are, if you like, US methods, redesignated via transnational approaches to capital formation and sporting accumulation – part of promiscuous commodification. When a betting scandal rocked Australian cricket in 1998, it was significant that the *Weekend Australian* called on American signifiers to lament the creeping monetarization of the game – the headline 'Say it Ain't So' consciously borrowed from the 'Shoeless' Jackson myth of the 1919 World Series fix, as troped in the 1996 film *Jerry Maguire* (Cameron Crowe). Here, the US was a tragic site for popular remorse. And the image dominating the article was a cricket ball resting on US dollars (Brearley, 1998: 19). As we shall see in Chapter 3, Australia itself has aggressively pursued globalization through the export of rugby league and rugby union. Even the ultimate in parochial nomenclature (Australian Football, or Australian Rules) established an International Australian Football Council and an International Australian Football Championship in 1995 ('Aussie', 1999).

It is quite apparent that American football, hockey, and baseball are simply not globally popular next to soccer, cricket, cycling, and tennis. These sports dominate internationally, while Formula One racing is excluded from the US because it does not make a profit for promoters. The supposedly waning state (for example, Malaysia) outbids US capital every time in this domain (Siano, 1998). As mentioned above, the *methods* for turning sports into commodities definitely follow an American model of managerialism and televisualization, while golf, originally British, has migrated in such a way that its origins are as misty for some as the sport's point of origin, the St Andrew's golf course in Scotland. We are told that 'local villagers watch The [US] Masters in the jungle with a dish and a Honda generator'. But although golf courses are virtually all designed by Americans, in American style, and the sport is dominated by US equipment, an oversupply of British professional coaches means that *they* are dominant across Europe, and US success in élite competition has eroded as the domestic market has reached saturation (Phillips, 1998). If this is Americanization, it is extremely uneven.

Peter Donnelly does not see this as American cultural hegemony, but 'a two-way process in which the recipients have interpretive and resistant powers'. Homogenization and differentiation are both at play (1996: 248, 250). Has the US, in fact, become globalized by sport, rather than the other way around? The 1998 men's World Cup of soccer in France gave US residents some excellent opportunities to think through how the most isolated sports culture in the world views the product of openly competitive sports-TV markets, where 'world champions' refers to more than the best amongst a handful of arbitrarily selected North American cities. Apart from the intrusive telegenics of English-language US coverage, such as laying a graphic advertising NFL games scheduled for three months later over the quadrant of the picture that contained the action, and thanking companies for bringing the game free of commercials when their logos occupied the screen throughout, we were treated to an updated Monroe Doctrine. That wonderful relic of the 1820s, revived by Reagan's 'backyard' rhetoric, supposedly justifies the United States' political destabilization and economic restructuring of an entire continent. Its durability was on display in the Entertainment and Sports Network's (ESPN) bizarre, resolutely repeated insistence that 1958, when Brazil won the World Cup in Sweden, was the only occasion when a team had done so outside its own hemisphere. In 1994, as we were told over and over this time around, Brazil won the World Cup in the United States. Aren't those two nations from different hemispheres? Perhaps the North American Free Trade Agreement (NAFTA) and Monroe cover Brazil, to the point where they have shifted its place on the globe. Is that right? Could a fact-checking reader help us out here? Or is this simply a throwback to Nelson Rockefeller's 'Good-Neighbor Policy'?

Today, foreign athletes playing for US teams are routinely rubbished by crowds (Authers, 1997) and the US pursues a policy of internal Americanization. When corporate sponsors expressed displeasure at the success of Kenyan runners in the mid-1990s, organizers of US distance meets either imposed limits on the number of foreigners permitted to compete, opening the field up to locals, or stopped offering prize money in the hope of ensuring an American winner (Bloom, 1998). And the Atlanta Olympics of 1996 were notable for the way that US television made it look as though American products and athletes dominated the rest of the world, a neat twinning of competitive success in the two domains (McAllister, 1997). No one who saw them will forget the time- and space-binding claims made by US products such as Visa and Coke in advertising shown during international sports events, where these commodities are said to be universal signage. But the power of deterritorialized populations to create and sustain nationalism should be a sobering counter-sign.

Nation-states, Past and Present, with a Future

Anthony Giddens (1985) and others have pointed out that nation-states have not been in existence for very long, and claim they may be in the process of decline and even disappearance (Held, 1989). This seems as excessive in its own way as the hopes placed in nation-states over the twentieth century. After the First World War, as national self-determination was proving to be panacea, placebo, and disorder all at once, Ernest Barker outlined three material bases to the nation: race, as a source of human identification; environment, as both physical border and internal geography; and population, as a set of statistical forms. Now whilst the first and second terms were conceived as natural divisions (although never encountered as such, given the political venality of racism and the inevitable struggles over resources) the idea of the population as an object of care, to be quantified and qualified, modelled and bettered, derived from social theory. Barker almost celebrates the fact that this last category, already muddied, is the only one really applicable to the architectonics of nations (Barker, 1927: 2–3, 12). As May Joseph says, '[t]here has never been a pure space within the nation-state' (1995: 3).

The demise of the nation-state and the emergence of international sovereignty have been routinely – and mistakenly – predicted over the past century. More and more such entities appear, even as the discourse announcing their departure becomes more and more insistent (Miller, 1981: 16–18). The internationalism of new communications technologies and patterns of ownership and control and increases in the variety and extent of global diasporas in fact extend the significance of the state as a regulatory and stimulatory entity, because their corollary has been a need to create national subjectivities from disparate identities. Internationalization is perhaps nowhere better exemplified than in the work done by states to build a sense of belonging amongst their polyethnic populations, and the labour performed by those populations to seek new forms of state representation. It is our contention that, while the nation-state is beset with problems caused by the pressure of ethnicity from below and supranationalism from above, pronouncements that nationhood is dead – the project of globalization – are seriously premature (Hirst and Thompson, 1996). A book like *The End of the Nation-State* (Ohmae, 1995) can be viewed in this context as a capitalist conceit, appearing as it did during the advent of a supposedly exemplary open market specimen (NAFTA) that needed a mere thousand pages of governmental rules to 'work' (Palley, 1999: 50).

There is a tendency in the social sciences to conflate the nation with the service of a centralized bureaucratic or capitalist state, thereby denying the force of local civility as separable from, but partially produced by, state power (Southcott, 1987: 51). Yet as Benedict Anderson reminds us, 'nation-ness is the most universally legitimate value in the political life of our time' (1983: 12). Even institutions such as the Olympics, which are allegedly built around universal humanism rather than nationalism, are shot through with national symbols, via flags, uniforms, and the customization of media coverage (Bourdieu, 1999: 16).

The nation is defined here as 'an imagined community – and imagined as both inherently limited and sovereign' (Anderson, 1983: 15). This concept gets around the debate about the diachronic and conceptual primacy of nation and state. Nations are distinct entities thanks to their presentation by the state system as geopolitically delineated groups of peoples and defined duties. Flattening out the citizenry leaves no room for division, 'regardless of the actual inequality and exploitation that may prevail in each' (Anderson, 1983: 16).

Nations are recent and popular, increasingly so. Although not as easy to identify as states, which can be marked out in legal terms, they are multiplying. We live in an international age, which by its very formulation decrees that we are also in a national one. The nation is a oneness of imagination that binds citizens to states, places, and people, transcending the everyday apparatus of repression. A means of identification beyond the horizon, it may be founded on genetics or policy, perhaps a postcolonial hangover of boundaries drawn to suit metropolitan bureaucrats and industrialists. It may be complicated by all of the above, and it can be a matter of settled agreement or collective anxiety. Given these differences, how can we render so slippery a term of belonging analytically useful? Why should 'everyone' want to form nations, just as the more duplicitous or utopian among us continue to insist on their obsolescence in a new era of global capital? As Tom Nairn paradoxically remarks of the break-up of states and their multiple splits, '[s]mall is not only beautiful but has teeth too (speaking both technically and politically)'. This is the difference between the apparently outmoded 'medieval particularism' of small nationalism that Lenin derided and the really rather modish 'nonlogical, untidy, refractory, disintegrative, particularistic truth of nation-states'; the revolutions of 1989 made medieval particularism the future (Nairn, 1993: 157–58). Our contemporary moment equally references intra- and trans-nationalism, with diasporic subjects and First Peoples gathering political momentum. Most studies of cultural nationalism have seen it as an excuse for state activity, a *raison d'être* for state-building. But the intensity of feeling generated amongst diasporas and non-state actors has drawn this into question (Hutchinson, 1999). Threats to secular modernity through the state come not only from economic change, but from religious opposition to representative government, as recent events in Turkey and India have underscored (Benhabib, 1999: 709).

Forming nation-states requires the establishment of both order and authenticity. The order may be new in its type and operation, but it must invoke an older connection to essences as part of its claim to be. The nation becomes a base for this claim. It is 'authentic', and cannot be superseded, because it represents a one, true culture. Yet the manifestation of fealty to culture is of course in the apparatus of the state. Any sense of the nation-state as a discrete entity selected by persons with a common ethnic and political heritage can be applied to half a dozen cases at most. The rest of us are testimony to massive migration and/or the cartographic fancies of colonial powers. And when groups claim a national identity that is not expressed in existing political arrangements, this is necessarily phrased in terms of the desire to have their own state. Clearly, then, most nations are formed inside the nation-state (Miller, 1984: 285 n. 1).

For the most part, the state articulates the nation as a spirit-in-dwelling that gives it legitimacy, but which it also reserves the right to name and monitor. For nations are always coterminous with existing or desired systems of government. This is a paradox. Even as the nation is manufactured, it is said to be an already existing, authentic essence of statehood and peoplehood, a one, true culture. Anderson argues that we can study nations as 'cultural artefacts' that draw on 'a deep, horizontal comradeship' (1983: 13, 16). This collective identity was initially achieved through the spread of the printed word using local forms of European language after the sixteenth century. It came to represent political sovereignty, displacing the religious authority which had been communicated via Christian Latin's previous monopoly on the book. There was a similar iconographic change. The era of sacred internationalism had produced images that elided time and space by denying the passage of history. They represented the foundational Christian myth as a spectacle that was always contemporary and local. Medieval European paintings of the crucifixion depicted medieval European people gazing at Jesus. For audiences such as these, time was coming to a rapturously cataclysmic end. Sacred power would be witnessed first hand, as at a Second Coming. For us, this is anachronistic. Our sense of the simultaneous is of events occurring at the same moment in different places. But this logic was not available then. Past, present, and future were essentially one. Now, we think we can distinguish between them, and do so to delineate a shared national cultural history. This change took place because two new forms of writing translated an older sense of time into a modern order that came to characterize European life in the eighteenth century: novels and newspapers. Anderson thinks they made it possible to imagine a nation through the invention of 'meanwhile', a term to describe action taking place elsewhere, but also now; part of our world as connected individuals looking at a text, but not available to us as connected individuals at a single site (1983: 24–25, 28–31). Sports events covered in the media are a contemporary equivalent.

As Philip Schlesinger sees it, national culture 'offers respectability and brand identification' for state actions (1991: 138). The expressive interiority attached to national sentiment legitimizes public education, displacing oral language by writing that spans distance and difference, in the very way that sporting culture binds people who have never met and do not expect to do so. Identity becomes transferrable through literacy and a formal method of educating people, once responsibility for this task shifts from church to state. At the same time, it would be silly to endow these developments with the happy face of functionalist sociology: industrial culture divides even as it rationalizes, creating diffuse collective identities as well as officially endorsed ones (Gellner, 1981: 757; Barker, 1927: 4; Kohn, 1945: 301–2; Schlesinger, 1991: 160).

The expansion of nationalism in nineteenth-century Europe encouraged writers to produce an edifice of ideal types, a list of components of the national machine that described a state of affairs even as they brought it into being: 'L'histoire nationale fortifiait la nation et la nation encourageait l'histoire nationale' (National history strengthens the nation and the nation encourages national history) (Delannoi and Morin, 1987: 5). The Janus face of national comradeship is alterity, the othering of those excluded. This may take destructive material and symbolic form, with sport a touchstone. But such processes ironically connect same and other.

Our touchstone in this book is Bruno Latour's observation that 'the words "local" and "global" offer points of view on networks that are by nature neither local nor global, but are more or less long and more or less connected' (1993: 122). Such terms are often binarized (and hence all-encompassing) in the globalization literature, where the plenitude of one becomes the lack of the other and vice versa: a graceless zero-sum game between national and international, public and commercial. In place of this logic, we follow the dictum that 'if one wants the great systems finally to be open to certain real problems, it is necessary to look for the data and the questions in which they are hidden' (Foucault, 1991b: 151). Sport undermines any claim that globalization is a totality: it is, rather, a series of discontinuities and continuities – as demonstrated, in particular, by post-Second World War developments.

So we do not argue that the nation-state has lost its potency and relevance, but instead assert that in a globalizing context, analysis must both encompass and transcend individual nation-states (Rowe and Lawrence, 1998). National governments increasingly struggle to control the impact of cross-border flows stimulated by transnational forces through a hollowing out of the state. While global integration is neither automatic nor unproblematic, its destabilizing effects require supranational agreements and bodies like the World Trade Organization (WTO), the World Bank, the International Monetary Fund, NAFTA, the European Union (EU), MERCOSUR, and the Association of South-East Asian Nations, which regulate the conduct of individual nation-states. Scott Lash and John Urry (1994: 308) argue that while a 'cosmopolitan civil society' has now supplanted much state authority, this does not mean that a global culture has superseded it. In going beyond the nation-state, we also need to acknowledge that global constructs are as arbitrary, artificial, and nebulous as those they replace. While some might consider the Olympics the quintessential global sporting phenomenon, the notion that audiences react to it in predictable and identical ways is quite implausible. Within and between nation-states, cultural data are decoded not according to fixed principles of meaning, but in a manner contingent upon local histories and competing ways of seeing and doing. The nation-state and its sub-groupings (including cities and regions) still provide particular contexts in which meanings are negotiated, no matter how self-evidently and compulsively global they may be.

Global tendencies foster uncertainty, disorganization, and consumption at the expense of production (Crook et al., 1992). Ultimately, they suggest the desirability of abandoning the grand narratives – including the earlier works of Marx, Durkheim, and Weber – which sought to explain both revolutionary and evolutionary change. According to Lash and Urry (1994), 'economies of signs and space' are defined by reflexive accumulation (where the growth of capitalism is increasingly premised on knowledge-based non-material production) and flexible specialization (where work is conducted in vertically disintegrated networks of small firms involved in 'transaction-rich' market-exchange linkages with larger – often transnational – firms) which have tended to undermine conventional notions of work, space, and time (see discussion of the NICL in Chapter 2). Paralleling changes in workplace practice, we now see 'global' citizens, mobile subjects (either literally, as migrants, or metaphorically, in relation to consciousness). They find new meanings and identities in information flows, media images, communication networks, cultural forms, and aesthetics (Waters, 1995; Maguire, 1999). Such people have corporate homologues: 1999 produced stark statistics on the gross domestic products of major countries *vis-à-vis* major US corporations – IBM matched Colombia, Spain and Microsoft were equal, and the same was true of Wal-Mart and Argentina, Hewlett-Packard and Greece, Lucent Technologies and South Africa, Qualcomm and Singapore, and American Express and New Zealand/Aotearoa (Morgenson, 1999).

Sociologists of sport can quite legitimately emphasize sport's role as a cultural adjunct to economic imperialism, acknowledge the power of the First World capitalist media in promoting spectacles such as the Olympics (see Gordon and Sibson, 1998) and the men's World Cup in the Third World – and note that US and Japanese sports are minority interests elsewhere, other than in parts of Latin America. While the nation-state still provides the space in which cultural meaning is negotiated, there are clear limits to its powers and considerable threats to its continued legitimacy in a world of instantaneous, transnational image exchange (through, for example, the internet). In relation to the role of the media in this context, Joseph Maguire asserts:

> The pervasiveness of (the) media/sports/capital nexus, inspired by American practice in sports such as American football, basketball, and baseball, has forced a range of sports such as soccer to align themselves to this model. Failure to do so would place in question their ability to survive in the global media marketplace. (1993b: 35)

Sport is increasingly shaped by the media, spectacularized by commerce, employed to deliver audiences to sponsors, and intimately linked to the technological opportunities afforded by various media delivery forms (satellite, cable, webcast, and microwave) but not in a manner that ignores dissent and resistance. As such, globalizing tendencies must always be viewed as mediated by local structures, including the nation-state. What remains problematic is the speed and ephemeral nature of global exchange, as well as the increasing reliance upon symbols and images, rather than physical commodities, in contemporary capitalist economies. These shifts of direction intensify and complexify the contest between the global and local dimensions of all cultural forms.

The IOC and Corruption/Corporatization

At the beginning of the new millennium the Olympic story has become one of 'tarnished rings'. A major bribery scandal was revealed in early 1999, when delegate Marc Hodler accused 25 colleagues of accepting cash and other financial incentives from bidding committees during the 1990s. Soon after the allegations were made, US officials began investigating the circumstances of Salt Lake City's successful 1995 bid for the 2002 Winter Olympics. It was revealed that, among other incentives, the bid committee had provided IOC members with prostitutes, bribes, college scholarships for relatives, and free medical services (Lusetich, 1999a: 1). When Switzerland applied to host the Games, the vote against was taken as a reaction to Hodler's whistleblowing.

Here is a good example of a supranational sporting body conducting its own internal regulation, largely outside the scrutiny of the nation-state. It is a sorry tale of greed and corruption, indicative of what might happen to sport when it is truly global but not answerable to representative global governance. In such circumstances it becomes a law unto itself. As the events of 1999 unfolded, it was revealed that 30 IOC members had received money from would-be hosts. Within a month of the story breaking, three IOC members had resigned, six were to be sacked, and at least another five were under investigation (Longman, 1999d; 1999e: D2).

So desperate was Australia to host the 2000 Summer Games that, along with the normal excesses and extravagances enjoyed by IOC delegates (such as dining on lobster and cognac and residing in five-star accommodation) officials had Sydney wired to coincide with Samaranch's visit. According to J. Lehmann (1999: 19) the

A$28 million spent directly on the delegates helped secure Sydney's bid, along with ancillary services:

> Traffic lights were timed to turn green for IOC members' limousines … Samaranch's hotel radio was 'fixed' so it could not pick up a programme likely to broadcast negative comments about the IOC boss; the … Australian Opera general manager ensured that shows never started until IOC delegates had taken their seats; [and] elaborately compiled dossiers detailing IOC members' personal tastes were put into action

What fun to be a Falangist! A final attempt to buy votes was initiated by Australian Olympic Committee (AOC) President, John Coates. Close to the final vote for the 2000 site, he detected a possible swing against Sydney. Coates promised sports grants to Kenyan and Ugandan IOC members. According to the Australians these were not bribes, but acceptable enticements. The preferred words are, in fact, 'customary exchanges' (Stevens, 1999a: 4). Coates received virtually no condemnation for providing these gifts – Sydney had, after all, won the right to host the Games. But another Australian, Phil Coles, was forced to resign from his position as AOC Director of International Relations when 'customary exchanges' afforded him came to light. These included lavish skiing holidays, care of the Salt Lake City organizers (Lehmann and Guinness, 1999: 1).

For W. Smith (1999: 21):

> Not since the Roman Catholic Church started selling indulgences during the late middle ages has such a force for good been so diverted from its course, so tainted by money…. Faced with compelling evidence that at least eight IOC members might have sold their votes to the 2002 Winter Olympics candidate city, Samaranch, the supreme pontiff of Olympism, is now steeling himself for an unprecedented act of mass excommunication

Samaranch came under pressure to resign. Yet, in a secret ballot, over 80 delegates endorsed him. He appointed a reform commission, comprising friends of peace and democracy like Henry Kissinger and 41 IOC members. It reported late in 1999. The IOC adopted its key recommendations – twelve-year term limits for presidents, an age limit of seventy years instead of the existing eighty, recruiting 15 athletes as members (out of an enlarged body of 130), opening financial records to public scrutiny, banning visits by members to cities bidding to stage Games, and generating a code of conduct and ethics commission – but none of these rules applied to him. Most of the delegates had been hand-picked by Samaranch, which explains their reluctance to undermine their patron. Princess Anne, who voted against reform, told the media: 'This is what you lot have asked for.' So grubby, those proles (Longman, 1999d, 1999e; Anne quoted in 'Steps in the Right Direction?' 1999). Meanwhile, fellow-travellers from the US Olympic Committee sent a cease-and-desist letter to a Utah ski resort that promoted itself for the winter 1999 season as entirely unrelated to the Games – the Committee deemed this unauthorized commercial use of the Olympic name (Branch, 1999). As if a company would want a free ride through association with graft and corruption!

Just as he had done twenty years earlier when Franco died, Samaranch called for an amnesty to absolve him of his acts (Copetas et al., 1999: A1). But his continued support was also connected to his 'legacy' – turning the Olympics into a cash crop for corporate interests. By 1994, for example, transnational companies paid more than US$100 million to the IOC for marketing rights, growing to US$400 million at the 1996 Atlanta Games. Television rights were well in excess of this amount. NBC is to pay US$3.5 billion for the rights to broadcast the Summer and Winter Games between 2000 and 2008. In fifteen years, the IOC has increased its asset base from US$240,000 to over US$100 million, with each Summer and Winter Olympics now worth US$10 billion (Zengerle, 1999: 19). The brief for the Sydney 2000 Games was to restore the name of the Olympics that had been threatened by the scandals of 1999.

The desire for total control by Samaranch's 'Olympic state' is shown in the figures above. Yet, not surprisingly, questions are being asked about the ability of an organization with such an eye for profit to ensure fairness in competition among athletes, and about its accountability as a global entity with no mechanism of democracy. The World Conference on Doping in Sport held in Lausanne in early 1999 unanimously concluded that the IOC was unfit to oversee a new global anti-drug authority. This would come as no surprise to ex-athlete and drug entrepreneur David Jenkins. He has provocatively stated that about 50% of the world's top athletics competitors have used illegal drugs at some stage in their careers (see Cashmore, 1996). With estimates that some 30% of Olympic athletes *currently* use illegal drugs to enhance performance (Zengerle, 1999: 19), confirmation of widespread drug use would greatly harm the Olympic movement. Why should the IOC be vigilant in its fight against drugs if it knew that by doing so it would expose the current meaninglessness of the Olympic ideal, and eventually undermine its own financial operations? M. Stevens (1999b: 19) notes that the Games' innocence was comprehensively compromised in 1984:

> The Los Angeles Olympic Games made money when television began desperately seeking new sports to provide cheap profitable entertainment, [and] when hosting the Games became a once-in-a-lifetime windfall for cities rather than loss-making urban chivalry.... In ensuring a financial future for the Games, Los Angeles created problems which the IOC had neither the means to recognise, nor to cope with. As money poured in, so corruption became endemic. Despite celebrated athletes such as Ben Johnson being disgraced in past drug scandals, too many competitors are now cheating by using drugs. And too many IOC officials have used the new leverage of their vote to select host cities by selling to the highest bidder.

As J. Zengerle (1999: 19) has lamented:

> Whereas the Olympics ... once stood for the ideal of excellence, today they are a money-making opportunity and stand for greed. Indeed, the Olympics are already so far gone that there's only one sure-fire way to fix them: abolish them.

This will not, of course, happen. Things have become too entrenched and there is simply too much money involved – the very week that IOC reforms were proudly trumpeted, *New York Times* travel-section readers were regaled with puff pieces on 'Australia: Olympus with an Ocean View' (1999) and the IOC hired public-relations experts at great expense to recover their post-1999 image (Kranhold, 2000). Meanwhile, old colonial bigotries and power patterns continue to influence the Games. Élitist minority sports like equestrianism and yachting feature, while *sepak takraw*, akin to a blend of soccer, volleyball, and gymnastics – played and watched by millions of South-East Asians – *wuhu*, a martial art, and *kabbadi*, a tag-team competition followed by billions in South Asia and South-East Asia, are excluded because they are not played across five continents (Beh and Leow, 1999). By contrast, *tae-kwon-do*, whose President was a Samaranch lackey, is accepted.

Resistance?

When the national ideological analogue of sport is factored in, fruitful tensions between the civil, commercial, national, and governmental realms *are* referenced at the levels both of cultural industrialization and of symbolic meaning. Consider this instance. In 1995, the New Zealand/Aotearoa Rugby Football Union appointed John Hart as coach of its national side, the All Blacks. An executive from one of the country's premier corporations, Hart had not coached for years. His 'corporate-based approach' placed the 'accent on management rather than coaching *per se*' (Thomas, 1997: 41). Hart offered as his goal 'transforming the All Blacks into a great international sporting brand. At present, the All Blacks are a great international rugby brand: notwithstanding the talk about rugby's global reach, the two are poles apart' (Hart, 1997: 7). When winger Jonah Lomu had a McDonald's hamburger named after him in New Zealand/Aotearoa (Jackson and Andrews, 1999: 37), this was hailed as market customization. Hart's next step was to transcend localization rituals for foreign MNCs and make 'his' team into its own global sign.

Rugby, an amateur game until 1995, is played at a competitive international level in Fiji, Australia, South Africa, Argentina, England, France, Ireland, Romania, Japan, Western Samoa, New Zealand/Aotearoa, Papua New Guinea, Tonga, Wales, Italy, and Scotland. But that status was not enough for Hart. He had in mind the sign value of Manchester United and Brazil in soccer and (until 1999!) Chicago in basketball, a value that transcended the material coordinates of their particular sports to stand for something known and appreciated by those who would not profess to know or appreciate soccer or basketball (Manchester United has 100 million fan-club members worldwide and is 'the most recognized sporting brand in the world': see Chapters 2 and 3 and Larsen and McCann, 1998). Of course, in the process of attaining that cosmopolitanism, teams lose first their regional and then their national identities – just as the Chicago Bulls won with an Australian and a Croatian in their starting lineup, so Brazil's top footballers all play for clubs outside their country of origin, and Manchester United team members may have as little relationship to England as to Manchester (Hobsbawm, 1998).

How did the New Zealand/Aotearoa coach/manager hope to achieve equivalent recognition for his team? 'Great international sporting brands are created by consistent success … but it must be success with style…. The team become [*sic*] synonymous with excitement, with glamour, with class.' To this end, Hart knew the necessity to 'globalize rugby'. He understood that 'many people are uncomfortable when they hear the All Blacks talked about as a brand and rugby described as a product', because of the threat this posed to 'New Zealand culture', but rejected the notion that 'rugby can quarantine itself from economic and commercial reality'. The cultural aspect could be preserved if professionalization nurtured junior and amateur play rather than striving after profit for its own sake (Hart, 1997). By expanding beyond New Zealand/Aotearoa's limited business and consumer base, the game, the All Blacks, and their followers would see a huge world of money (Thomas, 1997: 301–2).

Following the publication of Hart's autobiography, dissent in the dressing-room accompanied repeated losses, as players found the demands of this corpo-ratization beyond them and in conflict with their sense of the sport. The US *Worldpaper* noted that to stay on top of rugby union, the All Blacks 'must play their toughest opponent to date, global capitalism', because the newly profes-sionalized sport saw leading coaches leave New Zealand/Aotearoa for more lucrative locations, in accordance with the NICL (Gray, 1998). After a dismal performance at the Rugby World Cup of 1999, Hart resigned, just as his politi-cal counterpart, ex-Prime Minister Michael Moore, was about to run the WTO into global disrepute (a Geneva-based bureaucrat who couldn't speak any lan-guages of the country he lived in, leading a group of unelected mavens working in secret to determine the world's trading framework). Anyone for the supply-side NZ revolution?

The All Black players' feelings may be transitional – a throw-back that will not be experienced by workers who are *formed* under the sign of global capital rather than being *trans*formed by it. But the story references many of the tensions we address here. Specifically, it captures a moment of change for a traditionally amateur sport, one imported from a colonial power and then used to represent independence from – and even superiority to – the former ruler. New Zealand/ Aotearoan rugby drew great patriotic fervour from its amateurism. Now that commodification and televisualization are under way, along with the imposition of governmental norms to prescribe conduct (part of GGATaC) rugby is in crisis. A sport which relied on a mythic, disinterested masculinity standing for a tiny country – producing remarkable international sporting success – had taken the promise of commodifying itself offered by a deregulated television system, and then encountered the disciplines expected from such a shift.

The question is: are these processes globalizing ones, or do they generate local forms of engagement and interpretation, including resistance? Do we live in a 'McWorld of homogenizing globalization', or one in which, to use a Sartrean phrase, local and regional areas are 'condemned to freedom' (Robertson, 1995: 39)? Regions are obliged to interact with wider forces to maintain their economic future. But they do so in differing ways, and under an array of conditions. If this is so, the local is not the other of the global. With time-compression of the global economy, the local dialectically absorbs, shapes, alters, and opposes wider tendencies while creating and promulgating its own. These, in turn, contribute to the eventual shape of macro or global forms. Jan Nederveen Pieterse (1995) rejects any view that globalizing processes necessarily make the world uniform. There may be some synchronization brought about by technological, economic, and cultural flows, but the effect is hybridized.

Yet, with free-to-air and pay-TV sporting coverage bringing diverse audiences closer by shrinking both time and space, some homogenization is occurring. Of course, how such events are read will be determined to a large extent by local histories, ideologies, and cultures. More difficult to interpret are the pay-TV fillers which allow viewers throughout the world to choose between watching US college basketball, Canadian lacrosse, or rugby from a South African province. Whether such globally available sports represent a realistically alternative local space for viewers remains open to question. But if satellite TV can enhance the ability of those in local settings to follow their teams on a week-by-week basis, or to follow individual, idiosyncratic sporting interests, it may enhance local forms of engagement.

In terms of resistance, we might consider the Global Anti-Golf Movement (GAGM), which works against a business/state carve-up of Asia into lawns for Euro-American and Japanese golf-cart-driving businessmen (Donnelly, 1996: 240). GAGM's World No-Golf Day (29 April) attracts a great deal of attention. Founded in Penang in 1993 by activists from Japan, Thailand, Malaysia, Hawaii, Hong Kong, India, Indonesia, and the Philippines, GAGM is a model of Southern civil society assaulting Northern despoliation and capital plus the emulation effect of a cosmopolitan bourgeoisie (Chatterjee, 1993). As *The Economist* ('Asia in the Rough', 1997) puts it, golf in Asia is 'a status symbol' – the meeting of the heads of government at the Association of South-East Asian Nations regularly schedules a gentlemanly wander around the links. GAGM highlights the impact of golf-course pesticides on human mortality and genetic disorders, the advertising message to the Third World of an unattainable lifestyle, the need for public recreational space rather than private links, sexual harassment by male golfers of female caddies (it is common for each male Thai player to be 'assisted' by four women), water wastage, and soil erosion. The Movement has succeeded in preventing golf-course development in several parts of Japan. In addition to GAGM, there is an anti-golf movement in Mexico, where indigenous peoples' land has been expropriated for the sport. Again and again, governments are key participants in the destruction of the environment as they search for foreign exchange – but are also key sites of appeal for activists (Avery, 1996; Chatterjee, 1993; Klein, 1999; Robbins, 1998). On the Right, upper-class Hindus, who have benefited most from globalized commerce in India, are the most trenchant nationalists where cricket is concerned, deploying this as a test of others' loyalty, even as their pleasures are sponsored by Coca-Cola and Pepsi and their avowed goal is global expansion of the game (McDonald, 1999). Meanwhile, cricket itself, perhaps the sport with the most fetishized/storied history and self-textualization, appointed its first global 'Development Manager' in 1998. The International Cricket Council (ICC), formerly the Imperial Cricket Conference, announced that the game 'must move rapidly to take up opportunities of global expansion'. It divided the world into five regions, each of which was allocated a full-time 'Development Officer', charged with the mission to 'take the sport to 2020 and beyond' by increasing participation in 'emerging cricketing nations' and bring as many of them into the one-day international fold – the biggest TV moneymaker – as possible ('Media Release', 1998).

John Sugden and Alan Tomlinson conclude their study of world soccer with the following: 'FIFA can be viewed *both* as a transnational body which promotes globalization (and transnational capitalism), and as a locus of resistance to entrenched forms of imperialist domination, and emergent forms of international and capitalist power' (1998a: 228). If the 1998 men's World Cup saw Adidas beat Nike in the Final (in that those companies sponsored the French and Brazilian teams respectively, just as each of the 32 national sides was 'owned' by a transnational (Endean, 1998)), the massive expense seemed worthwhile because of the enduring sign value of the nation as something that continued to appeal beyond the brand loyalty of capitalism. Pelé gained massive media attention when he accused Nike of corrupting soccer in Brazil (LaFeber, 1999: 144). The reassertion of ethnic specificity and older traditions of autotelic sport, such as the Highland Games in Scotland, Native-American lacrosse, and Atlético Bilbao seeking a distinctively Basque mode of soccer, are important ripostes to the juggernaut (MacClancy, 1996: 9–10). And on the Olympic front, the Catalans who spoke up against Fascist dictatorship in the 1970s were not forgotten, as Samaranch and his ilk might hope. Norwegian cross-country skier Vegard Ulvang was chosen to take the Oath at the Lillehammer Games. Ulvang went public in early 1994 about the exclusion of working athletes from IOC deliberations and the undemocratic nature of Samaranch's second career powerbase, linking these tendencies to 'His Excellency's' dark past. This led to a remark by an apparatchik, IOC Director-General François Carrard, that told the public all it needed to know: 'IOC does not care what Norwegians think. The opinions of four million people in a small province in Europe about the IOC do not concern us' (quoted in Klausen, 1999b: 43). Just in case anybody wondered.

We have argued in this chapter that discussions of modern sport should be framed with reference to global trends, tendencies, and structures. Global theorization, in turn, needs to address the ways in which transnational capital is commodifying and corporatizing sport, evaluating the attempts of nation-states – successful or otherwise – to control capital and information flows, including the pressures on them to adopt neoliberal policies. It should be sensitive to the growth of extra-state bodies that monitor and regulate production and exchange in sport. At the local level, it is essential to acknowledge differentiated impacts in the face of global culture. The interconnectedness of locations around the world reduces the importance of space and time and allows for an increase in the flows of people across national boundaries – a process of major significance for sport. Consumer consciousness of the international culture industries also needs to be taken seriously if we are to understand how sporting products and events become embedded within the psyche of sports fans. We have also argued that it is important to be sensitive to counter-knowledges based on national interest. Finally, we should constantly remind ourselves that, while globalization is more than a brand-name for sociologists and business leeches, and assuredly describes and explains 'real' processes, its provenance as a transcendental signifier is problematic. When the national ideological analogue of sport is factored in, we see fruitful tensions between civil, commercial, national, and governmental realms, both at the level of cultural industrialization and of symbolic meaning – the basis of our remaining investigations of GGATaC and the NICL.

2

National Symbolism and the Global Exchange of Sporting Bodies

> The irrepressible conflict between Labor and Capital [is] asserting itself under a new guise.... Like every other form of business enterprise, Base Ball [*sic*] depends for results on two interdependent divisions, the one to have absolute control and direction of the system, and the other to engage – always under the executive branch – the actual work of production. (Albert Spalding, quoted in Marcano and Fidder, 1999: 518)

Far from the musings of a latter-day Marxist, these words were spoken a century ago by a powerful industrialist involved in building both MLB and his own sporting-goods firm. They capture the central issue of this book. Globalizing sport necessitates twin tasks: securing an efficient division of labour, and manufacturing an efficient consumer base. This chapter deals with the first of these tasks, and Chapter 3 addresses the second.

Labouring bodies are the principal objects of sports. They are selected, trained, disciplined, bought, sold, monitored, invaded, celebrated, desired, and despised. Sporting bodies are taken to represent the condition of the nation through racial 'integrity', the 'health' of the economy, the rate of technological progress, the nature of appropriate gender identities, and any other symbolic role that can plausibly be deployed. Maguire (1993a; 1999: 67–68) typifies the sporting body as a model of discipline, a mirror, a site of domination, and a form of communication. The disciplined body is modelled through diet, training, and technology. The mirroring body functions as a machine of desire, encouraging mimetic conduct via the purchase of commodities. The dominating body exercises power through physical force, both on the field and – potentially – off it. Finally, the communicative body is an expressive totality, balletic and beautiful. These taxonomies bleed into one another, and can be internally conflictual or straightforwardly functional. They are carried by human, commercial, and governmental practices, increasingly across international boundaries.

The sporting body bears triumphalist national mythologies in a double way, extending the body to encompass the nation and compressing it to obscure the social divisions that threaten national unity. The value of this sporting body is, therefore, maximized through the successful accomplishment of metonymy – that *a* body can stand for all the common and noble characteristics of the citizenry – at least long enough to discipline the paying spectator, the television viewer, the newspaper reader, the aspiring school-age athlete, and so on. This control of the gaze is achievable only by careful management before major sports events and spectacular occurrences on the field of play. Sporting bodies can simultaneously connote agency, individuality, freedom, and resistance, while also producing a *habitus* characterized by self-surveillance, obedience, and social control.

The bodies of 'active' spectators, who expend energy in physically attending sports events, are preferred to those of 'passive' media spectators, who are routinely depicted as flaccid, corpulent, and decadent. These spectating bodies, no less than their athletic counterparts, are also subjected to regulating processes, because the successful production of sport must be mirrored and, indeed, measured by its consumption. For this reason, the consuming/viewing sporting body must be in the right state in the right place at the right time to complete a circuit of cultural, economic, and ideological exchange – a Leavisite fantasy of sorts! Somewhere between the commodified bodies of sports producers and consumers lie the non- or semi-commodified bodies of amateurs and schoolchildren, for whom the discursive prescription is predominantly moral and ethical. While this latter representation of sporting bodies is not entirely innocent of economic imperatives – it is claimed that public health, military training, and law-and-order costs will be reduced by expanding the size of the sports-participating general population, as noted in detail in Chapter 4 – it has drawn rhetorical strength from keeping sport-related commerce at a distance. Today's division of labour problematizes this distinction. Eight-hundred metre world champion Wilson Kipketer, for instance, was born and raised in Kenya, is a Danish citizen, and spends much of his time training under a Polish coach in Switzerland (Ibsen, 1999: 84). But the story is not always so cosmopolitan, and it sits inside a grand narrative that is very troubling – the NICL.

The New International Division of Cultural Labour

John Wiseman vividly details the implications of globalization for labour:

> Globalization is what happens when you lose your job ... because the company for which you work has been bought out by the Australian subsidiary of a Dallas-based transnational company that has decided to relocate production of its T-shirts to Mexico because of cheaper wage costs and lower health and safety standards. It is what happens when you get a job in Brisbane under a new employment contract that lowers your wages and conditions and your boss explains that this is essential to compete with Mexican, or Indonesian, or Chinese, workers. It is what happens when your sister is sacked from her hospital job because of budget cuts by a State Government that defends its actions by saying it must meet the demands of credit-rating agencies for balanced budgets and lower taxes. And it is what happens when you get skin cancer because of the hole in the ozone layer created by chemicals released by refrigerators and aerosol cans all over the world. (1998: 13)

This statement captures the pervasive effects of global processes, including how the state responds to an increasingly externally imposed neoliberal agenda aimed at 'freeing' the labour market to allow further penetration by corporate capital. Philip McMichael (1996) views globalization as a project driven by transnational capital that produces uncertainty and a crisis of legitimacy for the nation-state, creating a worldwide labour surplus and provoking global migrations.

This follows a longstanding pattern. In the fourteenth and fifteenth centuries, a mercantile system arose from business-driven calculations and manipulations of climate, geography, flora, and fauna. The exchange of goods came to be matched by an exchange of labour. As food commodities made their way around the globe, so did people, often as slaves. When machinery was developed, work split into an industrial mode. Cities grew into manufacturing sites and populations urbanized as wages displaced subsistence during the sixteenth, seventeenth, and eighteenth centuries. This is the moment of Adam Smith's famous text on pinmaking:

> One man draws out the wire, another straightens it, a third cuts it, a fourth points it, a fifth grinds it at the top for receiving the head; to make the head requires three distinct operations; to put it on is a peculiar business, to whiten the pins is another; it is even a trade by itself to put them into the paper.... The division of labour ... occasions, in every art, a proportionable increase of the productive powers of labour. (1970: 110)

As developed countries moved on to the global stage, new forms of labour were institutionalized in empire. In the eighteenth and nineteenth centuries, manufacturing went on at the centre, with food and raw materials imported from the periphery. Today, divisions of labour occur via sectoral differences in a national economy, the occupations and skills of a labour force, and the organization of tasks within a firm. Life-cycle models of international products suggest that they are first made and consumed in the centre, in a major industrial economy, then exported to the periphery, and finally produced 'out there', once technology has become standardized and savings can be made on the labour front. Goods and services owned and vended by the periphery rarely make their way into the centre as imports (Lang and Hines, 1993: 15; Strange, 1995: 293; Keynes, 1957: 333–34; Cohen, 1991: 129, 133–39; Evans, 1979: 27–28).

The idea of the NICL (Miller, 1990, 1996, 1998b, 1998c) derives from retheorizations of economic dependency theory that followed the inflationary chaos of the 1970s. Developing markets for labour and sales, and the shift from the spatial sensitivities of electrics to the spatial insensitivities of electronics, pushed businesses beyond treating Third World countries as suppliers of raw materials, to look on them as shadow-setters of the price of work, competing amongst themselves and with the First World for employment. Any decision by a multinational firm to invest in a particular national formation now carries the seeds of insecurity, because companies move on when tax incentives or other factors of production beckon. This development broke up the prior division of the world into a small number of industrialized nations and a majority of underdeveloped ones, as production was split across continents. Folker Fröbel, Jürgen Heinrichs, and Otto Kreye (1980) christened this the New International Division of Labour (NIDL). We suggest that just as manufacturing fled the First World, cultural production has also relocated, though largely within the industrialized market economies.

This is happening at the level of popular textual production, marketing, and information and high-culture, limited-edition work. In sport, labour market slackness, increased profits, and developments in global transportation and communications technology have diminished the need for co-location of these factors. Fragmenting production depresses labour costs and deskills workers (Browett and Leaver, 1989: 38; Welch and Luostarinen, 1988; Fröbel et al., 1980: 2–8, 13–15, 45–48).

As G. Teeple argues: 'with the coming of computer-based systems, capitalist production became less constrained by large-scale, long-term investments, and with the continued diminution of national barriers it could increasingly be "sited" in regions or countries with the most favorable conditions for accumulation (for instance, proximity to markets, types of labor force, and state concessions)' (1995: 65–66). By 1994, half of the 100 biggest economies in the world 'belonged' not to nation-states, but to MNCs (Donnelly, 1996: 239). Four hundred of the latter accounted for two-thirds of fixed assets and 70% of trade (Robinson, 1996: 20). With control of the economy in the hands of MNCs, some common elements appear to be gaining hold. One is the view that the unmitigated rule of corporate private property must be sacrosanct. Another is that the welfare state should largely be dismantled. Teeple suggests that 'the same changes wrought by globalization are the rationale for neo-liberalism' (1995: 6). The rise of neoliberalism is a key feature of globalization – the state has not disappeared, but become an aid to accumulation (Robinson, 1996: 19).

Neoliberalism is associated with individual freedom, the sanctity of the marketplace, and minimal government involvement in economic matters (Overbeek, 1990). It provides an intellectual excuse for a comparatively unimpeded flow of capital across national boundaries and the rejection of corporatist or tripartite approaches to solving economic problems, where labour, capital, and the state work together. Subordinate groups are now given little or no credence. On behalf of capital, the state actively undermines the union movement through policies designed to 'free' labour from employment laws. The Keynesian welfare system, which helped to redistribute funds to the working class, is dismantled in the process. As C. Hamilton has noted:

> The preferences of citizens expressed through elected governments take second place to those of international financial markets. When unemployment increases, the markets generally rally because higher unemployment reduces the likelihood of inflation. If governments increase spending on social welfare they are in danger of being punished by capital withdrawals, driving up interest rates and causing exchange rates and incomes to fall. The effect is reinforced if the new spending is to be financed by increased taxes on capital or wealth. The wishes of the citizens cannot be fulfilled. (1996: 5)

Ralph Nader refers to this as 'a slow motion coup d'etat', as the historic gains to representative discussion and social welfare made by working people and subaltern groups are problematized and rejected by corporate power (1999: 7).

The issue is the extent to which the historic promises made by established and emergent governments after 1945, to secure the economic welfare of citizens and their political sovereignty, can still be kept. Neoliberalism is the latest lever for these guarantees, and the one that has gone furthest towards breaking them. Governments want to secure ongoing sovereignty and controlled financial markets, along with international capital markets – what *The Economist* magazine calls an '[i]mpossible trinity' ('Global Finance', 1999: 4 Survey Global Finance projection).

The promise of economic welfare initially seemed locally workable, via state-based management of supply and demand and the creation of industries to substitute imports with domestically produced items. The second promise, sovereignty, required concerted international action to convince the colonial powers (principally Britain, the Netherlands, Belgium, France, and Portugal) that the peoples they had enslaved should be given the right of self-determination via nationalism. The latter became a powerful ideology of political mobilization as a supposed precursor to liberation. When this second promise was made good, the resulting postcolonial governments undertook to deliver the first promise. Most followed import-substitution industrialization, frequently via MNCs that established local presences. But Third World states suffered dependent underdevelopment and were unable to grow economically. Their *political* postcoloniality rarely became *economic*, with the exception of those Asian states that pursued export-oriented industrialization and service-based expansion. With the crises of the 1970s, even those states which had bourgeoisies with sufficient capital to permit a welfare system found that stagflation had undermined their capacity to hedge employment against inflation. We know the consequences: 'the space of economic management of capital accumulation [no longer] coincided with that of its political and social dimensions' (Amin, 1997: xi).

Import substitution of the 1950s and 1960s was progressively problematized and dismantled from the 1970s to today, a tendency that grew in velocity and scope with the erosion of state socialism. We have reached a point where it is said that 'the state remains a pre-eminent political actor on the global stage', but 'the aggregation of states … is no longer in control of the global policy process', which is fundamentally non-normative and is run by banks, corporations, and finance traders (Falk, 1997: 124–25, 129–30). In the new system, core and periphery are blurred, the spatial mobility of capital is enhanced, unions are disciplined, the strategic strength of labour is undermined, and the power of the state is circumscribed by the ability of capital to move across borders – a fundamental shift in the bargaining and power relations between capital and labour, facilitated by transportation and information technologies, but still displaying the traces of specific national modes of integration into the NICL (Ross and Trachte, 1990: 63; Thompson and Smith, 1999: 197).

This era is known as the 'Washington Consensus'. Dominant since the late 1970s, it favours open trade, comparative advantage, deregulation of financial markets, and low inflation. The 'Consensus' has, of course, presided over slower worldwide growth and greater inequality than at any time since the Depression, with job security and real wages down, and working hours up in the industrialized market economies, while the world's richest 20% of people earned 74 times the amount of the world's poorest in 1997, up from 60 times in 1990 and 30 times in 1960. The manifold catastrophes of the Consensus in the late 1990s – Mexico, South-East Asia, Russia, and Brazil – were explained away as aberrations by neoliberal apologists (Palley, 1999: 49; Levinson, 1999: 21; Galbraith, 1999: 13).

We now have firms which view the world as a 'mosaic of differentiated sites of potential investment' (Ross and Trachte, 1990: 223). Because of their mobility, MNCs can discipline both labour and the state, such that the latter is reluctant to impose new taxes, constraints, or pro-worker policies in the face of possible declining investment from those firms. Post-state-socialist labour movements are advised on 'appropriate' forms of life by the American Federation of Labor – Council of Industrial Organizations, in keeping with its strong opposition to Marxism-Leninism over many decades (Herod, 1997: 172, 175). The 'uncompetitive' countries of the Arab world and Africa have their labour forces bracketed by MNCs as a reserve army of low-cost potential workers who will be imported to the North if required (Amin, 1997: ix), while throughout the world, 'household and informal sector activities' increase 'to sustain global reproduction' (Peterson, 1996: 10).

There are two difficulties with the NIDL and the NICL. First, they aggregate investment and trade data, assuming a necessary correlation between the movement of capital and the division of labour that is not always accurate, especially given the role of the state. And second, privileging production and distribution in the cultural arena may negate the importance of meaning in the circulation of texts. So the model is tentative (Miège, 1989: 41–43; Cohen, 1991: 130, 132; Beaverstock, 1996). At the same time, it closely parallels the political moves made by ruling capitalist classes across the world in the 1970s in opposition to income redistribution achieved by unions and social movements.

The global economic system that evolved from the mid-1970s saw Northern class fractions support a transnational capital that displaced non-capitalist systems elsewhere (Robinson, 1996: 14–15). Regulatory and other mechanisms were set in place to liberalize world trade, contain socialism, promote legislation favourable to capitalist expansion, and aggregate world markets. The last of these, which included the formation of the EU and other trade groupings, was crucial for the promotion of free trade régimes in the 1980s and beyond (though trade since then has not exceeded that of the post-war quarter century: Hirst 1997: 412). As we have seen, it also undermined state sovereignty. The growth of corporate power had provided enough strength for corporations to demand the removal of national barriers to trade, as the spread of foreign capital and currency markets meant that economic decisions were taken outside the context of the nation-state, in ways that favoured the market. The 'relationship between capitalism and territoriality' shifted (Robinson, 1996: 18).

But it was still governed by inter-state bodies as much as ever, dominated by the G7 (Hirst, 1997: 413; McMichael, 1996: 177). Capital markets, for example, operated internationally but with national supervision and regulation; all conceivable plans for dealing with their transnational reach still involved formal governance ('Global Finance', 1999). Rather than 'a borderless world, this might best be construed as a shift from states managing national economies, to states managing the global economy' (McMichael, 2000). Workers have dealt with these changing conditions via international trade secretariats, with many US unions following the very logic of Manifest Geo-Destiny that animates their bosses. Transnational worker solidarity has tended to apply only at the grass-roots rather than the peak level, and is severely compromised by an isolationist labour stance that romanticizes national glories in opposition to a globalizing managerialism – a gruesome business-leech discourse that has displaced international working-class solidarity as the prevailing international utopianism (Herod, 1997: 168, 171, 185; Amsden and Hikino, 1999: 7).

In rendering problematic both space and time, globalization confuses identity – one effect of which is to question the meaning and efficacy of nationalism. National sporting teams (such as recent English cricket sides comprising players of South African, West Indian, New Zealand/Aotearoa, Indian, and Australian descent) blur the meaning of 'us' versus 'them', the traditional core of nationalist sentiment. For Joseph Maguire and John Bale (1994) the latter issue is of particular pertinence in understanding global sport. They highlight the trans-continental movement of soccer players, the growing Afro-Caribbean involvement in British soccer, and the presence in the US of athletes from many nations, stimulated largely by generous college scholarship programmes. They report the summer 'invasion' of Australian, New Zealand/Aotearoan, South African, South Asian, and Caribbean cricketers to play in England's domestic competition, and comment upon the lifestyles of a host of élite golf, tennis, and rugby players, harnessing Arjun Appadurai's (1990) notion of global cultural flows to identify 'mediascapes' (global flows of film, television, video, and newspapers) and 'ideoscapes' (the flow of ideas about the role of the state and its significance in furthering globalization).

Labour mobility is not at the wage-earning end of the sports labour force, but amongst the salariat. At the top of certain sports, rates of pay for workers who compete internationally have combined with a deregulated world TV market to create labour cosmopolitans across soccer, ice hockey, motor-racing, basketball, track, cycling, golf, tennis, horse-racing, and cricket. They may migrate on a seasonal, residential, or comprehensive basis (Bale and Maguire, 1994; Maguire, 1996). This pattern is very much in keeping with other new professional diasporas (Cohen, 1997: 155–76). Secondary labour markets overseas also provide a place to test home-grown players – more than 130 NFL footballers in 1998 had played in League-sponsored competitions outside the US. Canada has always been the largest foreign supplier, but the 1999–2000 season featured 50 foreign players from 23 states (Buckley, 1999; 'NFL International', 1999; 'NFL Full', 1999).

At the opposite end of the scale, foreign recruiting is designed to circumvent the historic gains made by local athletes to secure income redistribution. Between 1974 and 1991, the proportion of revenue spent on MLB players' salaries increased from 17.6% to 42.9%. The free agency achieved by baseballers following court and union action had the effect of producing wealthy clubs able to buy great players and poor clubs unable to purchase equivalent success. So in 1999, the New York Yankees' payroll was US$85 million, whereas the Montréal Expos paid out just US$16 million. The two sides performed as those figures would suggest (Marcano and Fidder, 1999: 517–18).

MLB teams set up baseball academies across Latin America in the 1980s in search of young men (defined as aged 11+) who will sign up for much less than equivalently gifted players domiciled in the US, because the former are outside the amateur draft's protection of wages and conditions – just like MNCs in other activities, sports corporations are uninterested in applying labour laws and conditions from where their executives live. Few clubs comply with local government regulations for baseball hiring. Teams discourage young boys from attending school and require them to avoid agents (whose bargaining skills have been so important in the domestic arena). The biggest source for the pros now after California is the Dominican Republic, with Puerto Rico, Venezuela, and Mexico of increasing importance. A quarter of Major League players are Latino and 147 men on the 1998 roster were born overseas, while there are now US amateur coaches in 30 nations. It is especially significant that these programmes are exclusively aimed at Third World states. The First World has an entirely different type of aid, based on developing an interest in baseball rather than schooling stars (Japan, not the Dominican Republic, was the first place outside North America to host an official MLB series, in April 2000). When US-based players seek to play off-season back home in Latin America, MLB blocks them, lest there develop an alternative baseball system. There was great irony and symbolic violence in baseball's nomination of March 2000 as 'The Month of the Americas', in recognition of Hispanic contributions to the sport. As if in mocking preparation for this, *Sports Illustrated* magazine offered a photo-essay of young boys in the Dominican Republic using makeshift equipment in the dirt as satellite dishes for US games overlooked them (Chass, 1998a, 1998b; Winegardner, 1999; Marcano and Fidder, 1999: 512, 518; 'MLB Honors', 1999; 'Leading Off', 2000).

Officially binational leagues, where teams themselves come from outside the US, must comply with multiple legal systems. North American pro leagues in baseball, basketball, and hockey are all subject to Canadian as well as US on labor law, for example (Jarvis and Coleman, 1999: 347). This has not been a problem in practice for baseball in its dealings with Latin America – no surprise, for as noted earlier, the Monroe Doctrine lives on in apparently licensing contemptuous US attitudes towards the legal framework of the region.

Aggressive recruiting activities are not restricted to pro sports. Consider efforts by US colleges to recruit athletes who can heighten their institutional standing as nationally prominent entities that do more than educate. The 'latter-day scramble for Africa', an unseemly search for track-and-field stars that started in the 1970s, resembled nineteenth-century imperial powers seeking new territory. In 1960, US colleges recruited 8% of their athletes from Africa. By 1980, the figure was 33%, following numerous Olympic successes by middle-distance runners. Once African student-athletes came to the US, they were brutally overworked to service boosterism, leaving with devastated bodies that allowed no room for further success on behalf of their own countries (Bale, 1991: 79, 74).

As noted in Chapter 1, pro sports have recently turned away from the provincialism of US TV and arenas because of the classic capitalist problem of overproduction. Having saturated the domestic supply of good athletes and reliable consumers, and increased local players' wages, the NBA went overseas during the 1990s in search of cheap talent and likely customers to maintain its business, opening offices in Switzerland, Spain, Australia, Hong Kong, and

Mexico during the decade. Just three international players were drafted into the NBA for the 1993–94 season. The number had increased to 12 four years on. Opening rosters for the 1999–2000 season contained 37 international players from 25 countries, compared to 29 players from 20 nations two years earlier (Jackson and Andrews, 1999: 34; Whitnell, 1999; 'Global Player List Grows', 1999).

This chapter focuses, then, on how sporting bodies have been implicated in some of the economic, political, cultural, and technological processes associated with globalization. We examine how the hegemonic, white, Anglo, heterosexual, male sporting body of the Victorian era was gradually decentred due to decolonization, commodification, and migration. Our argument is that the global traffic in sporting bodies has made it harder for the nation to be represented by traditional corporeal symbols. Yet we also maintain that schooling, commodification, scientization, medicalization, and surveillance have regulated all bodies in restrictive ways. It is necessary to examine how these interrelated processes were influenced by events in Victorian Britain.

The Victorian Sporting Legacy

The nineteenth-century British ruling class played a pivotal role in institutionalizing modern sports by codifying football contests between English villages. Conducted under rudimentary rules, these violent encounters had provided opportunities since medieval times for young men to settle scores in ways that would be considered savage today, with the participants (or perhaps more accurately, combatants) often crippled and sometimes killed (Elias, 1986). Around the middle of the nineteenth century, masters in the élite schools, seeing the potential of these brutal activities for inculcating discipline and morality in their pupils, began to standardize them according to middle-class sensibilities. Although neither monolithic nor uncontested, this hegemonic definition of sport – which emphasized homosocial heterosexuality, gentlemanliness, modesty, loyalty, fair play, bravery, self-control, a balance between mind and physique, sport for its own sake, patriotism, and Anglocentrism – had effects that reached far beyond the playing fields. The privileged graduates of these élite schools went on to participate in sport at ruling-class universities, becoming the 'old boys' who founded exclusive sports clubs. Along with language, armed force, religious education, and administration, British imperialism exported bats, balls, and a sporting ethos to the colonies. Hence the pervasiveness of such phrases as: 'The battle of Waterloo was won on the playing fields of Eton', 'It's just not cricket', 'Sound body, sound mind', and 'Sport builds character' in locales as diverse as Zimbabwe, Australia, Pakistan, Canada, New Zealand/Aotearoa, South Africa, Singapore, Hong Kong, Sri Lanka, India, and the Anglophone Caribbean.

The codification and appropriation of barbarous rustic rivalries by bourgeois-aristocratic classes in the late nineteenth century does not mean, however, that the genesis and development of modern sport can be explained as either the outcome of class hegemony or some male predisposition to violence. In addition to being shaped by social class, modern sport was both determined and deployed by a plethora of sports-related organizations, ideologies, and practices.

These include muscular Christianity in crusading commitment and belief in the need to discharge unhealthy impulses through physical activity; physical education (PE), with its state-sanctioned governmentality; physical culture and natural-beauty movements; gymnastics; imperialism's militaristic coupling of sports and battlefields and Eurocentrism; rational recreation; French neoclassical romanticism, symbolized by Baron Pierre de Coubertin's revival of the ancient Olympics as an international festival of male corporeality and diplomacy; and the interleaving scripts of Eurocentrism and social Darwinism, which both constituted and reinforced notions of white supremacy. Modern sport was also contoured by the concatenation of events in Western Europe during the eighteenth and nineteenth centuries: the historic shift from absolute monarchy to parliamentary democracy, rapid expansion of the global capitalist system, and social upheavals associated with industrialization and urbanization.

Michel Foucault (1977) has demonstrated how élites attempted to solve the interrelated problems of sustaining a productive and compliant labour force and maintaining social order during this turbulent period through 'biopower'. Bodies were subjected to external modes of regulation and more subtle forms of self-surveillance and self-discipline. This complex governmentalization was initiated in asylums, hospitals, prisons, and schools. In the latter sphere, school sports, marching, military drills, gymnastics, and PE were directly implicated in shaping bodily dispositions. David Kirk (1998) explains how the gendered régimes of corporeal regulation, individualization, and differentiation that underpinned PE programmes in colonial and postcolonial Australia intersected with the discourse of eugenics, anxieties over racial purity, and concerns about national efficiency and fitness. These disciplinary technologies continue to shape contemporary, substantially commercialized, activities like aerobics. Similarly, Jean Harvey and Robert Sparks (1991) use a Foucauldian perspective to show how the popularity of PE and gymnastics in the late nineteenth century dovetailed with the corporeal discipline and surveillance associated with the emergence of modern nation-states. John Hargreaves (1986) argues that the cardinal values of contemporary school sport and PE programmes – 'effort, discipline, achievement, compliance, co-operation, harmony and role competence' – are condensed in the 'mesomorphic image of the body', while P. Vertinsky (1998) has highlighted the gendered assumptions that undergirded the medicalization of women's bodies in the Victorian era, which still permeate health-and-fitness promotion campaigns.

Equivalent patterns can be detected in the medicalization of sport. While it can be traced back to the late nineteenth century, both the aims and effects of sport science were relatively diffuse until after the Second World War. Since then, a variety of factors – the race for international sporting supremacy between the former protagonists in the Cold War; sophisticated developments in pharmaceutical research; the increasing commercialization of sport; and the hegemony of instrumental rationality – has caused the techniques of biomedical science to be applied systematically to sport for the explicit purpose of enhancing performance. According to John Hoberman:

For the past century, high-performance sport has been a vast, loosely coordinated experiment upon the human organism.... Today's attempts by teams of athletes, trainers, doctors, and scientists to produce record-breaking performances have the quality of an obsession. The widespread use of drugs to boost athletic performance is only the most publicized symptom of this global mania to produce 'world-class' athletes, which is as excessive in China as it is in Germany or the United States, as fashionable in Morocco as it is in Kenya. (1992: ix)

As Cheryl Cole (1998) notes, one reason sporting bodies are such powerful symbols is that they articulate commonsense ideas about free will, self-control, health, productivity, and transcendence (e.g., 'Just do it'). Particularly in its élite, commercial form, sport has both reflected and projected a worldwide 'body crisis', a 'body panic' (Kroker et al., 1989). The seemingly natural boundaries of human bodies have been transgressed via scandals like the detection of performance-enhancing drugs and the threat allegedly posed by athletes who are HIV-positive. Commonsense notions about free will sit awkwardly with the fact that around the world, athletes with the requisite somatotypes are being identified as early as possible, then selected, trained, and monitored by psychologists, physiologists, biomechanists, physiotherapists, and international agencies responsible for drug testing and gender verification. The spectre of cryogenics is evident in a proposal by the Office of National Drug Control in the US to freeze blood and urine samples from athletes at the 2000 Olympics. According to its proponents, this technique allows tests to be conducted decades later in order to detect performance-enhancing drugs that current technology cannot identify (Bita, 1999). The scare of new tests led to the unexpected withdrawal of some 27 athletes and officials from the Chinese team before it left for Sydney. Nine other athletes were removed from the Olympic village before they had the chance to compete in their events. With numerous weightlifters also being stripped of their medals, it looked, to many, that Sydney would be remembered as the 'drug games'. Numerous athletes in the Sydney Paralympics also tested positive.

Athletes subject their bodies to inordinate levels of pain and injury and often over-train in distinctly unhealthy ways. Moreover, in the quest to improve performance, élite athletes from virtually all countries engage in blood doping; consume diuretics, hormones, steroids, and stimulants; adhere to ascetic dietary régimes; and use aquadynamic and aerodynamic clothing and equipment. Many high-level athletes train in national sports institutes that simulate climates and altitudes, elevating red-blood-cell counts. The Australian Institute of Sport even has a special facility known as Altitude House, where athletes sleep in chambers that simulate a high-altitude atmosphere. Far from being 'natural,' élite sporting bodies are akin to docile cyborgs. As Jacques Ellul presciently stated nearly forty years ago:

In every conceivable way, sport is an extension of the technical spirit. Its mechanisms reach into the individual's innermost life, working a transformation of his body and its motions as a function of technique and not as a function of some traditional end foreign to technique, as, for example, harmony, joy, or the realization of spiritual good. In sport, as elsewhere, nothing gratuitous is allowed to exist; everything must be useful and must come up to technical expectations. (1964: 384)

There is tension between the demands of sporting edification, expression, entertainment, and exploitation, especially in those contact sports now deeply reliant on televisual images, as well as in representations of sportswomen that emphasize their looks, emotional and physical fragility, and heterosexuality.

In keeping with this ambivalent displacement of social élites by cyborg élites, we turn now to the most international of sports – soccer – and trace its movement from English coding to universal signage, then look at how the NICL has both destabilized hockey's patrimony and facilitated the success of Nike. The results are politically ambiguous.

Making and Unmaking the Nation:
Soccer and the NICL

Most histories of association football describe Britain as the 'home' of the game. Indeed, in Britain the game generally bears the generic title 'football', whereas it is known as 'soccer' in those mainly Anglophone countries (like Australia, Canada, and the USA) where other football codes lay stronger claims to stand for the nation. Indeed, the historical association between Britain and soccer is so long established that, as early as 1860, an anonymous handbill was issued proclaiming itself to be an 'Obituary: Death of the Right Honourable Game Football' (1992) after two court cases prevented the citizens of Ashbourne, Derbyshire from playing an annual festive street game. In 1996, when the European Football Championships (given the predictably marketing-friendly title of Euro 96) were hosted by England, the chorus of the chart-topping song of the tournament declared that 'Football's coming home' (see discussion below). If soccer had 'died' at a time when most contemporary playing nations had barely encountered the game, it was soon resurrected in a much more rationalized and commodified form, recognizable as the forerunner of today's game in being played before present and distant, paying and non-paying customers (Mason, 1980). It is not possible here to do more than touch on the history of (British and non-British) soccer – its early relationship with the British Empire, growth beyond that realm, domination through FIFA by European and then Latin American identities and entities, and the return of power to Europe in 1998 based on the latter's status as a profit centre of the game (see Mason, 1980; Wagg, 1984; Sugden and Tomlinson, 1998b; Giulianotti, 1999; Coman et al., 1998).

As soccer developed first into a national pastime and then into an international sport, British hegemony became deeply entrenched. Its migration coincided and blended with the establishment and synchronization of the Empire's cultural mission. Regional variation meant that the game's 'domestic' development was patchy in Wales, parts of Scotland and Northern Ireland, and the west of England. One irony of this is that, as with rugby union (which produces an 'all-Ireland' team that crosses sectarian and national divides) but unlike rugby league and cricket (which made little domestic impression outside England) British soccer was split into separate and competing 'Home Nations'. As in other sites of national identity, there is a tension between 'Britishness' and 'Englishness'. In the case of hierarchical soccer ideology, this is clearly resolved in favour of the latter: 'Within the dominant ideas of Britain, and British character and culture, England and "Englishness" have always been allocated the leading role' (Clarke and Critcher, 1986: 120). But the pristine idea of soccer belonging to one nation was brought into question quite early. Signs of an international division of labour emerged when Mussolini promised to erect a stadium for the winner of the Italian Cup in the 1930s. Clubs sought new talent from players of Italian heritage from Brazil, Uruguay, and Argentina (Lopes, 1997: 67).

Here we can see not only the protean nature of the sporting nation – on occasion contained within the boundaries of the nation-state, on others overlapping them – but also the importance of international sporting competition as an ideological and cultural force capable of both reinforcing and challenging the national status quo (as was evident, for example, in the politically charged matches between England and Scotland in the now-discontinued Home Championship series). The national or quasi-national representative status of athletes and teams is, as we shall see below, especially crucial in the context of economic and political forces that have progressively deregulated national sporting competitions, problematizing, for example, the national character of soccer in England, Scotland, the Netherlands, and so on. Simon Kuper points to the decline in Brazilian soccer of the 'poor, dark-skinned' trickster *Malandron* (among whom he counts 'great dribblers' like Pelé, Didi, Garrincha, and Jairzinho) in favour of the more orthodox soccer demanded and produced by the 'rich, light-skinned people [who] live along the beachfronts' (1998: 197–98). The role of the sports media in negotiating between sport's competing cultural and identity formations is pivotal. This becomes more complex when local competitions are populated by foreign players, and international teams by diasporas that return home for a few matches a year.

The intense coupling of 'Englishness' and soccer relates to assertions of the game's paternity (the gendered term is used advisedly). The extent of this cathexis can be measured by the extreme local response when, in 1953, the English national team was beaten for the first time at its emblematic Wembley Stadium, by 'communist' Hungary. This was represented by the English media as analogous to the loss of the Empire and even of national sovereignty. The establishment newspaper of record, the London *Times*, noted:

> Yesterday by 4 o'clock on a grey winter's afternoon within the bowl of Wembley Stadium the inevitable had happened. To those who had seen the shadows of recent years creeping closer and closer there was perhaps no real surprise. England at last were beaten by the foreign invader on solid English soil. And it was to a great side from Hungary, the Olympic champions, that the final honour fell. They have won a most precious prize by their rich, overflowing, and to English patriots unbelievable victory of six goals to three over an England side that was cut to ribbons for most of an astonishing afternoon. Here, indeed, did we attend, all 100,000 of us, the twilight of the gods. (Green, 1992: 65)

Such profoundly mythified readings by sports commentators persisted throughout the twentieth century. When England won its only men's World Cup in 1966 (on that same 'solid English soil') both the popular and the élite media took the opportunity to metaphorize sport, war, national character, and cultural superiority. As John Clarke and Chas Critcher (1986: 120) state:

> the supremacy of England was confirmed not only by the fact but also by the manner and the bearers of victory. They had beaten the world, not by forsaking their English character but by exploiting key virtues to the utmost: discipline and organization, the sacrifice of individual needs to those of the team, a determination to overcome a better equipped enemy. Echoes of World War Two, most visibly in the recurrent comparison of the victory celebrations with VE day, were not entirely inappropriate, for the team was seen to symbolize English virtues which had purchase outside a mere game. As the *Times* had noted a decade earlier: 'the ordinary man finds the form of our professional footballers a more convenient indication of the state of the nation than all the economist's soundings'.

Of course, in the thirteen years between these two footballing events, the Suez Crisis had occurred and 'winds of change' had blown. Britain's colonies in Africa and the Caribbean gained independence, withdrawal from East of Suez was imminent, and Britain had already been vetoed from joining the European Economic Community – public signs of decay. A new global order had emerged, built around the Cold War, postcolonialism, and the spread of capitalism. The international British sports system remained intact symbolically, but thanks to the media, not government and empire.

In 1996, as the English soccer team prepared for a semi-final against its former adversary in war and now partner in Europe (once again on 'solid English soil') the *Daily Mirror* and *The Sun* tabloids competed in the patriotism stakes with continual war allusions, puns, and jokes about Germany (Maguire and Poulton, 1999). The *Mirror* placed the entire English team on its cover with lions' manes airbrushed around their heads, beneath the headline 'Pride of England', exhorting fans to SING THEM TO VICTORY with a free adaptation of the popular song (by Skinner et al.):

> Eleven lions in grey shirts
> Now we are dreaming,
> Tel's* boys are dead certs
> We'll send the Germans reeling
> It's coming home,
> It's coming home
> Football's coming home
>
> (*Tel refers to the England manager, Terry Venables)

Many academic sports and media analysts (such as Blain and O'Donnell, 1998) have noted that this nostalgic recreation of a half-remembered England (not unlike that of the 'lost America' symbolically found again in baseball films like *Field of Dreams* [Phil Alden Robinson, 1989; see Rowe, 1999]) is symptomatic of a conservative urge to ward off the foreign and the alien. Neil Blain and Raymond Boyle (1998: 369) point to the *Mirror's* 'Achtung! Surrender!' before England's match with Germany as an instance of the 'endless replay of the Second World War', while Ben Carrington (1998: 106) sees in the culture of English 'New Laddism' that enveloped much of Euro 96 not a 'harmless manifestation' of 'boys just having fun', but an attempt to 'redefine the limits of white English masculinity'. The home to which football is coming is being symbolically defended not only against an external threat, but also against the 'enemy within' – the Asian and Afro-Caribbean people who help make up the multicultural British nation, but who spoil the fantasy of a homogeneous national culture and history. The continued exclusion of South Asians from professional football, of course, marks the game as riven with bigotry, not to mention the treatment of black stars by fans and officials (Orakwue, 1999; Bains and Johal, 1999). While it would be misleading to lump together the circulation-driven jingoism of the British tabloid press with all manifestations of 'New Laddism' (with its ironic, tongue-in-cheek, *faux* working-class elements accompanied in places by more serious political interventions on subjects such as anti-racism) it is apparent that complex permutations of Englishness, class, and masculinity emerge in the light of systemic transformations to the nature of soccer both in Britain and beyond it.

The nation which claims a special foundational status in soccer has only won the sport's premier competition once in seventy years. England declined to enter the first three competitions, and took part for the first time only after the World Cup's post-war revival in 1950. The team failed to qualify for the men's World Cup finals in 1974, 1978, and 1994. The global development strategy of the game adopted by FIFA has seen organizational power and playing accomplishment (rarely, it seems, synchronized) spread out from its administrative base in Europe to Latin America (notably under the Presidency of the Brazilian Havelange, which lasted for almost three decades; he was succeeded by an apparatchik, the Swiss-German Sepp Blatter). Most recently, it has turned towards Africa and Asia (Tomlinson, 1986; Sugden and Tomlinson, 1998b). This trend is in step with England's decline as a football power – GGATaC has uneven effects.

The image of national homogeneity – itself a fiction, although one which can be suppressed through selection policies and de-emphasizing non-Anglo ethnic origins – has come under challenge with the emergence of black sportsmen and women in international teams and competitions. Before professional players from overseas started to populate English soccer, the children of post-war immigrants from the Caribbean began to make their mark on it. Cyril Regis, Laurie Cunningham, Viv Anderson, Garth Crooks, and others carved out notable national and/or international careers during the 1970s and 1980s. In the 1980s and 1990s, players such as John Barnes, Des Walker, Ian Wright, and Sol Campbell became regular members of the English national soccer team. In 1996 a black player, Paul Ince, was appointed captain of England. It should be observed, in the light of Clarke and Critcher's analysis of 'Englishness', that the qualities of bravery, determination, and patriotism ascribed to 'white' England were also those most frequently associated with Ince by the sports media. When England qualified for the 1998 World Cup finals in France after a drawn 'away' game with Italy, an agency report read:

> It was a particularly tough match, with plenty of harsh tackles and England captain Paul Ince finished literally bloodied but unbowed. He played both halves with a blood-spattered shirt, after an aerial collision with Demetrio Albertini, and ended up with a bandage around his head. Ince said: 'It's a great day for the English nation'. (Huggins and Balmer, 1997: 28)

Changes to the global ethnoscape precipitated by post-war labour shortages in Britain and recourse to the reserve army of labour from its Empire can be seen, two generations later, to have had a profound impact on its cultural division of labour and prevailing notions of British identity. Not only has this change made much more complex the imagery of 'Englishness', but it has also undermined the racial and ethnic stereotyping that Dave Hill describes as rife, for example, in the successful, Ulster-Protestant-dominated Liverpool team administration of the 1960s and 1970s:

> If the club's Orange foundations had never been flaunted or actively promoted, on the field of play the Protestant work ethic was alive and well: blood, sweat and discipline a plenty, with no unnecessary ritual – and, of course, home with the silverware year after year. Given the unyielding stereotype to which they were routinely compared, black players were assumed to be as suitable at Anfield [Liverpool's home ground] as a ham sandwich in a synagogue. They, like all those swarthy Continentals, were generally regarded in English football as flashy, superficial and untrustworthy. (1992: 271–72)

If such a perspective pervaded the administration and coaching of soccer, and could also be found in cruder form on the terraces of soccer grounds with routine booing and insulting of black players (throwing bananas onto the pitch) and the circulation of racist recruiting literature for neo-Fascist political organizations, then the emergence of players of colour in national and international soccer competitions represents a significant symbolic shift in national identity. Yet it would be a mistake to see such changes as the inevitable outcome of enlightened social policies. Instead, we suggest that this new cultural division of labour was created under circumstances where, through the media–sports–culture complex (Rowe, 1999; and see next chapter), the economic imperatives of team success and the political requirements of supra-state bloc consolidation combined to weaken strategies of exclusion and extend the concept of representativeness.

The size of the football market to the south and east has long been difficult to ignore for non-English inhabitants of the British Isles, just as followers of the Scottish national team – the 'Tartan Army' – seemed irresistibly drawn to the idea of England as the other (Giulianotti, 1991; Finn and Giulianotti, 1998). For much of the twentieth century, 'English soccer' was something of a misnomer, in at least one sense – many players in the professional leagues came from the 'home' countries. This large-scale importation of players from Scotland can be seen as a manifestation of colonialist power. Scotland's small, highly urbanized working-class population and correspondingly less wealthy soccer infrastructure supplied English soccer at many levels with relatively cheap labour, including players of world standing like Denis Law, Kenny Dalglish, and Alan Hansen. Wales and Ireland exported John Charles, Ron and Wyn Davies, Paddy Crerand, and George Best to the English league. Such contemporary notables as Ian Rush, Neville Southall, Mark Hughes, and Ryan Giggs came from Wales.

The balance of trade in soccer players was very one-sided until the 1980s and early 1990s, when former English captain Terry Butcher and mega-celebrity Paul Gascoigne (in the latter case via the Italian club Lazio Roma) transferred to leading Scottish club Glasgow Rangers. The magnetic pull of the English competition was not only economic in nature, but also cultural and ideological. It was widely felt in both England and Scotland that superstar Scots players like Charlie Nicholas or Steve Archibald – and later the likes of Gordon Strachan or Gary McAllister – could not claim to have 'arrived' until they had been more thoroughly tested in the English First Division and then the Premier League. This rather condescending attitude towards Scottish football neglected to recognize the tutelage that English players, coaches, and managers had received from their Scots counterparts and the ebbs and flows in the quality of the respective football competitions.

Scottish soccer was widely regarded in the 1960s and 1970s as more sophisticated than the English game. In 1967, Glasgow Celtic defeated Inter Milan to become the first British team to win the European Cup. The Lord Provost of Glasgow, John Johnston, was not slow to note the geopolitical significance of the victory as the United Kingdom sought to enter the European Economic Community: 'Like the rest of the city I am delighted. Celtic, the first British and non-Latin team to win the European Cup, have put Glasgow on the world map.... Celtic have beaten the central Government in that they have taken Britain into Europe' (quoted in Glasgow Celtic, 1999).

The widespread use of 'British' soccer talent in the 'English' game problematized the conceptual coherence of the latter. For example, Liverpool's Bill Shankly was a Scot who achieved great success in English and European competitions managing a team consisting of many Scottish compatriots. Yet the 'Britishness' of the Scots provided a cushion against overwhelming concerns that English soccer was being taken over from the outside, especially when team success secured lucrative crowds, sponsorship, and TV rights revenue. From the 1950s onwards there was also a modest 'export' of British and Irish players like Charles, Law, Jimmy Greaves, Kevin Keegan, Liam Brady, Gary Lineker, David Platt, Luther Blissett, Rush, and Gascoigne to continental Europe, especially the wealthy Serie A competition in Italy. Several were failures, their doughty but inflexible provincialism perhaps summed up by an ingenuous comment Rush offered about his time with Juventus: 'It was like playing in another country' (quoted in Kuper, 1998: 72). Aha.

The supply of sports labour was diversifying by the 1970s. Players from inside the EU and also from Australia (Craig Johnston) and Israel (Ronnie Rosenthal) were seeking and gaining British work permits. Changes in soccer's division of labour extended to include Riccardo Villa and Osvaldo Ardiles of Argentina, part of a tentative overseas 'advance guard' following the 1978 men's World Cup, to be followed in the 1980s and 1990s by Eric Cantona and David Ginola (France), Peter Schmeichel (Denmark), Jürgen Klinsmann (Germany), Mark Bosnich (Australia), Gianfranco Zola and Roberto Di Matteo (Italy), Juninho and Emerson (Brazil), Dennis Bergkamp and Mark Overmars (Holland), Celestine Babayaro (Nigeria), and John Harkes and Casey Keller from the US. The US saw a 336% increase in young people's participation in the sport between 1980 and 1995 (Black and Hebdige, 1999: 531), setting the preconditions for a significant contribution to this section of the NICL.

British clubs also began recruiting overseas managers (such as Arsène Wenger, under whom Arsenal achieved a rare League and Cup double in the 1997–98 season, Ruud Gullit, and Gérard Houillier, improbably at Liverpool) to coach local and imported players, so diversifying the executive ranks of its soccer petty bourgeoisie. The emergence of private ownership and the stock-market flotation of Tottenham Hotspur and Manchester United has further eroded the division of soccer by nations. In 1997, for example, the Italian club Lazio Roma sought a listing on the London stock exchange ('Lazio', 1997) – although it finally raised capital in its 'home country'. Five other Italian clubs and the entire German First Division were considering public offerings as the century ended (Croci and Ammirante, 1999: 500).

It is sometimes claimed that the cosmopolitan composition of teams leads to a footballing equivalent of the Tower of Babel. One journalist, for example, ascribed the weakness of Liverpool's defence to the difficulties of multinational, multicultural communication:

> The enduring strength of Arsenal's back five is that they have not only been together for a decade now, but are all English.
>
> The Liverpool five consisted of: Friedel, an American, Rigobert Song, from the Cameroon, Sammy Hyypia (Finland), Stephane Henchoz (Switzerland), and Steve Staunton (Republic of Ireland). Even before they conceded the goals they had looked vulnerable to crosses, their weakness for so long. (Clarke, 1999)

But the next year, Liverpool's continental defence was masterful. Resistance to the rise of cosmopolitanism in English soccer has prompted intemperate nationally protectionist outbursts, such as that by Butcher in the tabloid *Daily Mirror*. Just as Ince had spilt blood for the England cause, Butcher had also famously played through a match bleeding copiously from a head wound. Alongside a colour photograph of the bleeding interviewee was the headline 'Where Have All the Bloody English Heroes Gone? Our game will end up starved of home talent just like the Scots Says Terry Butcher' (Cross, 1999: 54–55). Beneath a list of 'Premiership foreigners 1998/99 season' and a series of pie charts revealing that the number of foreign players in the English Premier League is, in fact, smaller than most major European equivalents, the article opens with the statement that:

> THE MAN who gave blood for England on the battlefields of Europe, now feels the country's football future is haemorrhaging fast. Under the bandages and the badge of the three lions, few hearts beat more fervently for his nation's cause than Terry Butcher's. (Cross, 1999: 55)

Butcher also called for the reintroduction of foreign (that is, non-English) player quotas. This resurgent emphasis on 'blood, sweat and fear' (1999: 54) in defence of sporting nationhood (a patriotic mood strong enough even to stir the 'soft Left' government of Tony Blair to expend £60 million of lottery money in employing 600 full-time sports coordinators to 'rekindle the "killer instinct" in [British] sport': Sylvester, 1999: 6), suggests a need for more than the symbolic reclamation of 'solid English soil'. It advocates, instead, an ambitious rolling back of multiculturalism, and restrictions on internal trade-bloc labour movement.

Corporate Soccer Bodies

This was one of several dramatic transformations in soccer in the 1990s. Two others were caused by political and juridical change. First, the revolutions of 1989 overturned the state-socialist sports system in Eastern and Central Europe. ANNICL was very quickly established, destroying the club and national teams that state-socialist systems had built up over decades. Within two years, Torpedo Moscow, for example, had sold 23 players to Western clubs because the top talent was desperate to leave in search of higher pay and quality of life. Home sides were left with cash balances to pay inflated wages to second-raters (Kuper, 1998: 38). Second, Belgian midfielder Jean-Marc Bosman appealed to the European Court of Justice against his suspension by the Union Royale Belge des Sociétés de Football for seeking an overseas transfer. The right to freedom of movement for EU workers saw the Court decide in his favour in 1995. It determined that European soccer's restriction on foreign players constituted restraint of trade. The Bosman decision over freedom of labour within the EU has prevented the imposition of quotas on foreign players. The only formal barrier to labour-market entry is now the immigration authorities' power of decision over whether players from outside the EU have sufficiently scarce and demonstrable skills to merit a work permit. Even these rules can be circumvented through the accelerated awarding of dual citizenship and the use of European 'nurseries' to 'assimilate' young players prior to their formal entry into the football labour market (Greenfield and Osborn, 1998).

The essence of the decision was that soccer was a business like any other – as maintained by Bosman. The Union des Associations de Football (UEFA) had argued that true economic competition was impossible and undesirable, since the very viability of soccer rested on an ongoing number of equivalently strong clubs. This does not mean that the Court of Justice rejected the notion that soccer has non-economic, cultural aspects. It *does* mean that the Court is suspicious of this claim without supporting evidence that such aspects are not a cloak for economic gain via anti-competitive conduct (Beloff et al., 1999: 69).

Even as élite players celebrated this freedom, many also felt that they lacked a sufficiently powerful union to counter the continental and global organizational power of employers and administrators (Redhead, 1997: 27–28, 95; Closson, 1998). Facing the threat of fines from the European Commission, in 1996 UEFA discontinued rules restricting the number of foreigners who could play in national competitions (Ayoub, 1999: 1091). Within a few months, cross-European player mobility had increased dramatically, as the talent gap between wealthy teams and also-rans developed. Wage relativities between workers were unsettled, with top performers able to command unheard-of salaries and leading clubs getting rid of their youth teams (Giulianotti, 1999: 122–23). Widespread anxiety was expressed that clubs would buy teams rather than develop them, while the EU seemed to stick to its view that soccer was a commodity like any other. Rules of competition applied to the sport, and its players were workers like any others, with the right to work for whom they pleased. Meanwhile, Bosman's agent, Jean-Louis Dupont, broke new ground in 1999 when he sought freedom for players to leave clubs with two months' notice, regardless of their contracts – a true end to feudalism, as this would prevent teams from charging slave-like transfer fees (whose excuse is compensation for having developed players). The claim was a double-edged implement for workers, as it would also allow *clubs* to break contracts in the event of injuries or loss of form, and it decimated league competitions in poor nations such as Portugal (Ayoub, 1999: 1106; 'Dupont Victory', 1999; Croci and Ammirante, 1999: 502). The Bosman culture–commerce dilemma neatly summarizes one of the key debates about Europe more generally. Is unification a testament to the Enlightenment, to democracy, and human rights? Or is it a convenience for the Bundesbank to dismantle social welfare, via the Maastricht Treaty's insistence that member-states cut their budget deficits to 3% annually (Benhabib, 1999: 714)?

Late in 1999, the European Commissioner for Education and Culture, Viviane Reding, met with FIFA and UEFA to discuss these issues. The Associations stressed that soccer was principally of 'educational value' and needed to 'collude' (in neoclassical economic terminology) in order to keep the game viable. For these reasons, the sport should be exempt from competition law. The European Council acknowledged that soccer was important as a device 'safeguarding current sports structures and maintaining the social function of sport'. As such, it seemed likely that sport would be treated *sui generis* (as a case of its own kind) in Euro-law, with monopolies justified in terms of social cohesion (Ayoub, 1999: 1107–108; 'European Union', 1999; 'FIFA and UEFA', 1999; also see Chapter 4).

Today's unprecedented fluidity of identities, personnel, and boundaries is queried not just among officials, journalists, and football fans, but by some professional footballers and their representative organizations. When the British government streamlined the allocation of work permits to non-European residents, there were protests from its local Professional Footballers' Association (PFA). The PFA's Chief Executive, Gordon Taylor, stated: 'We are amazed and disappointed at the government's new rules. This will lead to more not less foreigners coming into British football and will open the way for cheap, foreign imports' (quoted in Chaudhary, 1999: 7). Brendan Batson, Deputy Chief Executive of the PFA, pointed to a linkage between labour mobility, the destruction of orderly career paths for English (and other European) footballers, and the erosion of national teams:

> Football should have a united front to say that we need to protect our domestic talent, not just in England, but all over Europe.... We have got a very exciting Premiership and the overseas players have contributed an important part in that.... But there is a heavy emphasis now on just a few clubs producing players for the England team and that is not good. (quoted in 'Batson Calls', 1999: 24)

The suggested reintroduction of quotas by European clubs is a response, as Richard Giulianotti (1999: 123) notes, to a régime of 'flexible accumulation', which involves the 'top clubs ... hiring players for one or two years to do specific jobs without the need to offer long-term security'. At the same time, clubs have used Bosman as an excuse to introduce a salary cap, a clear restraint on players' ability to sell their labour freely (Taylor, 2000: 48).

The quantifiable impact of the Bosman ruling is very difficult to establish, given the lack of research on the effects of the previous transfer system and the already discernible, long-term economic trends in football. While the decision has been accused of exacerbating the inequalities between clubs, H.F. Moorhouse (1999: 91) counsels 'extreme scepticism about attempts to justify any transfer system in soccer by a reference to its supposed functions of sustaining smaller clubs and rewarding talent development'. Yet accountancy firms like Deloitte Touche produce statistics about the growing disparity of wealth between the English Premier League and the lower leagues, including a 40% increase in player salaries in the Premier League in a single season (1998), attributing the cause to Bosman and the 'influx into the league of overseas players' ('Payments', 1999: 109).

One representative body of the likely beneficiaries of 'labour import dumping', the English League Managers' Association, is perturbed, with its Deputy Chairman Frank Clark stating: 'We are still hoping that the government will do more. As an organization we are very concerned about the number of foreign players currently in the British game. Ideally we would like to see a quota introduced but we realize that it is difficult given European regulations' (quoted in Chaudhary, 1999). The reasons for this protectionism among those who help select and manage Britain's soccer labour force are no doubt complex – the difficulty of team-building when there is a high level of labour turnover; pressures from the Board and shareholders to buy cheaply overseas; perhaps even the problem of learning foreign languages. No doubt labour-market competition with foreign managers is also an issue – in the 1998–99 season, for example, only one club managed by an English national reached the quarter-finals of the FA Cup. It is also reminiscent of the 'Little Englander' remarks we associate with British xenophobia. When famed manager Brian Clough learnt that Third World countries would gain one nation–one vote status in FIFA, he enjoined like-minded folk to revolt against 'a bunch of spear-throwers who want to dictate our role in football' (quoted in Kuper, 1998: 108).

For Giulianotti, Bosman brought 'the free-market benefits of higher income and the potential for international mobility, and the growing awareness that football celebrity has its own pitfalls' (1999: 124). Of course, the search for labour internationalized without Bosman. Africa, long expected to provide a World Cup winner, saw Nigeria and Cameroon qualify for the 1998 Finals – without a single Nigerian player based in Africa, and very few Cameroonians (Solaja, 1999: 26). The Cameroon team that won the Sydney 2000 Olympics football gold medal from Spain included several overseas-based players, including Real Madrid's Eto'o Fils. And while African nations have made it to the Finals of every FIFA junior championship, the senior teams have been unable to follow suit. Since Ghana won the initial under-17 event in 1991, that country alone has transferred over 150 young players overseas (Aggrey, 1999: 33).

This 'infiltration of unfettered market forces into sporting culture (especially soccer)' (Redhead, 1997: 27) has diversified the ranks of 'celebrities with problems'. While not an entirely new phenomenon (we need only think of iconic bad boy George Best in the 1960s and 1970s) new possibilities for pre- and post-retirement fame and infamy are presented by the accelerated circulation of soccer players as commodity signs. The strange case of Didier Baptiste is indicative of this post-modern turn in soccer. A fictional character in a BSkyB TV soccer soap opera called *Dream Team*, he was the subject of a hoax announcement in November 1999 that he was transferring to Liverpool. The news was treated seriously by club officials, then picked up and embellished by *The Times* newspaper ('Dream', 1999: 120). This bizarre blurring of the real and the fictive in the context of transnational soccer labour migration is symptomatic of the uncertainties – and sometimes absurdities – of the NICL. We turn now to the deterritorialization of a second sport – hockey.

The De-Canadianization of Hockey

> To spectator and player alike, hockey gives the release that strong liquor gives to a repressed man. It is the counterpoint of the Canadian self-restraint, it takes us back to the fiery blood of Gallic and Celtic ancestors who found themselves minorities in a cold, new environment and had to discipline themselves as all minorities must. But Canadians take the ferocity of their game so much for granted that when an American visitor makes polite mention of it, they look at him in astonishment. Hockey violent? Well, perhaps it is a little. But hockey was always like that. (novelist Hugh MacLennan, quoted in Frayne, 1990: 179)

> If you can't beat 'em outside in the alley, you won't beat 'em inside on the ice. (popular Canadian hockey adage coined by founding owner of the Toronto Maple Leafs, Conn Smythe)

> As much a national symbol in Canada as the maple leaf and the beaver. (journalist Eric Brady's description of Wayne Gretzky, arguably the greatest player in hockey history)

Although five northern European nations established the International Ice Hockey Federation (IIHF) in 1908, and incipient versions of modern hockey developed more or less concurrently in northern Europe, the northern US, and Canada during the late nineteenth century, the latter country has traditionally been considered as hockey's birthplace and the exemplary exponent of the sport. As the above quotations suggest, Canada's harsh, wintry climate, and the aggressive reputation of its players have meant that hockey has often been constructed as a symbol of Canadianness, in a decidedly masculine vein (Avery and Stevens, 1997; Belanger, 1999; Etue and Williams, 1996; Gruneau and Whitson, 1993; Theberge, 1997). Barthes regarded ice hockey as the national sport *par excellence*, in that it represented the transformation of 'the immobility of winter, the hardness of the earth and the suspension of normal life into a buoyant, vigorous and passionate sport' that was distinctively Canadian in connotation (1997: 81). In a country that has always been divided by strong ethnic and regional identities, hockey has frequently been hailed as the one arena in which Canadians transcend their differences by fiercely contesting for supremacy.

Like most modern Canadian sports, hockey became institutionalized during the late nineteenth and early twentieth centuries as part of interconnected demographic, social, cultural, political, and economic changes (Gruneau, 1999; Ingham and Beamish, 1993; Gruneau and Whitson, 1993). Although the traditional folk games from which modern hockey developed were still being played on makeshift outdoor surfaces in both urban and rural settings at the turn of the century, the sport had also commercialized and rationalized, with increasing competition for the best markets. Professional teams were formed before the First World War, with those in the major cities gradually squeezing out local and regional competitors because they could afford to build large indoor arenas and attract the best talent. The NHL, which was founded in 1917, eventually became the most prestigious competition in the world.

Originally all-Canadian, the League expanded into the north-eastern US in the 1920s. After some minor changes, between 1942 and 1967 the NHL consisted of two teams in Canada (Montréal and Toronto) and four in the US (Boston, Chicago, Detroit, and New York). The combination of monopolistic and monopsonistic practices and an intransigent anti-union stance meant that for decades a handful of autocratic millionaires – and the servile NHL presidents they appointed – ran the professional hockey market and its junior feeder system in North America as a virtual cartel. Until the NHL Players Association was established in the 1960s and the World Hockey Association (WHA) appeared in the 1970s to offer unprecedented salaries, NHL owners practically dictated how all players were drafted, traded, released, and remunerated (the WHA threat was eventually repelled via a merger). Although there were grumblings as early as the 1920s about the influence of the US on 'Canada's game', the fact that nearly every player and coach in the NHL was a Canadian soothed the discontented (Gruneau and Whitson, 1993: 99–100). When the NHL doubled in size in 1967 and awarded all six new franchises to US cities in order to tap into profitable live and TV markets, Canadians still had several reasons to be secure about their supremacy in the sport.

At first, the Montréal Canadiens and the Toronto Maple Leafs dominated competition. Between 1945 and 1969, Montréal won the league championship trophy, the Stanley Cup, on 11 occasions, including a still unmatched five consecutive victories in the 1950s and Toronto won it nine times, including three straight titles in the 1960s. The Canadian teams' ascendancy was facilitated by feudal NHL rules that operated until the 1960s. One regulation allowed all teams the automatic rights to any junior player within a 50-mile radius, which was irrelevant to the American clubs, but gave Montréal and Toronto effective monopolies over the two largest hockey-playing cities in the world. Until 1969, Montréal was also permitted to select the first two draft choices each year from the powerful junior league in its home province of Québec, which contains the vast majority of Canadian Francophones (about 25% of the population). These two rules, along with shrewd management and coaching personnel and an efficient feeder system, principally of Francophone players, enabled Montréal to win more Stanley Cups than any other team in the NHL, and earned it a reputation similar to that of other professional dynasties in North America (such as baseball's New York Yankees and basketball's Boston Celtics).

Although the IIHF and Olympic competitions never had the same stature as the NHL, Canadians took pride in the fact that, until the 1950s, their men's teams had either won or been placed highly in these contests simply by sending amateur teams (championships for women sanctioned by the IIHF and the IOC did not begin until 1990 and 1998 respectively). Finally, media coverage in Canada assured audiences that hockey 'belonged' to them. As Richard Gruneau and David Whitson (1993) point out, the publicly funded Canadian Broadcasting Corporation (CBC), an important custodian of national identity, was fundamental in this respect. CBC radio and TV broadcasts of *Hockey Night in Canada* developed into home-based spectator rituals. Male hosts, presenters, and actors who appeared in accompanying advertisements became popular icons.

This hockey hegemony did not remain uncontested. Canada's dominance in IIHF and Olympic circles was first challenged in the 1950s, when Soviet-bloc countries began to base their national sports development programmes on rigorous recruitment and training regimens. Some spectacular advances flowed from this new system, and the USSR won many Olympic and IIHF championships in the post-war era. Yet most Canadians never considered these international competitions to be a case of 'our best against their best', because Canada was sending amateurs to compete against so-called 'shamateurs' (professionals pretending to be amateurs through the connivance of the Soviet state). The real benchmark for Canadians was the NHL, which except for a rare American or European player was dominated by Canadian nationals.

Canada finally got the chance to assert its supremacy over the Soviets in 1972, when its best NHL players (under controversial circumstances all WHA players were excluded, despite entreaties to the organizers by the Prime Minister) competed for the first time against the USSR in a long-awaited eight-game encounter that lasted almost the entire month of September. The event was hyped in the Canadian media with terms like 'summit series', 'war on ice', and 'Cold war' (MacSkimming, 1996; Morrison, 1992). Prior to the arrival of the Soviets for the first four games in Canada, some Canadian pundits were predicting an eight-game 'sweep', believing that the 'Russian robots', with their antiquated equipment, would not stand a chance against the innate superiority, individual brilliance, and aggression of their hosts. However, the USSR stunned the Canadian players, coaches, and fans by compiling two victories, a draw, and only one loss in the first leg of the series. After losing the first game in the USSR, Team Canada faced the seemingly impossible task of winning the three remaining contests in order to secure the series. However, the Canadians won the next two games by one-goal margins, setting up a decisive eighth match. With the majority of Canada's population following the game via radio or TV, Team Canada rallied from a two-goal deficit in the final period and scored a dramatic, series-winning goal with under a minute left.

The victory precipitated an unprecedented orgy of patriotism and inscribed the event as an indelible signifier of Canadian nationhood. For instance, the Premier of the province of British Columbia proclaimed: 'the French couldn't do it, the Germans couldn't do it; now Canada has done it [i.e., conquer Moscow] and they had better get out of town before it starts snowing' (Earle, 1995: 127). The chief Canadian organizer of the series, Alan Eagleson, who was lionized for his boorish nationalistic behaviour in Moscow, enunciated the prevailing myth that the victory was attributable to unity in a multicultural nation (in a manner that presaged the celebration of the 'rainbow' men's World Cup winning French soccer team of 1998):

> Our team was made up of a cross-section of the Canadian ethnic mosaic. Team Canada was composed of players who were French Canadians, Ukrainian Canadians, Polish Canadians, German Canadians, Italian Canadians and other first-generation Canadians. We also had representatives of third- and fourth-generation Canadians. The mixture of our backgrounds was an important ingredient in the success of our team. (quoted in Morrison, 1992: 12–13)

Instead of seeing the narrow victory as a lucky escape and ominous harbinger, many Canadians regarded the outcome as proof of their inherent sporting and national superiority. The prevailing smugness was probably best encapsulated by the comments of folk hero Paul Henderson, who scored game-winning goals in the last three contests:

> Until I scored that [final] goal, I didn't know the difference between democracy and communism.... For me, by going to Russia, you learned to appreciate what you have as Canadians. People want to talk about socialism. Well, go over there and you'll realize what a great country we have. You learn to appreciate it. You hear all these minority groups going on all the time – well, I'd like to see them over there. We've got rights, and they've got the right to shut up about our country. (quoted in Morrison, 1992: 196, 202)

If Canadian hockey had symbolically repelled the Communist threat in the early 1970s, by the 1990s it paradoxically faced the challenge of how to prevent 'Canada's game' from being dominated by players from ex-Soviet countries, the US, and northern Europe. Moreover, Canadians also had to confront the question that has haunted their popular culture in general: how much longer could hockey credibly represent national distinctiveness in the face of escalating US control?

Since 1972, Americanization and globalization have seriously undermined the mythical nation-building functions of hockey in Canada. Although Montréal and expansion teams in Edmonton and Calgary captured the Stanley Cup many times in the 1970s, 1980s, and 1990s, no Canadian team won it between 1993 and the end of the century. By that time, the once omnipotent Canadiens were one of the worst teams in the NHL, even offering two tickets to a game for the price of one (Hackel, 1999). Since Toronto won the Stanley Cup in 1967, it has been one of the NHL's most mediocre clubs, and its recent return to form can be largely attributed to skilful European and Russian imports. While Canada ignored many valuable lessons that it could have learned from the series with the USSR, the Soviet bloc, as well as the Americans and Europeans, gained a great deal of knowledge which they subsequently used to elevate the calibre of their play. In 1980, a team of American college players took the Olympic gold medal; in 1994 Sweden won the Olympic gold medal; in 1995 Finland won the world championship, followed by the Czech Republic in 1996; at the inaugural 1996 World Cup of Hockey tournament, Canada's best professionals won only one of four games against the underdog and eventual gold medal winner, Team USA; and although Canada's NHL players were allowed to compete at the Olympic Games for the first time in 1998, they proceeded to lose a gold-medal qualifying game to the Czech Republic and were then defeated by lowly regarded Finland in the bronze-medal match.

Although a number of internal factors certainly account for Canada's decline in international men's hockey circles, no explanation is complete without considering the supranational forces that have irrevocably reconfigured the 'natural' correspondence between hockey and Canadianness. First, the collapse of the Soviet bloc drained many of its star athletes from hockey, soccer, basketball, tennis, and track and field to the West. This exodus was facilitated by the search for new talent by NHL agents and scouts, who looked beyond the traditional borders of Canada and began vigorously recruiting American, Czech, Finnish, Russian, Slovak, and Swedish players. Consequently, since the 1970s, the proportion of Canadians in the NHL has shrunk from almost 100% to around 60%. In recent years, Europeans and Russians, in particular, have become scoring leaders, members of all-star teams, and winners of prestigious individual awards. We return to hockey's transformation in Chapter 3.

How Nike 'Just Does It'

The globalization of labour applies as much to equipment as to play. Beyond the élite level of cosmopolitan footballers and hockey players lies a more sinister division of labour. The *Washington Post* dubs Nike the *ur*-text of globalization (LaFeber, 1999: 102). One of the most recognizable brand names in the world, Nike's corporate slogan – 'Just do it' – has become a maxim in both public and private life, and the swoosh logo is ubiquitous. Many people reading this book probably own running shoes, shorts, T-shirts, bras, or baseball caps sporting the Nike logo. According to Robert Goldman and Stephen Papson (1998), the company's spectacular success as a *commodity sign* is partially attributable to its advertising images of sporting bodies. These articulate a 'metacommunicative aesthetic' of irreverence and inspiration, integrating themes of authenticity, realism, personal transcendence, hard work, achievement, discipline, and individual will-power. By using anti-authoritarian pop icons like William Burroughs and Dennis Hopper, Nike has positioned itself as a rebellious, maverick business. Nike's ads are also sensitive to the sensibilities of specific sports – what works for viewers of pro football may repulse skateboarders (Frank, 1999). The firm differentiates itself from competitors by constructing a sense of hyperauthenticity in a world of standardized consumer goods. Like the line from the old Coca-Cola ad, Nike conveys the impression that it is 'the real thing'. Yet the ironic, cynical, and self-parodying mode of address also signifies that Nike does not take itself too seriously. Finally, and perhaps most importantly, the ads invite 'hip, savvy, and media literate' readers to make intertextual links betweeen advertising montages (Goldman and Papson, 1998: 27).

Sporting bodies are at the centre of Nike's commercials, which feature both male and female athletes (although the latter are much less prominent than the former) from varied generational, ethnic, racial, and national backgrounds (Wilson, 1997). Nike features 'the good' (Gretzky, Cathy Freeman and Mia Hamm) 'the bad' (Jimmy Connors), and 'the ugly' (John McEnroe and Charles Barkley). Such promotions are an everyday reminder that the American Dream is alive and well, irrespective of age, social class, gender, ethnicity, race, or bodily ability. However, these representations of sporting bodies also contain several tensions. For instance, Nike emphasizes self-empowerment and achievement via mental and physical effort with slogans like 'Just do it', 'There is no finish line', and 'You don't win silver – you lose gold'. This individualism rests on 'conformity of consumption preferences' and the 'globalization of commodity culture' (Goldman and Papson, 1998: 2, 4). It is difficult to sustain an ideology of individualism (and authenticity) when billions of people wear apparel made by Nike, Reebok, Puma, LA Gear, Converse, Fila, Adidas, Asics, New Balance – all of which are very similar. And despite Nike's accent on rebelliousness, its clients use 'logo police' (Goldman and Papson, 1998: 18) to ensure that the athletes and teams it sponsors display the swoosh – non-conformists are fined. In this case, the athletes' bodies are disciplined as commodities. At the 1999 Australian Open of Tennis, Nike planted a group of male university students in the stands in order to 'support' Mary Pierce, one of its high-profile clients; the fans gained global media coverage by donning blond wigs and wearing bright yellow dresses, which were imitations of the latest Nike line that the blonde Pierce was wearing (CNN/Reuters, 1999). Here, the bodies of the fans were disciplined as promoters of a brand-name product. Nike has also engaged in 'ambush marketing' (e.g., displaying advertisements adjacent to those of rival corporations that have signed official agreements for exclusive sponsorship rights to events).

Nike and other companies usually feature stars, who allegedly play for idealistic purposes rather than crass commercial motives ('I Love This Game'), and 'deserve' emulation ('Be Like Mike'; 'I am Tiger Woods'). But these celebrities are serving their own material ends via endorsement and sponsorship deals. Moreover, the number of sportsmen convicted for a wide range of crimes casts doubt on the plausibility of sports stars as figures that ought to be admired and imitated. Such ads frequently use black athletes, but they do not mention the enormous economic chasm between black and white Americans, or that the overwhelming majority of blacks (and whites) will never make a career out of sport. Nike ads ironically criticize the capitalist system for commercializing sport, while simultaneously contributing to this very process, right down to the grassroots level. Nike commercials also carry messages about female empowerment (Cole and Hribar, 1995; Dworkin and Messner, 1999; Lafrance, 1998). But the company derives its profits from exploiting labour forces composed predominantly of women and children from the Third World.

Nike's founder and CEO, Phil Knight, says: 'What we are all about is being against the establishment' (quoted in Egan, 1998: 69). He has also stated that '[a]ccess to play should be a kid's inalienable right'. But 7,000 Pakistani children get 6 cents an hour for making Nike soccer balls. Does this mean the 'establishment' is adult labour and 'access' is to a workbench? The situation in Pakistan became the focal point for the International Labour Organization (ILO) in the mid-1990s, as this controversy gained added light and heat. Along with UNICEF and the Sialkot Chamber of Commerce, the ILO signed an agreement in 1997 to eliminate child labour in the soccer-ball industry; but two years later, little had been achieved. Needless to say, such child labour is legal under the rules of the WTO (Nader, 1999: 9).

The contradiction of Nike being Goliath while trying to 'appear like David' (Goldman and Papson, 1998: 45) becomes especially glaring when we switch from sweaty, inspirational sporting bodies in Nike ads to sweatshop bodies that produce Nike's sportswear. Originally based in New Hampshire in 1974, Nike expanded to Maine in 1978, but shut its American plants in the 1980s to manufacture in countries with appalling records regarding industrial pollution, human rights abuse, working conditions, wages, and industrial accidents and illnesses (Sage, 1994). The firm has gone from (a) a US distributor of Japanese and manufacturer of American shoes; through (b) an off-shore manufacturer in Taiwan, the People's Republic of China, and Korea for shoes sold in the US; to (c) a company with vast international sales, half a million workers in Vietnam, Pakistan, Indonesia, Thailand, and earlier South-East Asian locales earning under $1.50 a day/12–14 hours a day/seven days a week (20 cents an hour in Vietnam), and a website that works like a TV network (Harvey et al., 1996: 265; McMichael, 1996: 3; Egan, 1998: 67; Ayoub, 1999: 409; LaFeber, 1999: 145).

Nike's top-line shoes contain over 200 components. These are produced in five countries, passing through more than 100 pairs of hands during production. Nike is the most profitable multinational corporation of its kind, grossing over US$9 billion in sales in 1997 (Goldman and Papson, 1998: 4). This is a model 'hollowed corporation', with production strictly a subcontracting task. The firm's official description of its business to government regulators makes no mention of shoe or apparel production – a manufacturing company *that doesn't make anything*. It simply manages, promotes, and distributes signs. Multiplying these signs into multifarious niches is crucial to the strategy, so Nike sells 1,200 models of shoes in 3,000 styles and colours – all of which are essentially identical, and frequently made by the same people who are manufacturing products for the firm's competitors Adidas, Puma, LA Gear, New Balance, and Reebok. Nike has successfully exported consumption, too. Non-US receipts from footwear and clothing grew from 27% to 37% of total revenues in the decade to 1997 (Goldman and Papson, 1998: 4–9). In the process, the company instantiated a global, gendered division of labour based on shibboleths of female docility and 'nimble fingers'. Unsurprisingly, Nike left Korea when women workers there organized (Peterson, 1996: 10; Enloe, 1995: 12). Throughout, it has sought to stem a backlash at home by encouraging US runners to see themselves as consumers rather than citizens (Barber, 1998: 34).

We noted international outrage over Nike's sweatshop conditions for workers. Nike's exploitation of about half a million mainly female labourers, who work in sweatshop conditions and are sexually abused and harassed while earning wages we have already spotlighted, has led to a proliferation of social movements protesting about its abuse of human rights and boycotts of its products (Sage, 1999; Ayoub, 1999: 409). Indonesia's INGI Labour Working Group has accused Nike-licensed factories of breaking 12 national laws, violating several basic human rights, breaching American law by buying products that are manufactured in contravention of laws on workers' rights, and damaging local and national development. It is a perversely postmodern irony that a First-World company exploits workers in the Third World, while deploying images of black men to embody freedom and individualism. The firm's 1997 annual report boasted: 'The "swooshification of the world" should more appropriately be deemed the Sportsification of the world.... We will mature in tandem with the inexorable penetration of sports into the global psyche.' But that hubris came only a matter of months before its profit declined by 49% and stock dropped by 50% (Egan, 1998: 67). Worker solidarity and the collapse of South-East Asian spending power had militated against the company (LaFeber, 1999: 150). As the century ended, workers stoned a factory in Indonesia that manufactured Nike goods.

Coda

We have shown how the hegemonic male sporting body of the Victorian era was decentred by decolonization, commodification, and migration. This global exchange of sporting bodies has made it increasingly difficult for the nation-state to be represented by conventional corporeal symbols, as the spread of schooling, commodification, scientization, medicalization, and surveillance as part of the NICL has reorganized sporting bodies. Bourdieu emphasizes that the champion athlete 'is only the obvious subject of a spectacle that in some sense is produced twice' – as a body *competing* in physical space, and as a body *represented* in virtual space (1998: 81). This is a shift from sport as a practice, to sport as a spectacle, to sport as a commodified spectacle, and then a televisual one (Bourdieu, 1999: 16). We turn our attention next to that mediated body.

3

Sports Media *sans* Frontières

God wore number 23. (*De Morgen*, Belgium)
The 'Michelangelo' of sport shoes will not return. (*Faz*, Germany)
His royal Airness will never fly again. (*Telegraaf*, The Netherlands)
God is going home. (*Yedioth Ahrnonoth*, Israel)
[B]asketball is alone. (*La Repubblica*, Italy)
The King is Leaving. (*Sport*, Spain)
Earthquake. (*El Mundo Deportivo*, Spain)
A myth that has gone beyond sports. (*El Periodico*, Spain)
Tell us it is not true. (*El Pais*, Spain)
[H]e's the greatest. (*Herald Sun*, Australia)
King Mike Abdicates. (*Age*, Australia)
God will never fly again. (*Asahi Shimbun*, Japan)
God finally to retire. (*Tochu Sports*, Jordan)
[His] name is engraved on the heart of everyone. (*Beijing Morning Post*, China)
Año Uno D. De J. [Year One After Jordan]. (*Ole*, Argentina) (quoted in 'The World Bids', 1999)

These responses to Michael Jordan's retirement testify to three things – his exceptional athletic ability, the success of Nike worldwide, and the spread of the NBA across TV screens: *Rafaga NBA* in Mexico, *La Magia de la NBA* in Argentina, *Give Me Five* in Belgium, *NBA Mania* in Japan, *NBA Jam* in Taiwan, and *Zou Jin* in the PRC (Andrews, 1999: 508). Just as Nike and the NBA built their strategies for growth around Jordan, so his career can only be understood in terms of those institutions. While this is perhaps the most spectacular instance of the media–sports link, TV in particular is inseparable from global sport, as both a marker of globalization and one of its prime movers.

IOC official history marks the Olympics in terms of broadcast revenues – a total of US$1.25 billion for the 2000 and 2002 Games – and their status as 'a social, even sociological event, which more or less reflects the state of the world' (Macleod, 1996: 23; Verdier, 1996: 34). This sense of sport standing for more than itself, always both representing and being represented, has a pre-commercial heritage. In its nascent medieval form, and as it matured in the moment of early modernity, sport was above all a local cultural pursuit, linked first to the 'rough play' of mainly young men in the festival seasons and later through more formal, regular contests between settlements in particular regions (Elias, 1986). While never disappearing entirely, local sport has progressively given way to regulated professional competitions organized on national and international lines. The forces that, above all others, have transported sport from local pitches to the global stage are the mass (and especially electronic) media (Cunningham and Miller, 1994; Rowe, 1996). If a professionally-based economy of sport was first established by the enclosure of sports grounds and charging for attendance at matches against visiting teams, then the capacity to carry sports action, advertising, and promotional messages enabled that economy to take on first a national and then an inter- and transnational character, as the game was transformed from a practice to a spectacle (Bourdieu, 1999: 16).

In this chapter we examine how contemporary sport articulates with advertising, promotion, and commodification as it connects, disconnects, and reconnects collective experiences of space and time within and between nation-states. We are concerned with how local, regional, and national cultures are projected by the sports media into the domain of the global and, in turn, how the reception of globally mediated sport affects those levels of culture. We have selected five sporting cases – black athletic protest, British (especially English) soccer, Canadian ice hockey, Australian rugby league, and women's tennis – to demonstrate how certain contemporary sports seek to accommodate, mediate, or resist globalizing pressures according to their specific histories and geographies, institutional frameworks, and structures of culture. Each site shows the influence of television and enduring and shifting patterns of identification.

Mediated Sports Cultures

Sports reporting in the print and electronic media is deeply reliant on imaging the body. Still photography provides a sense of 'having-been-there' (Barthes, 1977), often through minute attention to the bodies of athletes. Photographic presentations of sporting bodies are largely limited to rigorous motion (during competition) and inertia (for example, at a medal ceremony). The latter image carries most efficiently the idea of the nation. For many spectators, the medal ceremony at major international events like the summer Olympic Games epitomizes national identification and affect. Such rituals are tableaux of bodily dispositions. The athletes, their bodies draped in the colours and insignia of nation and corporation, are led to the ceremony by a functionary. The different heights of the blocks on which they stand spatially signify hierarchy. They bend to receive their medals as in a military service, then turn their gaze to their national flags, also hierarchically arranged, while the national anthem of the winning athlete/team reinforces visual supremacy with aural presence. Apart from flags fluttering in the breeze, the moment is still. At this point, athletes frequently cry – moved perhaps by a sense of individual and, heavily imputed by television and radio commentary, national achievement and responsibility. The stately nature of the ceremony demands that spectators and viewers be serious. It is not unusual for patriotic viewers at home to stand for their national anthem, disciplined, as Foucault (1977) argues, most effectively not by external repression but through externally induced and internally accepted discourses of the social self. If tears well up in their eyes, this discourse of nation has become powerful enough to produce involuntary physiological responses in those subject to it.

National mythologies prosper when internal fissures – class, gender, race, ethnicity, locality, age, sexuality, and so on – are submerged. The risk of displaying differences and divisions to a global audience, rather than asserting the existence of a unified nation, makes the medal ceremony and other less formal aspects of major sporting events subject to strict official control over communication in all its forms – verbal and non-verbal, abstract, and corporeal. Athletes are pressured by national sports committees and media organizations (especially those who have paid for privileged access to them) not to be controversial about issues 'back home' – to preserve the illusion of the united nation for the duration of the event. The IOC, state-licensed and -funded national sports bodies, and the sports market's lucrative sponsorship and endorsement contracts, are decisive in disciplining athletes. The sporting body's marketability is significantly, but not exclusively, influenced by its degree of political quiescence. Race, gender, and sexuality also have a substantial impact on its place in the international cultural economy of sport. We shall examine now the vast and complex infrastructure that is hidden behind these sports tableaux of winners and losers.

Modern sport and the media developed simultaneously and symbiotically, supplying each other with the necessary resources for development: capital, audiences, promotion, and content. The sports media emerged out of a need, first, for the reporting of sports information through the print media and, later, through presentation of sports events via the electronic media (Rowe, 1992a, 1992b; Rowe and Stevenson, 1995). In Britain and Australia, print sports journalism developed from notices about the time and place of forthcoming local sports events, match descriptions, results, and, rather quaintly, the hospitality (usually by 'the ladies') afforded to visiting players (Brown, 1996). As sport became increasingly professional and commodified, it did not disappear from the local print media, but became secondary – even in provincial newspapers – to national and international sport (Rowe, 1999). This progressive detachment of sport and place was first supplemented and then accelerated by radio and television. National public broadcasting organizations like the British Broadcasting Corporation (BBC), the Australian Broadcasting Commission (later renamed a Corporation) and the CBC used such major sporting occasions as the FA Cup Final, the Melbourne Cup horse race, and the Stanley Cup play-offs, to develop outside-broadcast techniques and to engage in state-sanctioned processes of nation-building (Gruneau and Whitson, 1993; Hargreaves, 1986; Haynes, 1999; Whannel, 1992). Once the nation could be reached through the public and commercial sports media (Wilson, 1998), its boundaries could be exceeded as those media carried the nation to distant and dispersed sports events, further building a sense of national identity by encouraging readers, listeners, and viewers to support their national representatives in international sporting competitions.

There has been a dramatic shift in the nature of world television over the past decades. It has been transformed from a comparatively scarce resource to a common one in most parts of the world, moving from a predominantly nation-based and state-run medium towards internationalism and privatization. The global fashion for neoliberalism has: (a) cut down cross-ownership regulations (encouraging capitalists to invest in various media); (b) reduced public-sector budgets (drawing labour, product development, and technological initiative to profit-centred services); (c) opened up terrestrial TV to international capital (undercutting local production); and (d) attacked the idea of public broadcasting as élitist (blurring distinctions between education and entertainment) and ineffici-ent (crowding out investment in the private sector).

Sport has been crucial to these recent developments. As the idea of a universal service that provides broad coverage of news and drama is displaced by all-entertainment networks, sport turns into a cheap source of hours and hours of TV time. At the truly expensive, top end of TV sport, it offers a method of enticing viewers to make the massive monetary and technological shift to digital television (thereby rendering consumers' personal archives obsolete and making them guinea-pigs in the search for economies of scale) by showing favoured sports only on digital systems. France's Canal+ estimates that 40% of its subscribers pay their monthly fees purely to watch soccer (Williams, 1998: M3; Williams 1999: 104). In 1999, the rights to cover European soccer on television cost over US\$2 billion as part of this enticement (Croci and Ammirante, 1999: 500).

The IOC (n. d.) proclaims television as 'the engine that has driven the growth of the Olympic movement'. Just as shifts in capitalism are associated with new technology (early nineteenth-century national capitalism and steam, late nineteenth-century imperialism and electricity, twentieth-century multinational capital and electronics: Jameson, 1996: 3) so we might write a history of sport connected to technology – wire reports and the radio describing play across the world from the mid-twentieth century and television spreading cricket, soccer, and the Olympics since the 1960s, communicating ideologies of nationalism and the commodity. At Sydney 2000, not only was the internet popular, but TV placed moving images of Olympic winners from seconds before into commercials. The satellite and digital era promises to erase and rewrite relations of time and space in sport once more. This latter-day profit-making targets audiences defined and developed as part of nation-building by public services.

From the BBC's beginnings in the 1920s, its distinctively public mission has been to unite the nation through live coverage of sport. Quality control in early radio times even included a visually disabled person alongside the commentators who could vouch for the vividness of description (Crook, 1998: 85–86). At the same time, the BBC's payment of £1,500 to telecast the 1948 London Olympics set in train an entirely new relationship between sport and the audiovisual media; a precedent that has grown to consume the resources of its originator ('Sport and Television', 1996). Half a century later, the BBC's 1998 decision to commit vast resources to digitalization caused it to lose the rights to cover English inter-national cricket, leading to Cabinet discussion and public protest. The choice between technological upgrading and a traditional part of the national service was painful. In earlier times, it would not have *been* a choice – both innovation and national service would have been funded from tax revenue.

Sport has long been at the leading edge of TV and technology. When the Com-munications Satellite Corporation broadcast the 1964 Olympics, a new era began

(Kang, 1988) – the very name embracing the technological and the commercial as inseparable technical and social relations. Expansion has continued apace. The number of TV hours watched globally tripled between 1979 and 1991, while more than half the 30 billion people who watched the 1990 men's World Cup did so from Asia, never a football power. The 32 billion viewers of the 1994 event spanned 188 nations, and the 1996 Olympic Games drew 35 billion. The third most significant event is the Commonwealth Games, which draws 500 million viewers. US audiences for NBC's Atlanta Olympics coverage were offered more advertising time than game time, while Hollywood factors in a quadrennial over-seas box-office disaster during the weeks when people stay away from the cinema and watch the men's World Cup. And the move into TV time is massive. The NBA is now seen on television in 206 countries across 128 networks and 42 languages, and has its own cable and satellite network ready for digital interactivity – NBA.com TV. Its start-up operation, the Women's National Basketball Association (WNBA), was broadcast in 17 languages across 125 nations in 1999, its third season of existence. In baseball, MLB is seen in 215 countries. The 1999–2000 NFL season was telecast in 24 languages to 182 countries. Fans in Austria, the Netherlands, and Singapore, where no US football games are broadcast on Sundays, were offered webcasts from that season via broad-band. The NHL is also seen around the world, and has websites in France, Finland, Norway, Sweden, Germany, Japan, Slovakia, Russia, the UK, the Czech Republic, and Poland (Herman and McChesney, 1997: 39; Smith, 1997: 114; FIFA, n. d.; Muda, 1998: 223; McAllister, 1997; Pickard, 1997; Wise, 1999; Burton, 1999; 'New Television Deals', 1999; 'International Broadcasters', 1999; 'NFL Full', 1999; Dempsey, 1999a, 1999b; 'Country-by-Country', 1999). By contrast, Australian Rules Football's international circulation is mostly on highlights shows that are given away to networks ('TV Times', 1999).

No wonder that Rupert Murdoch refers to TV sport as News Corporation's 'battering ram' into new markets, while telecommunications corporation TCI calls it 'the universal glue for global content' (quoted in Herman and McChesney, 1997: 75–76). But the energies we identified in Chapter 1 with reference to the New Zealand/Aotearoa rugby team are also at play here. National and regional identifications bring into question the 'benefits' of new technology and global capital. Even neoclassical economists have argued against satellite exclusivity, on the ground that 'key sporting events, like the Olympics, the World Cup and the FA Cup ... generate positive social network externalities' when they are universally available. Folks talk to one another about the shared experience of viewing, which in turn binds them socially, and this 'social capital' may be lost if only a privileged few received transmission of such events (Boardman and Hargreaves-Heap, 1999: 168, 178).

The state has been bombarded by complaints about the takeover of sport by private networks. Citizens regard national sport as a public good (or at least one for which they only pay profit-making entities indirectly). In Germany, for example, it is likely that parts of the next two World Cups of soccer will only be available locally on pay TV, after the European Broadcasting Union, a consortium of public networks, was outbid by Kirch and Sporis in 1996, despite offering US$1.8 billion

(Hils, 1997; 'Sport and Television', 1996; Boehm, 1998a). When the plan materialized in Germany, there was immediate uproar, with politicians proclaiming free viewing of national-team games as 'a basic right of our citizens' (quoted in Hils, 1997). And when Vittorio Cecchi Gori outbid the Italian public broadcaster RAI for soccer rights in 1996, the Italian state moved in to declare the auction contrary to the public interest, legislating to preclude anyone holding more than 60% of the nation's rights to televise soccer (Tagliabue, 1997: D4; 'Flirtation and Frustration', 1999). Similar legislation was introduced in the UK and France, although cricket authorities persuaded the Blair government that 'their' sport did not belong on the 'A' list in 1998 (Boehm, 1998a; Boyle and Haynes, 2000: 216). But then Telepiu bought exclusive pay rights for the four leading soccer clubs in Italy, forcing audiences to make the digital move and making it harder for competitors to gain custom. When Murdoch announced a second digital platform in Italy for 1999 via partnerships with local football clubs, Mediaset, and Telecom Italia, he was also preparing a US$2.5 billion offer for six years' exclusive coverage of Serie A and B football, countering pay-per-view arrangements between Canal+, its Italian subsidiary Telepiu, and top clubs. Then he purchased a quarter of Kirch, staking out its non-broadcast rights (Williams, 1998: M3; Zecchinelli, 1998; 'Flirtation and Frustration', 1999; Boehm, 1999; Boyle and Haynes, 2000: 210). The criterion of national interest was being circumvented.

The Olympic Charter, which guarantees 'maximum presentation of the Games to the widest possible global audience free-of-charge' (IOC, n. d.) may eventually be interpreted to mean that the Third World will receive analogue signals and the First World digital. Watching the Olympics on television is meant to be a similar experience for all, as host broadcasters produce the visual text (except for the US, which has its own feed, camera angles, and commentary position). Countries then reterritorialize the text with their own verbal track (Pujik, 1999: 117, 119). Exhaustive studies of the Games as 'a communication phenomenon ... initially produced in a city, but then "reproduced" in multiple places', suggest that locally modulated coverage constructs very different texts and generates very different responses. Local cultural policy regulated by the state also plays a part, notably the insistence by Arabic countries that women's events not be broadcast and that they hence pay on a pro rata basis (de Moragas Spà et al., 1995: xvi, 22).

Disney/ABC's subsidiary ESPN has been a trendsetter in the televisualization of sport. ESPN International, which began in 1983, telecasts in 21 languages to 182 nations and 155 million households. It has 20 networks across Asia, Australia, and Latin America (the latter has four networks of its own) in addition to syndication deals. A single executive sent to Hong Kong to cover Asia in 1993 is now one of 300 employees based in Singapore at a major production facility (Fry, 1998b: A4; Sandomir, 1999). In 1998, ESPN struck a programming arrangement with the Argentinian military to broadcast in the Antarctic, which had long been a target in order for the company to claim a truly global reach (Fry, 1998a: A1; Fry, 1998b: A4). That reach permits Disney to address a social sector that has conventionally eluded it – middle-class men – and even to penetrate public TV: the PRC's sports network draws half its content from ESPN. The company's slogan is 'Think globally, but customize locally.' That means a degree of local coverage, such as table tennis in East Asia and cricket in India, while Latin American services produce 20% of their programmes (Grove, 1998: A6). But from 1996, ESPN offered 'global buys' to advertisers – the global commodity sign could be attached to the local sports referent (Herman and McChesney, 1997: 83, 63). The network uses Princeton Video Imaging to edit computer-generated visuals advertising goods and services onto real-life stadia, streets, and public space, making it appear as though purely televisual billboards are present at the site of live action (Williams, 1998). As a wonderfully doublespeaking ESPN executive puts it, 'When we say "local" we don't mean that it has to be from that locality, it can be programming from half-way around the world' (quoted in Grove, 1998: A6). Canal+ describes ESPN as 'one of the leading entertainment companies and brands in the "global information society"' (Lescure, 1998).

Given the crucial role that multinational media-entertainment companies now play in marketing all sports, it is not accidental that a recent NHL expansion franchise in Anaheim was awarded to the Disney Corporation, which also owns the ABC network, MLB's Anaheim Angels, 80% of ESPN, and partial rights to telecast NFL games for eight years. It is not surprising, then, that the 'Official City of Anaheim Web Site' lists Disneyland alongside the Mighty Ducks in projecting its civic profile. Wayne Huizinga, the owner of Blockbuster Video (which subsequently merged with Viacom) bought another new franchise in Miami via the Florida Panthers Holdings company. The Atlanta Thrashers, the NHL's most recent expansion team, belong to the largest media corporation in the world, AOL-Time Warner, which also owns NBA and MLB teams in Atlanta, TNT Sports, the Goodwill Games, World Championship Wrestling, the CNN/SI sports network, *Time*, and *Sports Illustrated*, and is the NBA's cable partner.

This trend toward the vertical and horizontal integration of hockey in the sports-entertainment sector is part of a general process by which a small group of sport-loving millionaire cronies who owned teams as a hobby are being supplanted by a conglomerate of global communications MNCs (Bellamy, 1998). Besides Disney/ABC and AOL-Time Warner, the other major players in this new oligopoly are: Cablevision, the majority owner of both the NHL and NBA franchises in New York and Madison Square Garden; Comcast, owner of NHL and NBA teams in Philadelphia; Adelphia Communications, with 34% of the NHL's Buffalo Sabres; and Murdoch, who is never far from view in the sporting mediascape. In addition to his global media empire of newspapers (over 100 Australian newspapers; UK publications like *The Times*, *The Sun*, and *News of World*; and the *New York Post* in his adopted country), books (HarperCollins), films (Fox), broadcast television (the Fox network), and satellite services (British Sky Broadcasting [BSkyB], Star), Murdoch has telecast rights to about two-thirds of the nearly 80 MLB, NBA, NFL, and NHL teams in North America via complex joint ventures between Cablevision and Liberty Media, and his Fox Sports Net, which consists of over 20 US regional cable channels with access to about 62 million households.[1] Murdoch recently purchased MLB's Los Angeles Dodgers and also has a 20% share of the new Staples Center in Los Angeles, 40% of the New York Nicks (NBA), 40% of the New York Rangers (NHL), and options on 40% of the NHL's Los Angeles Kings and the NBA's LA Lakers. He has a

40% stake in Canada's newest sports channel, CTV's Sportsnet, which began broadcasting NHL games in 1998, thus giving him regional telecast rights to the 1999 Stanley Cup finals. When the Dodgers operated at a loss in his first year of ownership, and played very poorly, it really didn't matter – amortization of costs lay in programming for Fox and future use in Murdoch's Asian territories (M. Williams, 1999; Dempsey, 1999c; Harper, 1999). The rationale for this corporate strategy is obvious: by controlling both the content and distribution of programming, a scheme that is increasingly popular with all major TV networks, companies can slash costs by eliminating third parties and cross-promoting their other commodities for free while securing much tighter control over the entire circuit of sports production and consumption.

The NICL is partly formed through the increased significance of the media in funding and displaying sport. Whereas soccer players and other athletes are currently sold as screen actors by governing sports organizations to television broadcasters and advertisers, they may soon be more directly employed as TV talent by sports that will simultaneously run and control the electronic distribution and display of competitions and events. Sports are engaging in the vertical integration pioneered by sports management companies like the International Marketing Group, which has simultaneously represented players and staged, promoted, marketed, televised, and secured advertising and sponsorship for designated sports events (Barnett, 1990: 188; Rowe, 1995b: 112). Given satellite TV's cross-border capacity, we may see more sporting competitions and events shaped by the reach of media technologies, rather than by the boundaries of nation-states and their contained audiences. New media technologies always provide a stronger and more immediate sense of 'having been there' – in the 1930s by simulating actuality radio commentary on cricket matches in England for Australian audiences, and in the 1970s through vivid satellite coverage of global mega sports events (Real, 1989, 1996). In the late 1990s, a CBS internet affiliate was providing US cricket fans with a high-quality website for play-by-play information on matches around the world ('SportsLine USA', 1999) and one-day cricket internationals involving South Asian teams were available on pay-per-view TV.

This does not mean an end to national identification. In Ireland, Sky and CNN beam foreign sports in, but RTE and the BBC continue to cover Gaelic games, while Setanta Sport and Tara TV provide worldwide coverage to the Irish diaspora, and there are additional highlights on airline video programming (Cronin, 1999: 68). Diasporic spectatorship sees fans double-declutching between their nations of origin and domicile and between regions. Since 1994, 14 MLB teams have offered domestic Spanish-language broadcasts. In summer, New York City-based Dominicans congregate at a sports bar that provides simultaneous coverage of all games involving the two most prominent Major League sluggers from the Republic, Sammy Sosa and Manny Ramirez. Their US team affiliations are overwritten by their homeland in the eyes of spectators. Bulgarian viewers of NTV tune in to the WNBA to watch the Houston Comets' number-one draft pick, expatriate Polina Tzekova. Dozens of reporters from Germany covered the 1999 NBA game between Seattle and Dallas, which featured their countrymen Detlef Schrempf and Dirk Nowitzki (Cooper, 1999; Marcano and Fidder, 1999;

Dempsey, 1999a; Whitnell, 1999). This form of identification is also a site of resistance to *le défi américain*, the cultural imperialism of American sports TV exports.

The Media–Sports–Culture Complex

Television was the prime motor in the development of post-war sport and its mutating NICL, helping to constitute a sports/media complex (Jhally, 1989) or media–sports–culture complex (Rowe, 1999) of sports organizations, media/ marketing organizations, and media personnel (broadcasters and journalists). The future of a sport relates, in large part, to its place within the complex. Dependency of sports organizations upon the media is due to the importance of continued revenue for national or international competitions. The direction of sport incorporation might be viewed as: media exposure → increased revenue → professionalization → more competitive and spectacular play → larger television audiences → further media exposure, and so on. As the media become increasingly important in this cycle, they dictate what they want from the sport (in terms of selling the product to advertisers). Prescribed innovations may be more colourful uniforms, the use of space for advertising on jerseys or the centre of the field, greater flow of play, breaks for advertisements, and other 'improvements' (Maguire, 1993b, 1999; Lawrence and Rowe, 1986; Goldlust, 1987; Cashmore, 1996). Peak sporting organizations find it difficult to resist the changes demanded by sponsors and the media.

This complex places the media at the very heart of sports structures and practices, because without the media's capacity to carry sports signs and myths to large and diverse audiences across the globe, sport would be a relatively minor and increasingly anachronistic folk pursuit. Television coverage, especially in its satellite form, has become the prime unit of currency in the cultural economy of sport. It can be capitalized in many ways – through paying and non-paying viewers, advertisers, sponsors, sports management companies, sports clubs and associations, news organizations, and so on. Most people most of the time encounter sport through the media, no matter how committed they may be as fans, while large sections of potential and intermittently contactable sports audiences are entirely dependent on media coverage for any kind of sports 'fix'. Without significant television coverage, individual sports are widely seen as moribund. The economic infrastructure of professional sport would collapse without the media's material and cultural capital.

This world of televisual sport is intensely competitive, not only between sports but also between sport and other news and entertainment programming. So sport on television is becoming more telegenic – lively, dramatic, digestible, and readable. A tension clearly exists not only between traditional and new telegenic procedures and forms of sport (for example tie-breaks in tennis, shoot-outs in hockey and soccer, and one-day cricket competitions) but also between smaller, traditionally sports-committed television audiences and those which are larger, fickle, and unconstrained by sports 'heritage'. The need for individual sports to sustain and expand their television audiences frequently leads to changes that not only undermine the game but, in nationalist terms, compromise the homogeneity of sports competitions. British soccer demonstrates that a drive for television revenue (especially from satellite and cable) and the need to glamorize the competition, when coupled with the requirements of EU membership and a more thoroughgoing commodification of leisure, changes the game's televisual representation and role as a signifier of nationhood and manhood. With globalization, both sports *covered* and TV companies *covering* have been transformed, as we shall see. But first, we detour to moments of fissure, of shock.

Consider Barthes' account of one such occasion:

I am at the barber's, and a copy of *Paris Match* is offered to me. On the cover, a young Negro in a French uniform is saluting, with his eyes uplifted, probably fixed on a fold of the tricolour. All this is the *meaning* of the picture. But, whether naively or not, I see very well what it signifies to me: that France is a great Empire, that all her sons, without any colour discrimination, faithfully serve under her flag, and that there is no better answer to the detractors of an alleged colonialism than the zeal shown by this Negro in serving his so-called colonial oppressors. (1973: 116)

Barthes is commenting on nationalist rituals that suture divisions within nation-states. These are especially charged when people marked out by their appearance, and linked to current or former colonies, participate in an apparently enthusiastic and consensual way, so demonstrating fealty to the national 'family' and rendering the abstract concept of the nation in concrete, myth-laden form. The sporting nation is seen to be truly transcendental. All people, including those once conquered by an imperial power but now consenting to its historical legacy, are united under the flag of an international sports contest.

Just such a highly charged, mythical scene inheres in the globally circulated images of the 200-metre track medal ceremony at the 1968 Olympics in Mexico City, when the African-American athletes Tommie Smith and John Carlos received their gold and bronze medals respectively. Images of their protest continue to surface, resonating in very different cultural and geographical contexts. The protocol of Olympic awards ceremonies demands precisely the same psychic and physical dispositions displayed by Barthes' soldier. The blighted legacy of slavery must be occluded, like the North African wars, by a celebration of the nation through the body of the subaltern athlete. In this instance, a simple adjustment to the draping of the body and the attitude of its limbs facilitated an exchange of subversive meaning across many cultures. In Jock Given's description:

the three place-getters walk to the dais where they are presented with their medals by Lord Exeter, the President of the International Amateur Athletic Association. The two Americans are wearing black scarves and black stockings without shoes. The Australian, like the two Americans, is wearing an Olympic Project for Human Rights badge, and has agreed not to shake their hands on the dais. Three flags, two American and one Australian, are raised in honour of the medallists and the *Star Spangled Banner* strikes up in honour of the winner. Suddenly, two arms are raised again – Smith's right, Carlos's left, each with a black glove enclosing a clenched fist. Two heads are bowed, as the Americans avert their eyes from the Stars and Stripes. (1995: 46–7)

Smith subsequently explained the meaning of the defiant gesture as follows:

> My raised right hand stood for the power in black America. Carlos' raised left hand stood for the unity of black America. Together they formed an arch of unity and power. The black scarf around my neck stood for black pride. The black socks with no shoes stood for black poverty in racist America. The totality of our effort was the regaining of black dignity. (quoted in Matthews, 1974: 197)

As rendered through sporting spectacle, the nation is heavily dependent on disciplined, scripted athletic bodies. When these rules are broken, the recalcitrant sports body is immediately subject to censure – in this case, expulsion from the Games and condemnation in the mainstream American media for being 'un-American'. Brent Musberger, who went on to become a leading TV sports commentator, dismissed the protest as a 'juvenile gesture by a couple of athletes who should have known better', and declared that Carlos and Smith were 'a pair of dark-skinned stormtroopers [who] should have avoided the award ceremony altogether' (quoted in Hartmann, 1996: 555). Ironically, this act of defiance can be seized and reinscribed by other, unlikely discourses – for example, as Jim McKay (1995) notes, almost thirty years later, images of the Mexico protest were used by corporate leisurewear manufacturers to symbolize the reconciliation of militant *négritude* with consumer capitalism, exploiting the black male body as an object-sign of style through consumption. Such techniques of advertising and promotion operate in the spaces between 'feel-good' associative messages and spectacular, perhaps confrontational, ploys to secure attention (cf. Benetton's advertising images: Murray, 1989). As Pasi Falk argues:

> the overall shift towards good experiences, characteristic of modern advertising specifically during the last decades, does not, however, imply that the representations produced operate solely within the positive register. The scale of positive experience goes far beyond unambiguous images of pleasure and happiness (beautiful bodies, smiling faces, sunny skies, etc.). Contemporary adverts – posters and especially TV-spots – are filled with dramatic spectacular elements, touching mini-stories of life which may bring tears to one's eyes and, of course, spiced with humour of different kinds. In other words, today's advertising exploits/uses the same themes as other contemporary experiential goods such as fiction film and music videos. (1994: 179)

The imaged male (especially black) sports body moves easily between these different media forms and sites, in many cases quite literally. African-American basketballers become pop singers (Shaquille O'Neal) and film actors (Jordan and Dennis Rodman). The apparently seamless transposition of 'attitude' from sport through product endorsements (not only for sport-related operations like Nike, Reebok, and Converse, but fast-food corporations such as McDonald's and KFC), promotional appearances, video performances on MTV, and so on, provide possibilities for attention-inducing, even transgressive image projection. Rapid-fire editing, grandiose individualist sloganeering, and the relentless juxtaposition of socially and historically diverse images plundered from the library of historical events thoroughly decontextualizes and reconfigures political protests like those of Carlos and Smith. As we saw in Chapter 2, black liberation is presented as the desire for overpriced leisurewear produced on behalf of white-dominated corporations by exploited people of colour in South-East Asia (McKay, 1995), while: 'The recurrence of nigga imagery through the game of basketball is another indication of the way in which contemporary popular culture has found profitability through the selling of the most strident forms of African American discourse' (Boyd, 1997: 140).

The requirement to foreground national loyalty is temporarily suspended in a depoliticized gesture of individuality and insouciance, marketable both within and outside the US and counterbalanced by intense and apparently spontaneous displays of patriotism in post-Olympic triumph salutes through the joyful brandishing of the Stars and Stripes by the likes of Carl Lewis, the Dream Team, and Michael Johnson at the 1984, 1992, and 1996 summer Olympics respectively. In the contemporary semiotic economy of the media–sports–culture complex, national, deracialized sports bodies coexist with 'black attitude'. The threat to traditional patriotic identification posed by black others in the UK, for instance, is neutralized by their reassurances of national loyalty at each major international sports event. The ideological role of mega-media spectacles like the Olympics and the World Cup imposes an intermittent nation-based order on the sports world and its social meanings when, for much of the time, that world seeks to transgress significant racial, ethnic, class, and sexual boundaries in the service of consumption. These complex signifiers of nationalism are made more convoluted by the NICL. Here, we return to our soccer and hockey case-studies, this time shifting the lens to media coverage and influence.

'British' Soccer, 'British' TV

By the commencement of the 1997 British soccer season, an agency newspaper article could state:

> From Israel to Australia, Nigeria to Norway, Italy to Iceland, foreigners are signing fat contracts to play in the English Premier League. They are also prompting a heated debate as the 1997–98 season opens Saturday. Are all these foreigners – arriving in unprecedented numbers – killing English soccer?
>
> In the off-season, over 60% of transfers involved non-British players, guaranteeing that about 125 imports will grace the 20-team Premier League this season.
>
> Two London-based clubs, Chelsea and Arsenal [managed by 'foreigners'], could field a team without a single Briton.
>
> The influx has been prompted by rich television contracts, which have driven up transfer prices and salaries, and the Bosman decision, which has freed player movement. (de Carvalho, 1997: 20)

This quotation indicates how crucial the television subsection of GGATaC has been to the NICL. Revenue from the sale of exclusive and live rights to satellite and cable television, and secondary rights or lesser games to free-to-air TV and radio, have created a large pool of capital which increasingly flows, like its associated media technology, across national borders.

The media-centred turn in football has had other significant consequences. As Raymond Boyle and Richard Haynes (1996) have demonstrated, satellite TV has transformed coverage of Scottish soccer, preventing the insulation of audiences from English and other soccer zones, and leading, after a brief moral panic over the death of Scottish soccer, to a 1994 deal with Murdoch's BSkyB. The Scottish League had little choice but to fall into line, given pressures from other European competitions in terms of both player salaries and television coverage. The virtual impossibility of sustaining spatial televisual integrity with the development of satellite and cable saw assertions of Scottishness become little more than rhetorical devices in the TV contract negotiations – with all the artifice and 'made-for-external-consumption' deployment of Scottish iconography that such tactics imply (see Jarvie and Reid, 1999).

In crossing various borders, satellite sports TV has also deeply invested in their symbolic maintenance, as noted by Boyle and Haynes:

> Interestingly, satellite coverage of Scottish football also mobilizes signifiers of the Scottish character, but these are aimed at enticing a predominantly English audience. Thus Scottish football and its accompanying characteristics (according to BSkyB) of flair, grit and passion (with, of course, obligatory bagpipes, tartanry and Scottish scenery included in the programme titles) become synonymous with aspects of the Scottish heritage industry, projecting a partial, simulated view of the country which emphasizes the important position that football has in defining Scottish (male) identity. Satellite sport, therefore, needs nations as cultural entities to be semiotically viable just as much as it needs nation-states and their constituent, perhaps pro-secession parts, to be compliant in the 'spraying around' of its televisual content and subscribing viewership. (1996: 562)

Meanwhile, of course, sports teams are themselves becoming media entities. In October 1997, following successful flotation on the stock market and the receipt of US$1.1 billion over four years for TV rights to cover its matches, Manchester United announced the formation of its own satellite and cable subscription station (other soccer clubs providing such systems include Real Madrid and Marseille). In late 1999, Arsenal's millionaire striker, Davor Suker, admitted that he had bought £20,000 of stock in United, which did not trouble the authorities (Smith, 1997: 126; Tagliabue, 1997: D1; Dawtrey, 1997; M. Williams, 1999: 104; 'Diary', 1999: 9)!

One other investor (holding 11.1% of Manchester United) was BSkyB, which also owned substantial amounts of Leeds United and Manchester City (Freddi, 1999). BSkyB's 1992 purchase of Premier League rights was crucial to this world of flotation. The company had formed as a merged operation after a long, debilitating struggle between the Sky and BSB satellite services. Securing prime TV rights to Britain's national sport, with few of the legal restrictions imposed in Australia to prevent the exclusive siphoning of key sports of 'national significance' from free-to-air TV (Rowe, 1996), meant that a highly unprofitable satellite venture gained ready access to a large subscriber base.

It didn't take long for Murdoch to make the next obvious move. In September 1998, he offered US$1.04 billion to buy Manchester United (putting into perspective his record-breaking offer exactly a year earlier for the Dodgers, which was just a third of that figure). The cost of televising soccer is growing by 40% a year, with BSkyB having exclusive rights to show England's Premier League until 2001. The crucial question then was: what hope would there be of competition for these lucrative rights when the current holder owns the most valuable sports team they cover (Boehm, 1998b)? The threat of losing this contract to screen English Premier League soccer in June 1997 had caused a fall in BSkyB's share price of 6.5% in a single day. The stimulus was a report that the broadcast rights had been valued at twice the sum paid by BSkyB, and a claim in the *Financial Times* that 'the Premier League, which represents the UK's top soccer clubs, was advised to set up its own television service from 2001 rather than renewing its £670 million four-year contract with BSkyB to screen its games' (Brewster, 1997: 21). The key to buying Manchester United was to sidestep revenue-sharing of TV receipts between clubs – by televising their matches himself on pay-per-view, Murdoch could derive a direct correlation between spectatorship and earnings. Meanwhile, Murdoch's Fox Sports Americas was delivering a dedicated sports channel to Star Asia, a Spanish-speaking service in Latin America, and a joint venture with Globo in Brazil that could carry Premier League matches if he went on to buy worldwide rights in 2001 (Larsen and McCann, 1998).

A rival concern, the English National Investment Company, with stakes in Scottish, Czech, Italian, and Greek clubs and participation by TV interests, ran a counter-bid, claiming that Murdoch's BSkyB and team ownership constituted unfair trading (Garfield, 1998). There was widespread opposition to the move from fan groups, such as the Independent Manchester United Supporters Association, competing clubs, and, not surprisingly, other media enterprises. James Lawton, chief sports writer for the rival *Express* group, characterized Murdoch as manipulative, obsessed with the power of money, foreign, and ignorant of soccer culture (especially in its English form). The (no doubt apocryphal) anecdote below captured this unease concerning the crossing of boundaries – between media and sport, and between US-based capital and European soccer:

> Murdoch [has the] potential to follow the gaffe of the chief executive of New York Cosmos, a soccer club owned by Warner Communications.... The Cosmos – which knew huge but brief success in the Seventies and Eighties – had signed the great Franz Beckenbauer and the big man from Warner's came to see him make his debut before a 70,000 crowd at Giants stadium, a concrete pile off the New Jersey turnpike.
>
> Beckenbauer, as any casual football observer would have known, played exquisite soccer from deep in defence. But his new boss called the coach's dug-out and demanded: 'Tell the Kraut to get his ass up front. We don't pay millions of bucks for a guy to hang around at the back.' (Lawton, 1998: 10)

The hitherto Murdoch-friendly Blair 'New' Labour government referred the takeover to the Monopolies and Mergers Commission. In April 1999, the bid to buy United was blocked, on grounds of decreasing broadcasting competitiveness and not being in the public interest, as it would further entrench already huge inequalities between football clubs. Manchester United's share price lost £85 million following the decision. Meanwhile, the UK media firm Granada elected to invest in the Liverpool team (Rowe, 2000; Bose, 1999; 'Implications of the BSkyB/Manchester United Case', 2000; Boyle and Haynes, 2000: 208–9).

Like the Bosman decision, television has exacerbated material inequalities between clubs. Anthony King notes that: 'the favourable coverage which television gave to the big clubs, especially during the 1980s, made those clubs more valuable to their sponsors. Television coverage, therefore, added momentum to the big clubs' drift away from the lower divisions, which sponsorship, in itself, assisted' (1998: 52). Given satellite TV's cross-border footprint capacity, we expect more sporting competitions and events will be shaped by the reach of media technologies rather than by the boundaries of nation-states and their audiences (Maguire, 1999). For example, just as the 1998–99 European soccer season gathered momentum, a European superleague was mooted, in which the continent's top clubs were to play only each other, on the grounds that no single nation could guarantee a sufficiently high standard of competition. Once again, the development did not occur when first proposed, but there is continued manoeuvring, especially in southern Europe, to establish league rather than knockout competitions (as is the case with the new UEFA Champions League) in search of increased television revenues. The most striking recent demonstration of these globalizing pressures was the permission given by the Football Association to Manchester United to withdraw from England's 1999–2000 FA Cup – the oldest soccer trophy in the world – so that it could take part in the World Club Cup in Brazil. This extraordinary decision to downgrade a nationally based competition, that is also one of the world's largest annual sports television events, arose because the state asked for help in appeasing FIFA in order to secure a greater prize – England hosting the 2006 men's World Cup (Allison, 1999). The English club team that was being urged to pass up the English FA Cup was managed by a Scot, Sir Alex Ferguson, with a team composed of 'local boys' from northern England (such as Paul Scholes and the Neville brothers) alongside players from Sweden, Australia, the Netherlands, Norway, Wales, and Tobago.

We saw above that economic, political, technological, and cultural changes have produced new forms of (TV) sports nation based on a contest between entities that have local, regional, quasi-national, and national state identities and are subject to constant reformulation within the media–sports–culture complex. In our next case study – Canadian ice hockey – the sporting nation has confronted a range of pressures from within and across the border and the former Iron Curtain, as we saw in Chapter 2. The new pressure comes from the media.

'Canada's game', long driven by American corporate interests (Kidd, 1991), has become even more Americanized during the past two decades. As Gruneau and Whitson have documented, an important take-off point in the development of hockey occurred early in the twentieth century when the mass media popularized the game by articulating its 'natural' connection with Canadian nationhood and manliness. But they also note that the mass media played a paradoxical role in the development of the game:

> hockey didn't really begin to leave an indelible mark on Canadian culture until the means of symbolic production – telegraphy, magazines, radio, and finally, television – had become fully national in technical reach, thereby creating the possibility of national audiences. This nationalization of symbolic production occurred against a backdrop of

developments that were beginning to make Canada an extension of the American domestic market for cultural goods and entertainment. (1993: 274)

Virtually every aspect of hockey – the form and content of games, broadcasting style, personnel, franchise selections, and TV contracts – has been marketed to American audiences, advertisers, and sponsors. For example, although the number of NHL teams has more than quadrupled since 1967, only six of the 30 clubs are now located in Canada. Until the 1970s, Toronto and the four American teams were composed primarily of Anglophones and a few Francophones, while the situation was always the reverse in Montréal. Consequently, most Anglophone and Francophone hockey fans in Canada were, as noted in Chapter 2, divided along ethno-regional lines into Montréal and Toronto camps. For instance, although the two Canadian and four American teams had some followers in both communities, most Francophones revered the Canadiens. The few Francophones who did support a team other than Montréal were highly unlikely to be fans of Toronto, since it represented the White Anglo-Saxon Protestant (WASP) establishment (hockey remains the whitest professional team sport) (Farber, 1999). Contests between Montréal and Toronto, especially during the Stanley Cup play-offs, often symbolized underlying tensions between Anglophones and Francophones (Belanger, 1999). But in 1974, Montréal and Toronto were allocated to separate divisions, a move that ended one of the greatest rivalries in North American sport. Although the teams were back in the same division as of 1998, reconfigurations of the NHL during the previous twenty years had rendered the old rivalry practically meaningless.

Additionally, some traditional 'hotbeds' of hockey in relatively small Canadian cities have been overlooked or disbanded, with franchises granted or shifted to sunbelt cities that have no 'natural' affinity with hockey, but possess the right demographics for US owners, advertisers, sponsors, and TV networks (for example, Anaheim, Atlanta, Dallas, Phoenix, Miami, Tampa Bay, Raleigh, Nashville, and San Jose). After NHL franchise owners in the comparatively small Canadian markets of Québec City and Winnipeg failed to secure suitable financial guarantees from their local communities, the teams were moved to the more lucrative US markets of Denver and Phoenix. To many Canadian ears, teams with 'showbiz' names like the Anaheim Mighty Ducks and the San Jose Sharks do not have quite the same resonance as 'culturally authentic' appellations such as the Canadiens or Maple Leafs.

Like other North American major-league owners, NHL moguls are less concerned about sustaining the loyalty of grass-roots fans than with signing rich TV contracts or telecasting games on their own networks, selling the maximum number of corporate boxes, squeezing every subsidy possible out of local taxpayers, and securing monopolies over property, signage, advertising, naming rights, concession sales, sporting apparel, and myriad product tie-ins (Whitson, 1998; Whitson and Gruneau, 1997). In short, the NHL, along with other professional sports in North America, has been well and truly integrated into the American and global culture industries.

The threat posed by the American dollar alone became apparent in June 1999, when NHL executives, representatives of the six Canadian franchises, players, and local, provincial, and federal government officials met in Toronto for a one-day 'Hockey Summit' called by the federal Minister for Industry. The aim of the meeting was to discuss the financial crisis that Canadian teams claimed they were facing, including the C$170 million they had lost between 1996 and 1998. This large losing sum was attributed to: (1) costs incurred from a 1995 collective bargaining agreement that eliminated salary caps and raised the average annual player's salary from US$773,000 to US$1.1 million; (2) unfavourable exchange rates that had seen the Canadian dollar plummet from US84 cents in 1989 to only US66 cents in 1999; and (3) generous tax breaks and subsidies given to professional sports teams by American governments. The owners maintained that they were being out-spent and out-subsidized by their American rivals and would be forced to move south unless they received tax relief and government subsidies amounting to C$60 million, which could be skimmed off from provincial sports lotteries, a major source of funding for amateur sport. The owners' plea for corporate welfare came at a time when neoliberal governments had been consistently reducing their commitments to basic health, education, and welfare, as well as forcing amateur sporting organizations to form 'partnerships' with the allegedly more efficient private sector! Meanwhile, Ottawa Senators fans sued Alexei Yashin for C$27.5 million for failing to play when his request for a US$8 million salary was rejected by the team owner (El-Bashir, 1999; Beltrame, 1999). Dissatisfaction was rife. When the Canadian government announced a raft of reforms to keep teams local, public outrage at this projected use of tax revenue to pad the mansions of the wealthy saw an immediate reversal in policy (Sandomir, 2000). How did the media – who were deeply implicated in this transformation of Canadian hockey – interpret this corporate 'crisis'?

Media Responses to the 'Crisis'

This process of de-Canadianization (as well as the perennial, looming collapse of the financially plagued Canadian Football League, constant rumours of NFL franchises being set up in Montréal, Toronto, and Vancouver, and the establishment of NBA franchises in Toronto and Vancouver) has been framed by the Canadian popular media as both symptomatic and constitutive of the combined economic, cultural, and political crises that allegedly threaten Canada's already precarious national identity (Gruneau and Whitson, 1993; Nauright and White, 1996; Silver, 1996). In 1988, there was an outburst of anti-US outrage in the popular media when the aforementioned (and since retired) Gretzky, one of Canada's unofficial national treasures, was traded from Edmonton to Los Angeles (Jackson, 1994). By 1998, Canada's leading quality national newspaper, the *Globe and Mail*, was so concerned about the decline of hockey in Canada that it ran a 12-part, front-page feature entitled 'A Game in Crisis'. The series focused on how Canada had deservedly lost its preeminent place in world hockey and what was needed to remedy this situation. The fact that soccer had replaced hockey as the most popular participant sport among Canadian youth was an index of the 'problem'. According to the author of the series:

Canada still sends more players to the National Hockey League than any country, but most of them are second- or third-line performers – checkers and role players, the 'unskilled labor of the NHL,' former Hockey Canada head Derek Holmes calls them. The top talent, with the occasional exception, now comes from countries other than Canada. (Houston, 1998: 1)

Canadian hockey players were seen not just as losing their former dominance – in a manner that could be regarded as cyclical – but as subject to a perhaps irreversible proletarianization, their skills degraded to the unglamorous exertion of physical labour. Earlier, another *Globe and Mail* journalist wryly proposed that the rise of the Americans had shifted the traditional stereotypes of 'them and us' from Canada vs. the USSR to Canada vs. the USA – an unthinkable opposition at the time of the epic 1972 series:

What has finally kicked in is the realization that the Americans have become the enemy, and that losing to them would be infinitely worse than losing to any edition of the Big Red Machine.... The Soviets were certainly the Other. They, in the bad old days, were said to represent godlessness and oppression and a threat to our very lives.... What has emerged, though, is a very different kind of villain, a too casual threat, far more difficult to stomach since it is eminently clear that Americans, on the whole, have spent not a nanosecond worrying about their position in the hockey universe. (Brunt, 1996: 23)

As in the case of English soccer discussed in Chapter 2, the influx of foreign players has prompted xenophobic reactions in Canadian hockey. Perhaps the most prominent example is the histrionic outpouring of Don Cherry, a former professional player and coach, much sought-after banquet speaker, ubiquitous 'pitchman', entrepreneur, and right-wing populist on the 'Coach's Corner' segment of (the recently renamed) *Molson's Hockey Night in Canada* (Gillett et al., 1996; Knowles, 1995). Cherry is a self-proclaimed spokesman for the 'average guy', by which he means the white, working-class males who are an important target of Canada's two leading breweries – Molson's, which sponsors the Saturday night telecasts, and Labatt's, which backs mid-week matches. Cherry has received widespread coverage for his jingoistic attacks on non-Canadians and complaints about the demise of violent play. His reactionary call for a return to hockey as it was played by and for Canadians in the 1950s – that is, violently – underlines what is perhaps the most unpalatable aspect of contemporary hockey to some Canadians – the displacement of their traditional style of physical aggression by the skill and artistry of Americans, Europeans, and Russians. It is also important to note that, for all the concern in the Canadian media about men's hockey, little has been said about the outstanding achievements of the national women's teams, which have won all five IIHF championships since competition began in 1990, and secured a silver medal in the inaugural women's competition at the 1998 Winter Olympics. Women's hockey is the fastest-growing area of the Canadian game. Participation rose from 5,000 in 1988 to 30,000 ten years later. Increasing numbers of talented players are heading south to take up scholarships at US colleges.

Uncoupling the organic links between hockey and Canadianness, and the ensuing media-fuelled moral panic about Canadian nationhood and manhood, occurred through televisualization, Americanization, commodification, and globalization, which effected radical changes in the global flow of athletic talent and the game's form and content. In this regard, Canadian hockey is not alone. In other contexts – such as Australian rugby league – similar forces have precipitated even more dramatic controversies.

TV Rugby League: From Australia to (some of) the World

In rugby league, the impact of the forces discussed above was even more profound: a schism in the game in Australia, the production of new discourses of tradition and modernity, and contests over the right to national representative status. The immediate cause of these dramatic events was a struggle over pay and free-to-air TV rights between two media proprietors, Murdoch and Kerry Packer (Rowe and McKay, 1999). The longer-term explanation lies in sport's remarkable capacity to secure large, loyal, and committed TV audiences and subscribers, interpellated as local, regional, or national subjects. What is the archaeology of this loyalty and its commodification?

The Rugby Football Union was established in England in 1871. In line with the policies and practices of British colonialism, similar peak organizations soon appeared in Australia, Ireland, New Zealand/Aotearoa, South Africa, and Wales (Phillips, 1994). In the US, American football developed in the 1860s and 1870s from a combination of rugby and soccer. The early internationalization of the rugby code was based on the hegemonic position that Britain occupied in the nineteenth century. Packaged along with its capital penetration and military presence was an array of cultural goods on offer to its current and former colonies. Conforming to the ideals of muscular Christianity (that is, the supposed development of leadership, fortitude, courage, health, and selflessness through sporting endeavour discussed in Chapter 2) and fostered throughout the world by church organizations, rugby was embraced by those eager to build a manly generation for the worlds of work and war.

It proved to be a popular sport with players and crowds. But an issue remained to be resolved – was participation to be for love or money (Collins, 1998)? To those who believed in amateurism, such love should not be compromised by acquisitiveness. As Eric Dunning and Kenneth Sheard (1979) have argued, playing the game was its own reward, and far superior to the ungentlemanly pursuit of material benefits. As men and boys from the working classes began to play rugby, the physical cost of doing so resulted in loss of income among those who suffered injury. For others, the pursuit of sport limited their opportunity to make money through paid work. The desire for income from sporting participation – and for financial recompense following injury – confronted the ethos of amateurism, with the result that, the Rugby Football Union was split in 1895 between amateurs and professionals (Cashmore, 1996). The former continued to play rugby union and the latter became rugby league footballers.

Over time, the rules of rugby league developed to make the game faster and more spectacular. Players received match payments – a practice eschewed by rugby union until the 1990s. In Britain, as in the colonies, rugby union was favoured by a largely Anglo-Protestant conservative élite which had been privately schooled (although its class complexion was variable – in southern Wales, for example, the game also had deep working-class roots at least partially sustained by antipathy towards English political, capital, and sporting hegemony). Firmly linked to the ideal of loyalty to king and country, rugby union continued to derive support from the middle and upper classes.

In contrast, rugby league had more in common with soccer, drawing most of its supporters and players from the popular classes. Furthermore, in Australia rugby league was closely linked to a labour movement via Irish-Catholic antipathy to the English 'squattocracy' (Phillips, 1994). The game developed on a regional basis (as it had in England and France) and became the major male winter sport in the eastern states of New South Wales and Queensland. It took the development of terrestrial television to make the sport truly national. With the emergence of satellites and subscription television, the prospect of rugby league becoming a bona fide international sport to rival rugby union and soccer became technologically – if not necessarily culturally and economically – feasible. But television, which in the case of rugby league and many other sports had already remodelled the game, also acquired the power to induce chaos.

Black-and-white TV, introduced to Australia in 1956 because of the Melbourne Olympics, generated a good deal of interest in rugby league both in that country and overseas. But it had many powerful competitors in the sporting and entertainment worlds, and by the early 1970s the numbers attending rugby league games were disappointing. It was decided to make the game more entertaining through a compulsory hand-over of the ball to the opposition team after six tackles, increased value of tries, and changed semi-final play-off rules (Cunneen, 1992). Colour television's advent in 1975 gradually increased both crowds attending matches as well as audiences viewing at home and in pubs and clubs. In Britain and Australia, corporate sponsorship heralded the use of logos on players' clothing (Denham, 1998). By the 1990s, American practices like cheerleaders, corporate logos on the field of play, and electronic billboards were either introduced or extended.

The commercial advantages of selling such television audiences to advertisers were not lost on the television networks, and League became a staple of eastern-seaboard Australian television (Cunningham and Miller, 1994). In 1995, free-to-air television was supplemented by satellite and cable. Despite competition from Channel Seven, holders of the rights to the Olympic Games, and Channel Ten which covered Australian Rules Football, by the 1990s, media magnate Packer's Nine Network was the leading TV sports network in Australia, and had also transformed the economics, organization, and presentational style of cricket (Stoddart, 1986; Miller, 1989). In 1992, Packer, his sometime joint venturer and rival Murdoch, and the (then wholly) Australian government-owned telecommunications giant Telstra, put forward a bid for one of two new satellite licences. When the bid failed, the consortium dissolved. Packer negotiated with Optus, Telstra's foreign-owned rival in the area of telecommunications (Rowe and McKay, 1999). Both Telstra and Optus built optical fibre cable networks for telephonic and broadcast services. With rugby league as one of his key bargaining points, Packer signed a deal that allowed him to charge those connected to Optus Vision to watch league matches. Fearing that it would be outmanoeuvred in the telecommunications market, Telstra approached Murdoch with a deal that would see Telstra provide A\$4 billion worth of cable in return for programming. Handsome profits for Murdoch's News Ltd. seemed all but guaranteed (Colman, 1996: 42). The missing component, however, was sport – which Murdoch realized would be essential for the commercial development of new TV technology in Australia.

Packer had already spectacularized rugby league on his broadcast network. It proved popular with audiences and advertisers alike. His influence upon the TV presentation of rugby league was not, however, as notable as it had been on one-day cricket, with its introduction after 1977 of coloured uniforms and balls, new rules for bowling and fielding, and three-way international summer competitions. After buying key players who had previously been contracted to the Australian Cricket Board and to its counterparts in England, the West Indies, and so on, he was able to construct his own élite, highly commercialized international sport, until he gained his goal – exclusive TV coverage of the conventional game. With rugby league, however, there was only a desire to get rid of its more violent aspects, and to promote the game among women and the middle classes (Phillips, 1994; Miller, 1998a). As at the mid-1990s, there seemed no need to alter league in the interests of additional commodification and spectacularization. After all, the governing body, the Australian Rugby League (ARL), was favourably disposed to virtually all the commercial opportunities offered (only severing its lucrative sponsorship connection with a tobacco company following an Australian government ruling that sports were not to be funded by cigarette sponsorship and advertising) and the players were under contract to the ARL. With regional aggregation of television services in the early 1990s making national commercial networks possible for the first time in Australia, the development of rugby league into a genuinely national sport could also be envisaged. In 1995, just as the competition was expanded to Perth in the west and Townsville in the north, and even extended across the Tasman Sea to Auckland in New Zealand/Aotearoa, so becoming simultaneously national and international (Rowe, 1996), it began to fracture under pressure from a formidable sports media power – Murdoch.

The 'Dirty Digger', as he is sometimes known in the UK as a result of the tabloidization of the *News of the World* and *The Sun*, had relinquished his Australian citizenship in order to acquire broadcast media properties in the US. This act enabled his enemies in the ensuing media war over rugby league to represent Murdoch as a foreigner, even a traitor, to be contrasted with Packer, now repositioned as national hero (Rowe and McKay, 1999). Unlike Packer, Murdoch was very international. Ownership of BSkyB in the UK, the Fox television network in the US, and the Star satellite service in South-East Asia allowed him to circulate content across the globe. As we saw earlier, American football, hockey, basketball, baseball, and British soccer were Murdoch sports media properties amenable to global marketing. Ownership of and access to satellites, television stations, and cable networks promised the sale of electronic information to viewers lured by the staple subscription attractions of feature films and live sporting events.

Developments in Australian rugby league became crucial to Murdoch's business plan for the Australasian region. He favoured new competitions that were simultaneously national and international, with programming distributed across broadcast, cable, and satellite involving 10 or 12 teams drawn from the 20 then playing in the ARL competition. These would be converted into Super League franchises, with a presence in the hitherto unexploited markets of Melbourne and Adelaide. In Britain, the reorganization of clubs into 14 European Super League teams (with the 'European' title justified by the inclusion of a team from Paris) was under way in 1995, with a 10-team competition beginning in 1996 that grew to 14 clubs the following year. The London Broncos and Paris St Germain provided a semblance of regional and international dispersion (Denham, 1998). US-style marketing strategies, such as mid-game entertainment, were designed to spread the audience base from predominantly male to mixed-sex family. The change of team names (in Britain, unlikely entities were created like the Hull Sharks, the Castleford Tigers, and the Leeds Rhinos) was more about aggressive imagery than local identity. As David Denham (1998) has noted, the use of popular North American names such as wolves, cougars, chieftains, and braves appears out of keeping in a nation that boasts none of these beasts! Sacrificing national iconography was demanded in a game that sought global coverage. For the players, in particular, international exposure also brought higher pay, improved benefits, and potential careers as coaches, administrators, media commentators, and promoters.

But Australian rugby league's national controlling body and locally dominant media magnate were not to be easily supplanted by Murdoch's global vision. After the failure of negotiations between Murdoch and Packer in 1995, and the latter's warning to wavering clubs that entering into any additional broadcast arrangements would lead to litigation, a prolonged and debilitating struggle began between the Murdoch/Telstra and the ARL/Packer/Optus Vision camps. What transpired was as dramatic as any melodrama – backroom deals with coaches, long plane flights crisscrossing the country, the wooing of players at late-night meetings, offers and counter-offers, and Oedipal subplots involving managerial moves by the antagonists' sons, Lachlan Murdoch and James Packer (Rowe and McKay, 1999). Just as the 'Aussies for the ARL' and 'Stop Murdoch Committee' pressure groups mobilized a rhetoric of patriotism to defend 'our' game, the realization of Murdoch's Super League model in England and New Zealand/Aotearoa isolated Australia from international competition in the sport (Rowe, 1997).

Rugby union, played in many more countries than rugby league, was arguably underdeveloped as a sport. Union officially renounced amateur status in the 1990s and emerged by the middle of the decade as the more viable national sport. During this period the loyal 'Citizen' Packer had been advised that, were Murdoch to be successful in his Super League bid, an excellent counterfoil would be to commercialize and internationalize union. A proposal was put to the Australian Rugby Union for three conferences in the Pacific, Europe, and the US, comprising 30 teams (Fitzsimons, 1996). Just as with Murdoch's Super League, the winners in each conference would play off for the world title. Packer signed over 500 rugby union players from various countries to large contracts, with the proviso that payments would be made only if Packer's World Rugby Corporation was ratified by the governing body. What *hubris*! Packer was promoting his patriotic guardianship of Australian rugby league at precisely the time that he was seeking a deep involvement with its principal sporting competitor, using many of the tactics deployed by Murdoch and deplored by Packer himself, and having declared that no media mogul 'should run your game'. Murdoch, however, had moved just prior to the 1995 men's rugby union World Cup Final in South Africa to secure worldwide TV rights to the game in Australia, South Africa, and New Zealand/Aotearoa for ten years for US$555 million (Colman, 1996: 210). Packer's World Rugby Corporation was stillborn.

The various stages and outcomes of the organizational, emotional, and legal struggle for rugby league were convoluted (Rowe, 1997). In 1996, Packer/ ARL/Optus Vision persuaded a judge of the Federal Court to uphold the ARL's loyalty agreements for clubs and players and ban Super League until the next century. A player-organized Global League was proposed, but also banned, and virtually all the players who had signed with Super League returned to the ARL fold for the 1996 season. Later that year, the judgment against Super League was overturned on appeal, leading, disastrously, to rival competitions in 1997, *rapprochement* between rival moguls, and the formation of a hybrid National Rugby League (NRL) in 1998, committed to introducing most of Super League's reforms such as the truly national expansion of the game, with concomitant closures and mergers of economically non-viable clubs (now redefined as 'franchises') clustered in suburban Sydney (with only 14 out of 20 clubs making up the league by 2000). News Ltd. owns 50% of the NRL (Dempsey, 1999c: 103).

The outcome was hailed as 'peace with honour' and a victory for all. News Ltd.'s newly installed Chief Executive Officer, Lachlan Murdoch, proclaimed: 'This is the best outcome for all parties – clubs, fans, the players, the ARL, and Super League'. However, buried beneath the celebratory motifs were two dis-comforting consequences. First, the players' position in the league labour market was dramatically weakened, as the new administrators had imposed a A$3 million salary cap on each team, leading to a small number of unprecedented defections to rugby union (as opposed to the more usual move in the other direction) and a larger number of players departing the Australian game for Europe. Second, the real winners were Murdoch and Packer, who agreed to share the lucrative pay-TV rights via the Foxtel and Optus networks – the reason why this billion-dollar conflict began in the first place. The 'foreign' and 'patriotic' sports media magnates had discarded their public rhetoric, entering into a number of agree-ments on free-to-air and pay-TV broadcasts of rugby league and other sports (such as horse racing). It was revealed that:

> Mr Kerry Packer's Publishing and Broadcasting Ltd. ended five years of warfare over pay-TV yesterday by taking up its option to pay about $160 million for a key share-holding in Foxtel, forging a fresh alliance with an old rival, Mr Rupert Murdoch's News Ltd. PBL revealed it would buy half of News Ltd's 50% stake in Foxtel, the country's fastest growing and largest pay-TV operator. PBL is now expected to exercise a further option to acquire half of News's interest in Fox Sports. (Burke, 1998: 1)

Australian rugby league had, it seemed, been taken apart and put back together again by media capital. Several clubs had merged (St George and Illawarra,

Balmain and Western Suburbs, Manly and North Sydney) and others had been consigned to history (teams from Perth, Adelaide, the Gold Coast, Brisbane, and the Hunter region). The South Sydney Rabbitohs, a foundation club, were refused the right to play in the 14-team 2000 competition, and took legal action for reinstatement after a highly emotional public campaign involving local residents and media celebrities. The sporting nation had been revived, but only because a US-based proprietor and his local ally/competitor had said so, with their terms of trade worked out in the context of global ambitions for sport, screen, and business expansion.

Market research provides media networks with immediate feedback about public taste, drawing its authority from the measured responses of consumers. The media can, in this way, effectively dictate the terms under which national (and global) sporting competitions will be run. If they encounter a defiant organization such as the ARL, one option, in the absence of government intervention (and even more so with state encouragement) is to bypass it (as Murdoch found in the British newspaper industry during a union dispute over the introduction of proletarianizing technology during the mid-1980s). If the sport's organizing body can be disabled or fractured, the game can be controlled directly. Its development in the mode prescribed by its new bosses is then assured. Such control is necessary, it would seem, when the stakes are high. There would be no point in Murdoch dealing with an organization which, after the expenditure of considerable monies on the part of his own corporation, was uncooperative. The NRL was in this position – just as the Australian Cricket Board had been with Packer in 1979 – and the result in both cases was a successful challenge to the authority of the nationally based governing bodies which ran those games. Ultimately, the struggle is for sovereignty over the sporting nation – the conceptual entity that represents space and place in and through the symbolic landscape of sport.

Maguire (1999) makes the point that other commercial strategies must be considered, particularly where sport is part of a wider business network. In Murdoch's case, for example, not only is he capable of showing sport on his cable and satellite networks, and selling those images to broadcast stations, but his companies own newspapers and magazines which help to give sport its profile in the community (see Rowe and Stevenson, 1995) plus sports marketing affiliates, and has contracted players who are expected to represent the sport (and News Corporation) when required. Profit-making opportunities for this network of interests must be considered by corporate media owners when making decisions about televising sport. This explains why it was possible for Murdoch to invest money in a global Super League when it would seem, on the surface, that the sport appealed only to a small number of rugby-league-playing nations. The aim here is control – through newspaper and television reporting – of the development (style, form, overall popularity, and impact) of the game, and the generation of spin-offs such as cable subscriptions, satellite dishes, and telephonic services to offset the cost of broadcast rights.

Rugby league remains a sport which despite being largely *commercialized* (open to advertising and corporate sponsorship) is yet to be fully *commodified* (where all aspects of ownership and control are subject to the rule of the marketplace – a condition, it should be acknowledged, that is almost unrealizable in absolute terms given the necessary precondition of absolute economic determinism). While it might be *internationalized* (relating to competitions between nation-states) it is still in the process of becoming *globalized* (that is, where competition is organized beyond the nation-state via corporate control/influence) (Broomhill, 1995). Might there be any risk involved in taking on such a sport, seeking to commodify it fully, and to increase its global impact? If the capital is available, and the sport has a reliable following, the answer would seem to be 'no', providing that a tenable balance is maintained between tradition (retaining established sports fans) and innovation (generating new ones).

New techniques of sports presentation – close-ups of sweating faces, images of elation after scoring a try, and slow-motion replays of crushing tackles – spliced with music, lively commentary, and pre- and post-match interviews and analysis, have become a recipe for spectacularization and hence marketability (Rowe, 1999). The excitement and spectacle generated by media presentations may be linked unambiguously to hegemonic masculinity and the celebration of violence (Goldlust, 1987; Yeates, 1995), but if this is consumed and enjoyed by fans, then that is the compelling measure of success in economic terms. The advantage of such a package for a company like News Ltd. is that sporting contests have relatively low production costs, and yet generate high and reliable audience ratings (Maguire, 1993b). It is for this reason that Rowe (1996) speaks of the 'global love match' between sports organizations and television corporations, and John Goldlust (1987) and Ellis Cashmore (1996) consider it a 'match made in heaven'. Viewers, of course, are proficient in the game of sports interpretation, and it is essential to recognize that televised sport provides them with 'skilled, pleasurable consumption' (Maguire, 1993b: 42). But it is just as important to realize that there is an underlying political economy of sport, structuring what is seen and by whom (Barnett, 1990; Rowe and Lawrence, 1998). That world is one of corporate executives, shareholders, and governments.

Maguire (1993b, 1999) considers that a number of '-izations' – Africanization, Americanization, Europeanization, Orientalization, and Hispanicization – compete in the global arena. He proposes a regionalization of sport – producing particular styles, images, and local meanings. We argue that other processes – not confined to any particular nation-state or region – have been influential in reconfiguring sport: corporatization, commercialization, rationalization and, of course, globalization, with culture produced and sold to an international market in a way that renders the nation-state of decreasingly direct relevance, in part because of sport's ambiguous place in a para-state, para-corporate civil society. Satellite signals do not conform to national boundaries, and cable subscribers throughout the world watch a variety of programmes that would otherwise be locally unavailable. Such global reach, made possible by the new technology, might be viewed as an extension of the process begun with procuring rights to overseas drama series. With programmes such as *Friends, The Simpsons, Futurama, South Park, Neighbours*, and *Home and Away* being seen in many countries, there is a temptation to understand these texts – together with their sporting equivalents like Davis Cup tennis, Formula One, and World Series-style baseball, golf, cricket, and rugby union competitions – as part of a homogenizing process which incorporates peoples throughout the world. When the Olympic Games are broadcast, is this common experience part of a shared global culture? Will the satellite and cable era collapse time (the 24-hour channel) and homogenize audiences (exercising choice from an increasingly globalized menu) in a much more profound way than broadcast stations?

As we noted in Chapters 1 and 2, Lash and Urry raise the question of whether such a process can be construed as the production of mass culture for a mass global audience. They argue that, rather than viewing the products of cable and satellite TV as evidence of a world market in electronic entertainment, it should be viewed as the antithesis of uniformity, with technology creating opportunities for multiple sites and communities for niche-marketed entertainment products:

> These new global processes have two crucial characteristics.... [T]hey are autonomous from mere interstate relationships ... [h]ence we should employ the term globalization rather than internationalization since the latter implies exchanges between the nation-state.... Second, these global processes are dominant but in a different sense from that understood in much of the dominant ideology debate ... with postmodernity it is the global networks of communication and information that are crucial. This has a number of implications: that the symbolic forms transmitted by the technical media of mass communication are central to contemporary cultural forms; that these developments greatly expand ideological scope since they enable symbolic forms to be transmitted and to extended audiences dispersed in time and space; they permit new kinds of social interaction ... they produce ... images that are diverse, pluralistic and which overload the viewer. Such images may be used for oppositional movements. (1994: 306–7)

This is not a picture of a dominant culture flowing in a single direction to uncritical viewers, but of multiple forms and meanings given to messages by audiences. These 'imagined worlds' respond in various ways to 'global cultural flows'. But, as Appadurai (1990), Maguire (1999), and John Tomlinson (1999) have pointed out, the globalization of culture does not equate with its homogenization. In fact, at the level of the nation-state there is a 'repatriation of difference' in terms of goods sold, and the slogans, signs, and styles which help to distinguish one national (or subnational) group from another. This is why, for Toby Miller and Alec McHoul (1998), sport becomes a 'crucial site' of both solidarity and exclusion. For instance, despite the processes of Americanization/globalization associated with rugby league that we have described, an annual (best-of-three) State of Origin series between New South Wales and Queensland regularly tops Australian TV ratings and is (in much the same way as hockey and 'Canadianness' discussed earlier) a powerful signifier of both 'Queenslanderness' and hegemonic masculinity in Queensland (McKay and Middlemiss, 1995). This return to origins is a sign of continuity in the face of sporting entropy.

The globalization of rugby league can be understood as an attempt to exploit national-based affiliations through the incorporation of sport within media networks, undergirding their expansion through the distribution of televised images via cable and satellite. Another force is the breaking of protectionist and other trade barriers as economic integration of the world order penalizes those nation-states unwilling to engage in free (or freer) trade, along with the 'de-traditionalizing' of social life (Lash and Urry, 1994: 311). Tastes, attitudes, values, and behaviour are destabilized and reconfigured as a direct result of the exposure of culture to new images, ideas, products, and people as part of wider global flows. It is hard to imagine the emergence of today's NHL or NRL in earlier decades, when the people saw their identities and futures as principally bound up with the nation-state.

Key international media proprietors are actively remaking relationships at local, national, and global levels, in a world of disorganized capitalism where reflexive subjects look beyond the nation-state for new experiences, deriving their cultural capital not from identifying with the traditional, but by exploring the postmodern. In this context it is possible to understand Super League as something close to the consummate postmodern product. It was constructed as a competition and a spectacle by a media network which tried to build upon but undermine and transcend traditions associated with the game of rugby league; it challenged and beat legal attempts to restrict the flow of players, teams, coaches, and referees on a global scale; it became a vehicle for the promotion of the products of postmodern culture from Coca-Cola to Nike shoes to airline companies; it was a 'mobile object' (see Lash and Urry, 1994) – an image rather than a physical product, from which profits could be made; it helped to perpetuate masculinist ideals of body, speed, and strength, from which males secure cultural capital (Maguire, 1999; McKay, 1992; Yeates, 1995); and it allowed viewers to invent and reinvent a community (of dispositions over rugby league) in a manner involving aesthetic reflexivity.

Super League was one use of Murdoch's 'battering ram' in a global mediascape which relies on sport-as-spectacle to generate viewer interest, corporate sponsorship, and media profit. By taking teams from their local areas and repackaging them as representative of wider regions (even continents) it has been another, potent force for breaking (working-) class affiliations among teams (as in the aforementioned dismissal from the NRL competition for 2000 of South Sydney, the team with the most visible following among subaltern – including indigenous – peoples) and for making social class much less relevant to the sport (Rowe and McKay, 1999). It is even possible that one or other of the media barons will commission a soap opera about the drama surrounding the development of Super League. It could feature players, reconstruct events to ensure a sanitized (corporate) version of events, and be screened worldwide on affiliated networks. Its sale to advertisers might provide the income from which to make another foray into the globalization of sport.

'Other' Sporting Bodies

For a white sprinter in the U.S. it's very, very difficult. It's kind of a phobia, you just don't see any white sprinters, and coaches aren't interested in developing them.... Black athletes are naturally gifted; they make great sprinters and jumpers. Why should a coach work to develop a white athlete when he doesn't have to do anything with a black athlete? They just recruit them, time them, and they have a winning team. (White sprinter Sandra Myers explaining why she renounced her American citizenship and became a citizen of Spain in order to compete at the 1992 Olympics, quoted in Marable, 1993: 42)

In Britain, France, Germany, Canada, Australia, and the USA, the most valorized sporting body-as-national-exemplar is male, white and heterosexual, while black bodies are connected with 'natural' sporting ability (Carrington, 1998; Hoberman, 1997; Miller, 1998a; Rowe et al., 2000). What happens when one or more of these characteristics is manifestly absent in representations of the nation, or when subordinated female, coloured, or homosexual bodies behave transgressively? For instance, a Joe Louis, Jesse Owens, or O.J. Simpson (before his fall from grace) could be positioned as an unthreatening 'credit to his race'; Michael Jordan can be constructed as 'proof' of the great American dream of transcendence (Andrews, 1996a, 1996b; Andrews et al., 1996; Cole and Andrews, 1996); and Tiger Woods can be hailed as 'America's son' (Andrews and Cole, 2000). But Jack Johnson and Muhammad Ali (until being venerated after lighting the flame at the opening ceremony of the Atlanta Olympics) were positioned as 'uppity niggers', who violated racist beliefs about the servile ways in which African-American men have been expected to behave (Jaher, 1985).

Like race, gender and sexuality pose problems for constructing unified notions about the nation. In the Olympics there may be a more widespread acceptance of women (or people of colour) as national icons than in less highly charged types of competition. Ambivalence about the 'national sportswoman' among many male players and spectators is symptomatic of the gendered value structure of the sports body. When sportswomen represent the nation, tensions are evident in both individual and team sports. For instance, although there was a generally positive reaction to the American women's soccer team's victory in the 1999 World Cup Final, headlines such as 'Looking Good' (Penner, 1999) and '"Booters with Hooters" Are Showing Women Can Be Athletic and Feminine' (Longman, 1999a: B19) point to both the continued sexualization of women and anxiety about their strong and active bodies. Some journalists also attributed the American team's popularity to its 'sex appeal'. Brandi Chastain posed nude for a tabloid men's magazine, and then responded to her critics by saying, 'Hey, I ran my ass off for this body' (quoted in Lusetich, 1999b: 53). Chastain's act caught the attention of David Letterman, host of the internationally syndicated *Late Show*, who invited her on the programme and subsequently became an unofficial cheerleader for the squad each night by showing a signed photograph of the team in which the players were dressed like beauty pageant contestants, appearing to wear only *Late Show* T-shirts. He proclaimed them 'Soccer Mamas' and 'Babe City'.

After scoring the winning goal for the USA during a penalty shoot-out in the Final, Chastain engaged in what she later said was 'momentary insanity' by tearing off her shirt, clenching her fists, sinking to her knees, and screaming ecstatically in front of over 90,000 home-town fans and a national TV audience that exceeded 40 million. By exposing her Inner Active Sports Bra, Chastain gave Nike, which supplied the American team with its sportswear, an incalculable sales boost in the annual US$500 million sports-bra market, as well as enhancing its already widespread brand-name recognition. Although Chastain's behaviour may have been spontaneous, Nike's presence was not. At the time, the company had personal contracts with six members of the American team and ran several commercials featuring its players during the month-long World Cup. It negotiated to use photos of Chastain from the front pages of virtually every American newspaper, as well as the covers of *Time* and *Newsweek*. The predominantly white composition of the team also came under scrutiny, with the executive editor of HarperCollins, which published a book by one of the team's star players, Mia Hamm, commenting that: 'The question needs to be asked, would this team be receiving all this attention if they looked like the Brazilian women's national team – boyish, wholly unglamorous and black?' (cited in Longman, 1999b: C23). In both cases, we can observe how the always already sexualized female sporting body becomes more or less valorized according to its relationship to prescribed modes of Anglo hyper-femininity.

At the individual level, W.J. Morgan (1998) has noted the intricate body politics surrounding reactions in Algeria to 1,500-metre World and Olympic champion Hassiba Boulmerka. Despite receiving a heroine's welcome for her sporting victories when she returned to Algeria, Boulmerka's achievements occurred at a time when doctrinaire Islamic parties were on the rise, and she soon came under attack for violating orthodox dress codes and speaking out against conservative religious practices. Her body is a site of contestation, where postcolonial pride over a sporting accomplishment coexists uneasily with patriarchal structures. Similarly, Cathy Freeman, the twice world champion, 2000 Olympic gold medallist in the 400 metres, and 1998 Australian of the Year, represents the possibilities of achievement on the world stage for indigenous Australians at the same time as she connotes images of bodies that have some of the highest morbidity and mortality rates in the world: 'White Australia likes to appropriate Freeman, her victories and her cheerful optimism because amid an Aboriginal race so often full of grief she's such a joy because she's one Aborigine we unequivocally don't have to feel guilty about' (McGregor, 1998: 12).

In addition to the ethnic and racial politics of sporting bodies, tensions and ambivalences also surround subaltern homosexual bodies. This is a transgressive corporeality according to the established and predominantly homophobic norms of sport, especially of the contact variety (Messner, 1992; Pronger, 1990b; Rowe, 1995a). The linkage of 'approved' masculinity and sport has been a key element of many social institutions and practices, such as the 'man-making' role of school sport, the homosociality of the sports club and sports bar (Wenner, 1998), and the camaraderie of television beer commercials (notably, for example, in the sport-centred male bonding of Australia's Tooheys beer advertisements, with their hearty bar-room choir chorus of 'I feel like a Tooheys, or two!'). Homosociality among male players and spectators, then, is not only tolerated but actively encouraged, providing the context and atmosphere for the conversion of sports values into sports-related consumption. Overt homosexuality, however, is likely to provoke hostility, even violence in such circles, subverting as it does the legitimized contact and feelings between men in sport, symbolically compromising its hierarchical separation from femininity, and undermining its contradictory claim to a universality based on the selective appropriation of certain ascribed masculine values. If the female body operating on the global stage is demonstrably superior or a threat to male dominance in performative terms, then one coping strategy scrutinizes the body for signs of maleness or its positioning in language as male. We now explore this aspect of gender, sexuality, and sporting bodies in a case study of the French tennis player Amélie Mauresmo.

Women's Tennis and Rates of Bodily Exchange

The sports media are an important site for naturalizing, essentializing, and sexualizing bodies. A prominent example is the 'cheesecake' presentations in magazines and calendars such as the special swimsuit issue of *Sports Illustrated, Inside Sport, Sports Monthly*, the *Golden Girls of Athletics Calendar*, and *Golden Girls of Sport Calendar* (Davis, 1997; Mikosza and Phillips, 1999). As Helen Jefferson Lenskyj (1998: 31) notes, the formula in such publications is based on a binary antithesis of men's sports/women's bodies. This process can also be seen in instances like former figure-skating champion Katerina Witt posing nude for *Playboy*, and the frequent sexual objectification of sportswomen in general. The other side to this relentless construction of hyper-femininity is panic over lesbianism (Burroughs et al., 1995; Lenskyj, 1995) and the allegedly unnatural (for which read 'muscular') bodies of women who participate in sports such as bodybuilding, powerlifting, and rugby, as well as individual champions like runner Florence Griffith-Joyner and swimmer Le Jingyi.

There is a long tradition of media concern about the sexual credentials of women tennis players. Margaret Smith Court, Renee Richards, Billie Jean King, Martina Navratilova, and Mauresemo are all élite players who became the focus of moral panics in the popular media for 'playing like a man'. The latter four were framed by the media as doubly abject – Richards for being transsexual, and King, Navratilova, and Mauresmo for being lesbians (very openly in the last two cases) while Navratilova's status as a Czech defector and Mauresmo's as French made them additionally awkward for the Anglo sports world. The US Tennis Association and the World Tennis Association (WTA) disaffiliated some events in which Richards competed, and these tournaments were also boycotted by many players, while the WTA has routinely tried to downplay same-sex affinities of players. Much of the alarm in the media has been related to the alleged recruitment of young heterosexual women by 'predatory' lesbians. For instance, in 1990, Smith Court, a champion of the 1960s and later an ordained minister in one of Australia's conservative churches, held a press conference at which she told the media that women's pro tennis was full of lesbians who seduced young women into their ways – a 'group of lesbian-bisexual players on the circuit, and they're the ones who get at the youngsters'. The former US Open champion and hyper-feminine icon Gabriela Sabatini said, 'I don't even like to take my clothes off in the dressing room', and was joined in her critiques by Steffi Graf, Jennifer Capriati, and Monica Seles, while Hana Mandlikova said of Navratilova that she 'must have a chromosomic screw loose somewhere'.

The current exemplars of hyper-femininity in tennis are Anna Kournikova and Martina Hingis (named, ironically, after Navratilova) (Stevenson, 1999). During the 1999 Australian Open, it was said of Kournikova that her 'every match was attended by the hormonal frenzy usually reserved for your finer strip clubs' (Layden, 1999: 58). However, Mauresmo challenged the standards that Kournikova and Hingis set for both sexuality and style of play at the 1999 Australian Open. After defeating world number one Lindsay Davenport in the semi-finals, Mauresmo 'leapt into the arms of girlfriend Sylvie Bourdon and was cradled with hugs'. Throughout the match, Bourdon had been 'pumping her fists and yelling, 'Allez!' (Come on!). Following a whirlwind romance, begun just a month or two earlier, they had moved in together and embarked on a joint work-out régime of several hours' weightlifting each week. Now they were on tour (Leand, 1999: 29).

Davenport had attained the world number one ranking by using her 6 feet 2 inch frame and marked strength, only to be defeated at her own game. Although five inches shorter, Mauresmo prevailed due to her superb physical condition, a fast and accurate serve, and a hard topspin forehand (traditionally used only by male players). Until her victory, the media had barely noticed Mauresmo, even though she had been world junior champion in 1996. But after the post-match media conference, Mauresmo became front-page news, because Davenport said in a much-repeated TV clip:

> A couple of times, I mean, I thought I was playing a guy, the girl was hitting so hard, so strong ... she is so strong in those shoulders and she just hits the ball very well ... I mean, she hits the ball not like any other girl. She hits it so hard and with so much topspin.... Women's tennis isn't usually played like that.

In addition to this tacit criticism (or, at least, othering) of her opponent for dis-playing 'unnatural' power, Davenport also sparked speculation that Mauresmo might have attained her physique through drugs, commenting that her shoulders 'looked huge to me. I think they must have grown; maybe because she's wearing a tank top'. Mauresmo responded to Davenport thus: 'the fact that I'm strong physically is maybe impressing her. It means that I'm a very solid player, so I take it as a compliment' (quoted in 'Hingis, Mauresmo', 1999: B2).

Of course, Mauresmo's musculature is unexceptional next to such players as Mary Pierce and Venus and Serena Williams. This fact suggests that sexuality animated the controversy. Before their match to decide the Open, Martina Hingis said to reporters that Mauresmo 'came to Melbourne with her girlfriend, I think she's half a man'. Mauresmo exclaimed: 'On top of wanting to beat her, now I'm enraged!' Hingis apologized and supposedly discussed the issue with Mauresmo following the Final, but then told *Sports Illustrated*: 'I'm not regretting anything I said about her' (quoted in Layden, 1999: 58). Hingis informed a press confer-ence after the Open that 'it wouldn't be very healthy for all the girls to go through five sets' and referred to herself as 'one of the Spice Girls of tennis' (quoted in 'Mauresmo', 1999). The founding mother of women's professional tennis, Billie Jean King, said she was going to ask Chris Evert, Hingis' tour mentor, to counsel against this homophobic speech (Araton, 1999). Faced with critical French journalists in Paris, Hingis suggested she and Mauresmo face off: 'Maybe we should meet in a boxing fight and bite each other's ears' (quoted in Dillman, 1999b).

The Australian sporting media went into a frenzy over Mauresmo's lesbianism and body. Melbourne's *Herald Sun* featured her in pictures from the rear, on court, and necking with Bourdon, under the headline 'OH MAN, SHE'S GOOD'. Other press coverage indicates the depth of press anxiety and sensationalism: 'Bourdon works in a bistro near her St Tropez home called Le Gorille. Translation: Gorilla. Just don't tell Lindsay Davenport'; 'Women normally only play tennis against men in mixed doubles. But that all changed yesterday if you believe the world's number one player Lindsay Davenport', and 'shoulders like Lou Ferrigno – she is the French "incroyable hulk.".'... Where is women's tennis headed?; Mind boggles at the muscle monsters' ('Teenager', 1999: 1); '"Man" taunts fire up Mauresmo'/ 'Mauresmo out in the Open' (1999: 63); and 'Grace v Power: An Eternal Struggle' (1999: 50).

North American press comments on Mauresmo's body veered from surprise at 'her strong chin and muscular shoulders' (Clarey, 1999a); through analogy to 'the best 200-meter butterfly swimmers in the world' (Dillman, 1999b), 'huge line-backer shoulders' (Patel, 1999), and 'the shoulders of an Olympic swimmer' (Naughton, 1999); to discrimination, via critiques of her femininity as 'rather manly ... a bit butch, with masculine facial features' (Patel, 1999), and the Reuters News Agency query: 'Who is this guy?' (Naughton, 1999). Record ratings were posted for Australian TV's coverage, and the WTA announced it would continue with pre-tournament/pre-out plans to feature Mauresmo in a marketing campaign, even as fears were voiced about their search for a new sponsor (Weir, 1999; Young, 1999). Mauresmo practised on Melbourne courts with bodyguards, and French television satirists made a puppet with her head on Arnold Schwarzenegger's body and this voice-over: 'It's the first time in the history of French sport that a man says he is a lesbian' (quoted in Dutter and Parsons, 1999: 4). In summary, Mauresmo bore the brunt of critique and negative fascination, as if she were a grotesque whose sexuality was defined by her shoulders and jaw. Clearly, homophobia was also at work in the implication that Mauresmo – and not Davenport, Pierce, or the Williams sisters – pushed the limits of tennis' transgenderization.

However, fissures were also evident in this media coverage. For instance, the controversy was handled quite differently by sports cable network ESPN2's commentators Fred Stolle, Patrick McEnroe, Cliff Drysdale, Pam Shriver, and Mary-Jo Fernandez, and John Alexander of Australia's Channel Seven (coverage of 29 January 1999). Drysdale criticized the Australian media, describing Davenport's remarks as 'much ado about nothing' and agreeing with Mauresmo that 'to say that somebody plays like a man, I think that is a compliment'. McEnroe applauded Mauresmo's handling of the situation, paraphrasing her: 'I'm here with my girlfriend, what's the big deal?' Drysdale concurred, while Stolle stated matter-of-factly that 'she lives with her girlfriend down in St. Tropez – spends time in the gym with her'. In noting the power emphasis of her game, McEnroe admiringly acknowledged a change, that this 'may be the future of women's tennis'. Shriver and Fernandez previewed the Final without referring to the controversy, other than alluding to the supposedly male-like game of Mauresmo. Alexander expressed admiration for Mauresmo's hard work, physical condition, and dedication. During the Final, the cameras cut about equally between the play, Hingis' mother, and Mauresmo's girlfriend, but the latter was verbally identified less often.

At her press conference after the Final, Mauresmo talked about closeted players on the tour, saying that they 'had a hard time dealing with their situation ... I feel sorry for them' (quoted in 'Out in the Open', 1999: 174). She had decided before the tournament to come out, because she felt it would be a topic of debate and it was best to clear the air. Shriver, President of the WTA, said that 'if the commercial world embraces her, it's a different era', alluding to Navratilova's earlier history of sparse endorsements and sponsorships. Mauresmo said that she expected to maintain her clothing contract, and 'if they want to set me aside, there will be dozens more who will take me.... And if they let me go for that, they are jerks anyway' (quoted in Clarey, 1999b).

Four weeks after their meeting in Melbourne, Mauresmo and Hingis played again, in the quarter-finals of the Gaz de France Open, where the local media referred to Bourdon as her 'petite amie' (little friend) (quoted in Atkin, 1999: 17). This time, the result was reversed, with Mauresmo winning. Her home crowd hissed and booed Hingis during the introductions and the warm-up, constantly cheered Mauresmo, and held up banners reading 'We love you Amélie' and 'We're behind you Amélie.' Patriotism endorsed queerness.

Not surprisingly, Mauresmo has become a heroine in the lesbian media, receiving front-page coverage and accolades in *Curve* magazine. She appeared on *Stade 2*, a popular sports show on French TV, after her match at the Gaz de France Open; a few hours later she was the featured guest on French TV's most prestigious prime-time commercial news programme; shortly thereafter, Mauresmo and Bourdon appeared on the front cover of the highly popular glossy magazine, *Paris-Match*, followed by eight pages of photos and interviews; and when the French Prime Minister invited 100 women to a formal function to celebrate International Women's Day, Bourdon accompanied her.

It remains to be seen if Mauresmo (and other lesbians) will be embraced by corporate sponsors and the mainstream media. Put another way, what limits does Mauresmo's sexuality place on her capacity to exchange her corporeal prowess for commercial gain? The answer might lie in the fact that although Nike's trademark swoosh was visible on Mauresmo's singlet and shorts during telecasts of the Australian Open, the company has been uncharacteristically reluctant to position her as one of their sporting 'rebels', as it immediately tried to do with Chastain. In short, even the most 'progressive' mainstream advertisers seem unwilling to challenge the highly sexualized and hyper-feminine image of the female sporting body.

Conclusion

The above discussion has demonstrated the unifying and dividing power of the sport–media nexus in US athletics, British soccer, Canadian ice hockey, Australian rugby league, and queer international tennis. In all five sports, semi-institutionalized, male-only, local contests of the nineteenth century were gradually professionalized, rationalized, and commercialized, first on a national and later on an international basis. In the US, track has been a venue for supposed racial meritocracy. In England and Canada, soccer and hockey became significant sites for both symbolizing and generating popular myths about national unity and superiority. In Australia, rugby league was an important emblem of Irish Catholicism and the labour movement in the eastern states of New South Wales and Queensland. Across the middle-class world, tennis has emerged as the one sport where women have global status roughly equivalent to men's. In all these situations, a symbiotic relationship was initially forged between sport and the mass media, with the latter instrumental in both constructing and reinforcing taken-for-granted connections among sport, gender, and regional and national cultures. However, this synergistic arrangement has gradually shifted to the advantage of the media, particularly global TV networks, which now virtually dictate both the form and content of sport according to the wishes of multinational sponsors and advertisers. As part of GGATaC, the media have been fundamental in destabilizing the customary links among sport, hegemonic masculinity and place. Consequently, the connections between soccer and Britishness, hockey and Canadianness, and rugby league and regional, working-class Australianness, have become increasingly tenuous. This tendency extends to the very experience of liveness, with Berlusconi maintaining that the time is nigh when admission to élite soccer games will be gratis, so irrelevant will physical presence be to enjoying the game given new technologies for TV viewing (Giulianotti and Armstrong, 1997: 25). The preconditions seem to be in place – in 1997–98, Manchester United gained 66% of its revenue from merchandising and TV and now has mega-stores across South-East Asia (Beloff et al., 1999: 133).

We are seeing a televisualization of sport and a sportification of television. And all done under two signs – audiences built up by national services at public expense being turned into consumers by preying capital, and new technology that has not excited customers being pegged to the sports habit. In all locations, the popular media have also generated anxieties about the very destabilizing processes that they helped to create. In Canada and England, this has taken the form of xenophobic attacks on foreign players, while in Australia it has been framed as the betrayal of the 'working-man's game'. The profound masculinist and heteronormative biases of TV sports were problematized by the queer activism of Mauresmo. Despite these fundamental rearrangements of the media–sports–culture complex, it is clear that the male, homosocial régimes of sporting organizations, advertising and marketing firms, and media outlets have remained relatively intact. In media portrayals of perceived threats to identity in our case studies, the usurpers have been either domestic or foreign *men* and a woman who 'resembled' a man. The Soviet sports régime, once reviled as the antithesis of the capitalist system, has become an integral component of national sports development programmes, which often feature coaches from former Eastern bloc countries. This is also an instance of global flows shifting from the periphery to the centre, rather than the more conventional move in the other direction. If this media–sports–culture complex is so shifting, how and by whom can it be governed – and in whose interests? In our last chapter, we address these matters.

Note

1. In April 1999, media moguls Murdoch and John Malone struck the richest (US$2.1 billion) deal in the history of the media industry. It was expected to be a precursor to joint ventures on the internet between them. Malone would become the second largest shareholder (8%) in Murdoch's News Corporation via his Liberty Media's purchase of US$1.42 billion of preferred shares in the former company. In return, Murdoch would tighten his grip on televised sport in the USA by doubling his control of Liberty's sports programming network, Fox Liberty Media, from 50 to 100%. Liberty Media is the programming arm of the giant cable operator Tele-Communications Inc., which Malone sold in 1998 for over US$45 billion to AT&T, America's largest telephone company. Malone, who is known as the 'King of Cable' (described less charitably by Al Gore as 'Darth Vader') due to his formidable influence over cable TV, also has interests in AOL-Time Warner, Discovery Communications, USA Networks, and General Instruments.

4

Citizens of the World:
The Governance of Sport

> Sport, like culture, or other economic activities such as agriculture, cannot be reduced to a single commercial dimension without severe detriment... it is a fundamental feature of national identity that FIFA and UEFA are determined to safeguard. (FIFA press release, 'FIFA and UEFA', 1999)

This quotation – a reaction to the Bosman free agency decision discussed in Chapter 2 – took a sport that the two agencies have worked hard to commodify and claimed that it is not a commodity, then called for the preservation of national heritage, to be undertaken by undemocratic, non-state actors that are constitutively transnational because of their status as governing bodies or 'guardians'. Something similar occurred, albeit with links to democratic political representation, when the ICC announced a partnership with the United Nations in 1999 'as part of cricket's globalization programme' because 'cricket is an ideal vehicle to promote the values and principles for which the United Nations stands'. These principles were about the governance of the game, and its ability to operate with an ethos of fair play that goes beyond rules and into the life-world of players.

Clearly, new forms of international civil society are emerging, akin to the 'civilizing mission' and 'corporate citizenship' ideology of capitalism. What is the lineage of this governance? In search of an answer, this chapter moves through concepts of citizenship and governmentality to look at the history of governing sport and contemporary attempts to deal with two unruly figures of modernity calling for citizens' rights – women and minorities.

The Citizen

Since the Enlightenment, the citizen has stood as a champion of freedom, a subject whose materialization has unfolded over time and space to grant citizen rights to more and more categories of persons. Although we read about citizenship in pre-Christian texts, its modern manifestations are of greater significance. Starting with eighteenth-century North American property-owning adult white men utilizing the concept to protect their economic position, citizenship has expanded to include all adult subjects and developed as a concept offering democratic and social rights across the world. But its younger sibling, the consumer, has become more and more powerful, as is clear from the commodification and neoliberalism outlined previously.

In one sense, the citizen has always been a contingent subject:

> the American people did not exist as the American people before having signed the Declaration of Independence. And it is in signing that they conferred upon themselves the right to call themselves the American people and the right to sign. It did not exist before the signature. Thus, the scriptor does not exist before the signature. The signature itself, which imposes the law, is in itself a performative act which in a certain way produces its own subject. (Derrida, 1987: 200)

The citizen has been with us for millennia, but has undergone a major revival in the last decade. Social theorists and policymakers have shifted their attention from class to citizenship as a magical agent of historical change. More easily identified than class, and more easily mobilized to justify state action, citizenship has become a site of hope for a Left that has lost its actually existing alternative to international capital. Given the NICL, how citizenship is theorized and actualized matters enormously for working people/subaltern groups. Can their participatory rights be asserted in terms of: (1) where they live, were born, or work; (2) the temporary or permanent domicile of their employer; or (3) the cultural impact of a foreign multinational on daily life?

Most writers in political philosophy and theory (PPT) use ideal types that appear unanchored by history and space, but can have definite material effects, and not just in textbooks or curricula. Communitarianism has been adopted by 'welfare reformers', and liberalism circles politics all the time. In this sense, PPT is similar to neoclassical economics, which also takes ideal types as its point of departure and transforms ivory-tower speculation into policy inputs and outcomes. Ideal types have a history that repeats itself. A problem or structure is analysed via a theoretical construct that explains its origins and operation. This theory is then disarticulated from the material coordinates it was developed to explain, becoming a device that accounts for other phenomena that might otherwise have been subjected to local inspection and critique (Sacks, 1972a, 1972b, 1995). Such problems definitely apply to PPT's theorization of citizenship.

In PPT, the social contract is a mythic solution to three queries that flow from what Louis Althusser called a *'problem of origins'*: (a) which came first – the state legitimized by public will, or the public itself; (b) how could there be a public without a state; and (c) when did the citizen *become* a citizen (1977: 25, 125)? Or in Robert Michels' formulation, what is 'the nature of the act by which a people is a people' (1915: 236)? The mythic installation and iteration of tradition argues for a compact with the polity and fealty to the nation. A performative becomes a constative via the work of myth. '[M]aking men free by making them subject' is Jean-Jacques Rousseau's paradox that freedom is both a source of good government *and* the authority of that government over individuals (1975: 124, 123). Jürgen Habermas glosses the material manifestation of this conundrum:

> According to the official version, political power springs from public will-formation and flows, as it were, through the state apparatus via legislation and administration, returning to a Janus-faced public that takes the form of a public of citizens at the entrance to the state and a public of clients at its exit. (1989: 65)

Myths such as the social contract deny their own conditions of existence, as per the ideal types mentioned above. But this process could be reversed. Instead of a binding, but not freely made, agreement, there might be a different engagement between state and person, one that eschewed blood, soil, or travel – a quid pro quo [exchange] based not on the notion that people pledge allegiance and practise obedience in return for rights, but that they do so by giving and receiving things. *Population* becomes a master signifier, displacing the mythic compact, and *demography* succeeds PPT as its principal interpretative method. This is equally a means of getting away from thinking of people as consumers, and dealing with the complexities of the NICL's deterritorialization – we all end up in material space, however cosmopolitan we may be. Nor is this wish-fulfilment, for even under globalization, there is always already government. Even exploitative non-state actors, like MLB or Nike, may be accountable under international law for their human-rights abuses (Marcano and Fidder, 1999: 557). And when we look back with some measure of distance on Eastern European and Third World state socialism of the 1980s, it may be possible to acknowledge the critical role that these nations played in finally persuading the West to follow an all-sports boycott of apartheid South Africa because it did not permit universal suffrage (Booth, 1998: 85–122). These actions were feasible because of citizenship's uptake as a crucial site of governmentality.

Governmentality

Barthes coined the term 'governmentality' in the 1950s to describe market varia-tions and the state's attempt to claim responsibility for them (when the outcome was deemed positive) (1973: 130). It was an ironic neologism, and we use it with a similar doubleness. Foucault developed the idea to account for 'the way in which the modern state began to worry about individuals' (1991b: 4) by asking: 'How to govern oneself, how to be governed, how to govern others, by whom the people will accept being governed, how to become the best possible governor.' These issues arose as twin processes: the displacement of feudalism by the sovereign state, and the similarly conflictual Reformation and its counters. A devolved reli-gious authority produced a void via ecclesiastical conflicts and debates about divine right. Daily economic and spiritual government were up for redefinition, and the state emerged as a centralizing tendency that sought to normalize itself and others. The doctrine of transcendence fell into crisis. Royalty came to be man-agerial rather than immanent (Foucault, 1991a: 87–90).

With the upheavals of the seventeenth century, such as the Thirty Years War and rural and urban revolt, additional conditions for implementing new modes of social organization arose. In eighteenth-century Europe, the definitional field of 'the economy' spread beyond the domestic sphere. Modernity emerged. The government of territory was henceforth secondary to the government of things and the social relations between them. Government was conceived and actualized anew, in terms of climate, disease, industry, finance, custom, and disaster: literally, a concern with life and death and what can be calculated/managed between them. Wealth and health became goals to be attained through the disposition of capacities across the population: 'biological existence was reflected in political existence' through the work of 'bio-power', as we saw in Chapter 2. Just as biopower brought 'life and its mechanisms into the realm of explicit calculations and made knowledge-power an agent of transformation of human life', so these calculations became of interest to governance. Bodies were identified with politics and managing them was part of running the country. For Foucault, since that time, 'a society's "threshold of modernity" is reached when the life of the species is wagered on its own political strategies' (1991a: 97, 92–95; 1984: 143).

The eighteenth-century foundations of classical political economy are generally associated with a libertarian championing of the market. But as Michael J. Shapiro's study of Adam Smith has shown, the very founder of the discourse theorized sovereignty beyond the exhibition and maintenance of loyalty, as a way of managing 'exchange within the social domain'. Politics already centred productivity in place of monarchy (1993: 11). Foucault sees both the physiocrats and Smith as concerned with the transformation of sovereignty from legitimacy to technique: 'what is free, what has to be free, and what has to be regulated', with crime and health key sites for playing out this knowledge in the public realm (1994: 124–25).

The eighteenth century continued to wrestle with sovereignty, through the early career of public law, and the model of the household as an economic matrix thrived, despite its weakness in an internationalizing, post-mercantilist world. But with the externalization of the state, following a brief moment of territoriality that looked exclusively inwards, new industries and modes of production emerged. For Foucault, the arts of government were freed from empire and economy by the strictures imposed by sovereign and household motifs. Not only did 'population' displace 'prince' as a site for accumulating power, but 'home' was displaced by 'economy' as a dynamic of social intervention and achievement. The populace became the province of statistics, bounded not by the direct exertion of juridical influence or domestic authority, but by forms of knowledge that granted 'the people' a life that cannot be divined from the model of the family. City and country substituted for home, with all the hierarchical dislocation that implies (1991a: 98–99). Even as Revolutionary France was embarking on a régime of slaughter, public health campaigns were under way. This was the ongoing Janus-faced 'game between death and life' the state constructs for itself (1991b: 4). Out of that came the following prospect: 'Maybe what is really important for our modernity – that is, for our present – is not so much the étatisation of society, as the governmentalization of the state' (Foucault, 1991a: 103).

Clearly, the emergence of modern capitalism is linked to the rise of the nation-state, which is concerned to deliver a docile and healthy labour force to business; but not only to business, and not merely in a way that shows the lineage of that desire. Cholera, sanitation, and prostitution are figured as problems for government to address in the modern era, through 'the emergence of the health and physical well-being of the population in general as one of the essential objectives of political power'. The entire 'social body' is assayed and treated. Governing people means, most centrally and critically, obeying the 'imperative of health: at once the duty of each and the objective of all' (Foucault, 1991b: 277). This presents contradictions for the state–economy mix of contemporary cultural capitalism: enterprise is accumulable nationally, based on individual initiative, but morality remains tightly knotted inside mythic family arrangements. At least paradoxically, governments become, more and more, guardians of an economy that is meant to be self-actualizing, and a civics that is supposed to derive from the nuclear family. But the statistical functions of the state reveal societies that are just not right for the myths empowering ideological discourse. And the categories of knowledge informing and informed by the census – and related governmental programmes – reveal a split society. In this space, between the empirical knowledges of governmentality and the mythic ideals of sovereignty, creativity, and economics, the cultural politics of a counter-public sphere take place: the family is said to be 'a model', when it is really 'a segment'. This space permits inquiry 'into the forms of power and authority that the practices of the present help to sustain' (Foucault, 1991a: 100; Shapiro, 1992: 14).

When the British Parliament enacted legislation requiring smallpox vaccination for all children in 1853, this was simultaneously a landmark in the uptake of medical knowledge and in public regulation of the body politic. Science and government combined in new environmental–legal relations, under the sign of civic management and economic productivity. Two years later, Achille Guillard invented 'demography', merging 'political arithmetic' and 'political and natural observations', which had been on the rise since the first population inquiries in seventeenth-century Britain. The new knowledge codified five projects: reproduction, ageing, migration, public health, and ecology (Synnott, 1993: 26; Fogel, 1993: 312–13). Sport quickly became part of this process, and with colonialism, the 'white man's burden' took flight, with games utilized in order to 'civilize' and control populations. This has had some unintended consequences. Ashis Nandy calls cricket 'an Indian game accidentally invented by the English' (1989: 19), while C.L.R. James points to the appropriation of cricket from the master:

> we were a motley crew. The children of some white officials and white business men, middle class blacks and mulattos, Chinese boys … Indian boys… and some poor black boys who had won exhibitions or whose parents had starved and toiled on plots of agricultural land … yet rapidly we learned to obey the umpire's decision without question, however irrational it was. We learned to play with the team, which meant subordinating your personal inclination, and even interests, to the good of the whole. We kept a stiff upper lip in that we did not complain about ill fortune. We did not denounce our failures, but 'well done' or 'hard luck' came easily to our lips. We were generous to opponents and congratulated them on victories, even when we knew they did not deserve it.… Eton or Harrow had nothing on us. (1963: 34)

The critical shift here was away from an autotelic accumulation of power by the sovereign, and towards the dispersal of power into the population. The centre invested people with the capacity to produce and consume things, insisting on freedom in some compartments of life and obedience in others (Foucault, 1994: 125). Government wanted to make people manufacture goods by the most rational allocation of resources available. In sum, governmentality is destined for a place beyond sovereignty, in the social field. Its target is the whole population, and sport is a key symbolic and material method for turning leisure into practice, and pleasure into fitness.

Foucault proposes a threefold concept of 'governmentality' to explain life today. The first utilizes economics to mould the population into efficient and effective producers (the NICL). The second is the array of governmental apparatuses designed to create conditions for this productivity, via bodily interventions and the promotion of fealty and individuality (biopower). And the third is the translation of methods between education and penology that modifies justice into human 'improvement'. Put another way, we might understand this as the indoctrination of the state by the social and the infestation of sovereignty with demographics (1991a: 102–3).

The contemporary world is unthinkable without government. As several recent studies have shown, governmentality provides a useful way of pondering this complex relationship of consumption and citizenship by centring the population as desiring, producing, and committed subjects that manifest contradictions (Yúdice, 1995). Attempts to look at reproductive ritual in Egyptian villages or Brazilian cities, for example, must think through the meaning of custom in the context of experiments in birth control sanctioned by the nation-state, international state organizations, and scientists accredited by state policing norms, while the recent US adoption market in white babies has made Romania a key supplier because of governmental opposition there to contraception (Ginsburg and Rapp, 1995: 2; Barroso and Corrêa, 1995; Kligman, 1995). It may even be that a form of world society is at play, an international civil society that 'works' the state into compliance with certain associational norms of socioeconomic development, citizenship rights, national science policy, justice, public health, and universal education – in short, a sense of responsibility for the population's progress that is as much about meeting international expectations expressed by academia, the media, and non-governmental organizations, as it is to do with rational, purposive action that is in some way 'essential' to statehood (Meyer et al., 1997).

Governmentality and Sport

The unusual relationship between sport and nation, where the former has been more clearly part of popular civil society than, say, national museums, obscures both its history of colonialism and its somewhat more recent *étatisation*. A trend towards ruling-class control of sport is structurally homologous with, and histori-cally connected to, state monopolies on legitimate violence (Shapiro, 1989). As discussed in Chapter 1, CAS has an international code for deciding sport-related disputes over drugs, endorsements, and violence through on-site panels at each Olympics and permanent courts in Denver and Sydney that many states defer to (Nafziger, 1999: 231–32).

The work of governments in normalizing sports has been crucial: first, policing holidays to normalize vacations and regularize recreation as play and spectatorship; second, securing the conditions of existence for a partial commodification that still makes sport governed rather than classically competitive (anti-trust exemptions and the like); third, supporting the generation of a media–sports–culture complex by putting up the risk capital for a new genre over many years; fourth, allocating resources to sport as both a diplomatic symbol and a domestic training mechanism; and fifth, being the site of appeal by activists opposed to global capital as well as others using the courts to secure financial advantage. This is the citizenship-access side to sport.

Governments are usually concerned about sport as a route to improved urban public health, military fitness, and the diversion of rebellious class politics. Modern leaders from Hitler and Pétain to Carter have initiated physical fitness tests to invigorate and ideologize the young (Houlihan, 1997: 61–64). As sports commodities, television coverage, and international competitiveness have upped the ante, the state has stepped in on behalf of nationalist ideology (consider the Malaysian government's takeover of the 1998 Commonwealth Games from a quasi-private concern: Muda, 1998: 220). This trend hints that sport may be an early warning sign of transformations in the nature and relationships of government – that whereas the state formerly focused its search for and exercise of power internally, now it looks beyond. Territorialization and the generation of wealth have been supplemented, and perhaps supplanted, by a deterritorialized contest over resources and market share (Strange, 1995).

This sporting governmentality has manifested itself in compulsory schooling, moral uplift, and the 'Britishness' of the former Empire. Until late in the nineteenth century, government intervention in sport generally took the form of protecting ruling-class interests in hunting from other classes, or ensuring social control of pastimes such as gambling; but at that point, numerous voluntary associations were formed that codified and governed pastimes that had previously been organic forms of recreation. As these bodies extended their local hegemony, and a series of international sporting events came to parallel First World economic and political engagements, their relationship to 'legitimate' expressions of national interest and representation intensified (Houlihan, 1997: 47–48, 1) – a rare case of relative autonomy from the nation-state combined with the 'right' to stand for the nation. In their analysis of Australian nationalism and the Olympics, David Rowe and Geoffrey Lawrence explain why the media break out into nationalistic fervour when a new star emerges. First, the appearance of such a figure is an opportunity for the 'unbounded rather than qualified exultation' that accompanies winning an ultimate prize. Second, it calls up Horatio Algerish myths about a meritocracy in which all can rise to their deserved level of achievement and reward. And third, 'the hero or heroine embodies an abstraction … [the spirit of the nation] and so helps to heal concrete rifts … between competing social groups' (1986: 196–97). Of course, if the hero fails to appear, falls from grace, or is in some way compromised or rendered contradictory, these 'rifts' emerge anew.

Norbert Elias analyses sport and social structure synchronically and diachronically, coining the term 'figuration' to designate how people inhabit social positions. The figural keys to sport are exertion, contest, codification, and collective meaningfulness. Without these, its magic attractions – tension and catharsis – cannot be guaranteed. Elias asks why there is such fascination with rule-governed contests between individuals and teams, evident in a trend that fanned out from the European ruling classes after the sixteenth century. Sentiment and behaviour were codified to supplant excess and self-laceration with temperant auto-critique. The displacement of tension and the search for ordered leisure allocated to organized sport the task of controlling and training gentry, workers, and colonists alike. High tension and low risk blended popular appeal with public safety in a utilitarian calculus of time and joy. An example from eighteenth-century England was the brutal enclosure movement's policy of destroying free peasants, which saw the aristocracy adopting and codifying organic sports (Maguire, 1999: 81). Of course, this was subject to local customization and struggle. There were contradictory, non-linear shifts in European sport between the thirteenth and nineteenth centuries, with enclosure and the open air in an ambiguous relationship. Sometimes, sealed-off spaces were deemed appropriate for ruling-class privacy, with field-like surroundings suitable for school exercise. The spatial separation of sport from nature in late nineteenth-century industrialization marked a trend. Bodies in motion were progressively contained, enraging hygiene movements but permitting surveillance, spectacle, and profit (Elias, 1986: 165, 173–74, 150–51, 155, 159). This is Foucault's policing role of governmentality at work.

Sport became a crucible of nation. Metaphor's role in sporting allegory has traditionally reinforced masculinism and patriotism, especially at times of great conflict or formal celebration. Consider the history of soccer in Africa, where the Cup of Nations saw the 'Winds of Change' generate symbolic and monetary capital exchanges between emergent states and soccer. As soon as Sudan gained independence in 1956, the government constructed a stadium and negotiated to start the Cup via a continental federation. Ghana's new nation determined to support soccer from its first days of freedom, in 1957. When Egypt and Syria merged to form the United Arab Republic that same year, the new ruling officer class identified its factions with particular clubs and sought to run soccer through control of local associations, while delegations to FIFA were decided by high-level discussions involving presidents and generals. In the 1960s, the Congo/ Zaire government intervened with massive subvention to aid the national team (Mahjoub, 1999).

The First World abounds with similar, if more mediatized, examples. Former US Secretary of Defense Melvin Laird euphemized the mining of Haiphong Harbour and increased bombing of North Vietnam as 'an expansion ball club', the Nixon White House staff called itself 'operation linebacker', and Tricky Dicky's own nickname was 'quarterback'. During his Presidency, Reagan regularly cited the role he played as footballer George Gipp in the 1940 biopic of a Notre Dame football coach, *Knute Rockne, All American* (Lloyd Bacon). This was supposed to stand as a universal sign of Americanness. He also repeatedly quoted Gipp's dying words inspiring the side to new heights – 'win one for the Gipper': in his 1981 Commencement address at the University commemorated in the film, opening the 1984 LA Olympics, as a rallying cry during the Nevada Senate race in 1986, and at Bush's nomination two years later. He referred to Walter Mondale in 1984 as 'Coach tax-hike'. Promotions for the 1991 rugby league series between New South Wales and Queensland after the Gulf War dubbed the players 'scuds' and 'missiles' (Shapiro, 1989: 80, 87; McKay, 1992: 256; Reagan quoted in Monnington, 1993). Reagan's metaphorization associates romantic male sacrifice with national glory through classic second-order meaning – the mythic last words of an historical character as replayed in a film. Four decades later, the actor playing him redisposes the words for political purposes, cleaving to himself the persona of the original speaker. Enunciation loses historical specificity.

That set the scene for a century of 'an invention of tradition' in the name of 'straightforward revivalism' (MacAloon, 1999: 10) that characterizes the intersection of sport and government. The Mexican Revolution moved quickly to institutionalize sport in the 1910s as a sign and source of national unity, and the same moment saw the British government encourage the National Rifle Association to use human-figure targets as military preparation. When the Argentine Olympic Committee was founded in 1922, it promised to work for 'the perfection of the race and the glory of conquering what is noble, worthy, and beautiful'. The successes of physical-education movements and Western European Fascism inspired the British to institutionalize gymnasium curricula in order to meet any armed challenge. The US Peace Corps argued in *Sports Illustrated* in 1963 that sports were more productive terrain for its mission than teaching because they were 'least vulnerable to charges of "neo-colonialism" and "cultural imperialism"'. John F. Kennedy established the President's Council on Youth Fitness to counter a 'growing softness, our increasing lack of physical fitness', which constituted 'a threat to our security'. From a very different angle, the Sandinistas abolished professional sport in Nicaragua, focusing instead on nation-building through a large-scale sport-for-all policy (Arbena, 1993: 110–12; Shapiro, 1989: 71, 74; Kennedy quoted in Lasch, 1979: 183; Skillen, 1993: 350; Corps quoted in Kang, 1988: 431).

Colonel Gaddafi's *Green Book*, which lays out the basis for Libyan revolution, is opposed to sports spectatorship, calling instead for sport to be 'practiced by all and not left to anyone else to practice on their behalf' (Gaddafi quoted in Shropshire, 1999). A recent Aotearoa/New Zealand Minister of Recreation and Sport referred to his portfolio as a route to 'social and economic prosperity' through the promotion of 'active, physical lifestyles'. He identified an additional benefit: 'being *into* sport' ensured being 'out of court'. This longstanding criminological obsession deems familially-based and formal sporting activities to be worthy, integrative norms, whilst informal leisure is demonized. Even the former Jamaican Socialist Prime Minister, Michael Manley, also a distinguished historian of cricket, pushed such a line: male violence is a danger that can be pacified and redirected into an appropriate sphere – literally, national fitness. Sovietism saw sport as a means of socializing the people into new values and away from capitalistic self-indulgence. The German Democratic Republic sought to integrate sport and its cultural history into the everyday life of the citizenry, a means of writing socialist physicality over Nazi brutality. For colonial powers in the Anglo-Caribbean, it marked the power of the English over the locals – something successfully protested against in Africa and a later site of protest against repressive postcolonial rulers, notably in Cameroon. Just as schools have often used the gymnasium for discipline, so too the nation. Come on down, Matthew Arnold. But more than that, sport becomes inflected with an ethnocentric notion of correct behaviour, and delinquency associated with racial minorities and youthful muscularity. Given diminished employment prospects in the latter half of this century, such moral panics are as much to do with governments preparing people for a leisure-defined poverty as with training them to work (Minister quoted in Volkerling, 1994: 8; Agnew and Petersen, 1989; Magdalinski, 1999; MacClancy, 1996: 10–12; Nkwi and Vidacs, 1997: 124; Leseth, 1997; McMurtry, 1993: 422; Griffin, 1993: 119).

The nation-state is concerned to deliver a docile and healthy labour force to business; but not only to business, and not merely in a way that shows the lineage of that desire. The 'emergence of the health and physical well-being of the population in general is one of the essential objectives of political power'. The entire 'social body' is assayed and treated for its insufficiencies. Governing people means, most centrally and critically, obeying the 'imperative of health: at once the duty of each and the objective of all' (Foucault, 1978: 277). This governmentality can be *both* a state exercising power over its citizens *and* a form of resistance – the 1884 formation of the Gaelic Athletic Association marked, and has remained, a critical form of opposition to British rule in Ireland. The Association promoted hurling and Gaelic football over cricket and soccer and came to be a site for Republican politics as well (Houlihan, 1997: 41–42). When the Bosman ruling erupted on the soccer landscape in the late 1990s, the German government formally protested that soccer was about culture, something inalienable by commerce, and that it should have a special exemption from the ordinary rules of the economy – governed, but governed as a public good (albeit with huge profits to private firms!) (Arnedt, 1998: 112).

Sport has long been an arm of US foreign policy, as illustrated by the Executive's hectoring of the US Olympic Federation to boycott the 1980 Moscow Games and Congressional censure of Beijing's 2000 Olympic bid, while the Treasury denied ABC a licence to telecast the 1991 Pan-American Games because they were held in Havana, and the US government opposed MLB's attempts to open up Cuban links until 1999 (Nafziger, 1992: 495; Chass, 1999; Carter, 1999). As part of international relations, sport can also be a subtle means of parastatal diplomacy: for example the table-tennis matches between the US and the PRC in 1971, set up after border skirmishes between China and the USSR, tennis contests between the Koreas in 1984, Taiwan first accepting the moniker of 'Chinese Taipei' rather than 'Republic of China' at the 1984 Olympics, Pakistani President Zia-ul-Haq's 'Peace through Cricket' mission to India in 1987, and Mu'ammar Gaddafi, Jr's attempt to make Olympic participation mark an end to Libya's pariah status in 2000. The Iran–US wrestling engagement of 1998 marked the first time the US flag had flown in Tehran for almost two decades. An American competitor held up a picture of Ayatollah Ali Khomenei to the crowd. This gesture of reconciliation was achieved through a patchwork of civil-society activity brokering the two states (Nafziger, 1992: 496–98; 'Zia', 1987; Singh, 1987; Mangan, 1999; Marks, 1998; Shropshire, 1999; 'Old Glory', 1998; K. Cooper, 1998). Of course, the outcome is not always successful – it has been claimed that fighting between Tamil Tigers and the Sri Lankan military lessened as Sri Lanka set a run-scoring record in a 1997 cricket match, but that was the very year when the soccer match between Red Star Belgrade and Croatia Zagreb, hailed as testimony to the peace process in the region, turned into a vicious encapsulation of wider struggles (Bairner and Sugden, 1999: 8).

Karl von Clausewitz described a trinitarian form to war and the state: material enmity, military presence, and political leadership. Sport's version would be a national divide, team competition, and management. Pierre de Coubertin founded the modern Olympics to follow the example of British muscular Christianity and redeem French masculinity after the shocks of the Franco-Prussian War, while the Boer War saw British imperialists clamouring for physical education of the working class to improve fitness for military service (Birley, 1995: 1–2). Famous Dutch soccer coach Rinus Michels coined the expression 'Football is war.' The 1969 Central American Soccer War broke out when the Honduran government expelled all Salvadorans following a match between the two countries, and the Biafran–Nigerian civil war the following year was halted for a day so the combatants could watch Pelé. The Brazilian junta took the national team's 1970 World Cup song for itself. In 1978, the Fascists running Péru helped out the Fascists running Argentina during the World Cup. The hosts had to beat Péru by at least four goals to nil in order to qualify for the second round. With the help of 35,000 tons of free grain and US$50 million in credits, they did so. Four years later, the Argentinian generals used the 1978 team song during the struggle for the Malvinas. The events of 1989 in Central and Eastern Europe were character-ized by intense passions associated with sport. Steaua military athletes shot at the secret police in Romania, Dinamo Club players defended their patrons, the Securitate, and the captain of the national rugby union side died in battle. (The Dinamo teams throughout the continent were all KGB-backed. One of their sides encouraged George Orwell to call sport 'war minus the shooting'.) When Georgia achieved its independence from the USSR, almost the first act of its new govern-ment was an application to join FIFA. In East Germany, skater Katherina Witt and swimmers Roland Matthes and Kornelia Ender had their homes sacked. That reaction repeats the treatment of the athlete Astylus when he switched nationali-ties prior to the 480 BC Olympics: his old house was destroyed (Michels quoted in Kuper, 1998: 5; Orwell quoted in Birley, 1995: 1; Beloff et al., 1999: 2; Kuper, 1998: 1–2, 175, 179). Today, US aircraft carriers have their own signal to carry live NFL games to sailors on ship through the Armed Forces Radio and Television Service, and the President of Belarus promises successful Olympians 'an apart-ment and dozens of dollars.... I'll buy anything you need, be it guns, boats, swimming trunks, even undershorts' ('NFL Full', 1999; President quoted in 'President', 1999).

At times, the narrative of sport codification and expansion also encounters critique and engagement from those who have only been granted full citizen rights gradually. Consider the US version of governmentality. In the seventeenth century the north-eastern Puritans devoted great efforts to quelling the pleasures of the lower orders, such as cock fighting and horse racing. This spread to the classically modern abhorrence of cruelty to animals across the country in the nineteenth century, with associated state intervention. The push towards Americanization of new immigrants in the late nineteenth and early twentieth centuries was embodied in the formation of voluntary sporting associations. In the two decades from 1881, the US set up national bodies to regulate tennis, golf, and college sports. Over the next twenty years, baseball, hockey, and football professionalized. The First World War saw a major articulation of sporting values with militarism and citizenship – an internal Americanization equating national sports with patriotism. The American Legion sponsored baseball to counter working-class radicalism and to encourage social and migrant integration. When feminist criticisms of sport emerged in the 1960s, part of their force concerned the claim to equitable public funding promised by the modern. Hence the Title IX Educational Amendments, which forced US colleges that were in receipt of federal funds to allocate them across campus in proportion to the number of men and women they enrolled. These were among the first legislative gains for women in the contemporary era, and they addressed the expenditure of state money on the body as a source of fitness (Houlihan, 1997: 62, 56, 63).

But governmentality is not solely the prerogative of states – civil society is part of it. Away from élite spectacle, everyday sport is influenced by the policing rites of the IOC and FIFA and by intergovernmental policies, as parlayed by the Commonwealth of Nations, the United Nations Educational, Scientific, and Cultural Organization, and the Council of Europe, as well as social movement manifestos such as the 1994 *Brighton Declaration on Women and Sport* (see Appendix 4.1), while Swiss law is part of international sport, because it partially governs the activities of the Geneva-based IOC, FIFA, UEFA, and the CAS (Harvey et al., 1996; Houlihan, 1994: 90–91; Beloff et al., 1999: 36). Although the quadrennial Commonwealth Games have long been its most visible sign, the Commonwealth, keen to separate sport from state, only established a Working Party on Strengthening Commonwealth Sport in 1989. Its goal was more equitable levels of sports participation and success. The Games routinely see the handful of white-settler nations overwhelm the formerly British Third World in competition, highlighting old colonial inequalities, while male competitors have outnumbered female four to one and only the Kingston Games had been held outside the UK or its old dominions until Kuala Lumpur in 1998. The Working Party has followed FIFA and the IOC into civil society governance, via Street Kids International, a community-based youth project across Papua New Guinea, Tanzania, Zambia, Pakistan, and India (McMurtry, 1993). So we should regard with no surprise the commitment of FIFA since 1995 to an SOS Children's Villages programme, which it calls 'private welfare' (FIFA, n. d.), and also acknowledge that the professionalization of sport represents a further govern-mentalization, as managers replace volunteer administrators and specialist lawyers and accountants emerge (Horne et al., 1999: 277). How accountable is this model of international civil society?

In the 1978 World Cup in Argentina, advertising boards covered the grounds for the first time – what FIFA referred to twenty years later as 'the foresight' of Adidas. By the 1982 competition, the shadowy International Sports and Leisure (ISL) Marketing firm was promoting the Fédération and the IOC (FIFA, 1997; Nafziger, 1992: 502). FIFA's key 1998 World Cup sponsors were Adidas, Budweiser, Canon, Coca-Cola, Fuji, Gillette, JVC, MasterCard, McDonald's, Opel, Philips, and Snickers. Most of those companies are domiciled in countries that perform pitifully in men's soccer. Sporting failure is irrelevant, however, to the business concerns of such MNCs. As members of what FIFA calls its 'small and select family', they are encouraged to 'be more than merely the names on the advertising boards around the world's most famous football stadia'. FIFA wants 'ideas and initiatives from the corporate world which may serve the future of the sport' (ISL, n. d.). But FIFA also claims that it is 'important for the sponsors not to influence – or even try to influence – the game itself' (1997) even as 44% of seats at France '98 were reserved for corporations (Endean, 1998).

One factor changed: Budweiser was removed from the list of sponsors because of local French legislation. Again, the state complicates the narrative of absolute globalization. Many local advertisers were more prominently displayed than major international sponsors, leading FIFA to require the Japanese and Korean hosts of the 2002 World Cup to give it control of all signage (Tomlinson, 1999). The contradictions are clear – a quasi-religious authority invested by billions of people in FIFA is jeopardized by commodification, even as that very process 'helps' to bring them closer to the world of their favoured sport. In this sense, the Fédération combines the moral suasion of a non-government, non-profit organization with the reach and capitalization of a multinational (Sugden and Tomlinson, 1998b: 300).

This blend of governmentalization and corporatization applies just as much, of course, to nation-states. Consider the example of Australia. When England sent sports teams there in the mid-nineteenth century, the local attitude was supine, in keeping with the belief that a combination of working-class convict ancestry and life in the southern hemisphere would produce racial impurity. Slowly, connections came to be adduced between vitality, rurality, and the whiteness of Australian-born males ('cornstalks'). Local virility was much remarked on in the newspapers, especially with the advent of organized sculling in the 1850s and the popularity of swimming from the 1890s (Cashman, 1995: 73, 76–77, 87). Colonial manliness made sport a key arena for differentiating the white Australian nation from Britain and then from the rest of the world, a differentiation that has been carried forward since by public mythology, governmental programmes and propaganda, media attention, and everyday talk. Sport has evidenced manliness, and manliness has made sport crucial to national identity. As sporting self-confidence grew, so did pressure for federation and independence – a nice case of sport helping to produce nation and governance. This obsession with sport continued in Australia, with great success in the amateur international domain for almost a century. A key component was the maintenance and development of racial continuity with Britain – the cornstalks became almost a higher point of evolution. The exclusion of Aboriginal Australians from sporting bodies was vital to this project for at least a century from the 1870s, while the 1982 Commonwealth and 2000 Sydney Olympic Games have seen extensive forms of repressive and ideological policing in the interest of stilling local racial politics during times of global media exposure. Like Australia, Canada dedicated many resources at the moment of federation to incorporating imperial sports and native ones into a white-settler amalgam. Snowshoe racing and lacrosse became Euro-Canadian, their indigenous origins a mere trace. The 1860s and 1870s marked the formation of national sports associations to govern recreation, just when political self-government was arriving – a clear structural homology (Houlihan, 1997: 27–28, 34–36).

As sports around the industrially advanced world professionalized and corporatized in the last third of the twentieth century, Australia's self-image as omniscient, nourished by success at postcolonial sports like athletics, cricket, tennis, and swimming, was threatened by the state-socialist sport systems of Europe and China, college 'socialism-by-stealth' from the United States, and the emergence of South Asian and Caribbean nations. The response from successive Australian governments combined varied strategies. On the one hand, what had been a comparatively organic, civil society model of amateur sports (albeit with a relationship to the school curriculum) became a quasi-moral imperative in terms of national fitness, peaceable everyday life, and full personal development, with associated programmes by the state and increased intervention in the running of previously voluntary associations (many of which encouraged this; they corporatized and drew on state assistance even as they underwent regulation). Since the 1980s, both the Australian Labor Party (ALP) and the Liberal-National Party have radically transformed amateur sport. In 1981, the Liberal Prime Minister, Malcolm Fraser, opened the Australian Institute of Sport (AIS), which is often referred to as 'the gold medal factory'. The Australian Sport Commission (ASC) was created by the ALP government in 1984 and incorporated the AIS five years later. Today, the ASC has a multimillion-dollar budget and is responsible for the national planning and funding of amateur sport, including gender equity. Like virtually all federal policies implemented by the ALP during its reign from 1983 to 1996, the planning and funding of amateur sport were shaped by neoliberal discourse and practice (see Beeson and Frith, 1998; Pusey, 1992). The conservative coalition which has been in office since 1996 has followed this trajectory. Like Australia, Canada's increasingly poor performances at the Olympics led to much soul-searching about the need for increased commercial and state input to ensure élite success at the same moment as the population was being subjected to biopower in horror at its sedentariness. The blend of settler nationalism and British ties shifted further with the powerful influence of US commodities (Houlihan, 1997: 62).

This transformation of sport from a relatively amateur-based pastime to a full-blown corporate entity exemplifies Foucault's concept of governmentality, as sporting metaphors and images are frequently invoked by politicians (and business leaders) to exemplify neoliberal slogans such as 'excellence', 'enterprise', 'the level playing field', and 'no pain, no gain', as well as the principles of social Darwinism, self-discipline, scientific management, competitive individualism, and the need for a fit and healthy population (McKay, 1991; McKay et al., 1993). Consequently, nearly all 'amateur' national sporting organizations (NSOs) now have CEOs and managers for advertising, marketing, and public relations, and are dependent on the private and/or the state sector for support.

In an age of privatization, corporatization, and deregulation, where the state has increasingly withdrawn resources, sport has received unprecedented state interest and involvement. The ASC was almost alone in being cushioned from 1996 budgetary cuts, and Sydney's hosting the 2000 Olympics guaranteed even more state funding (Cashman and Hughes, 1998). In a policy that underlines the anachronistic nature of 'amateurism', the ASC's Olympic Athlete Programme supports 33 national sports foundations through an annual budget of about A$25 million, partially on the basis of likely success at the 2000 Games (in 1996 the Australian Olympic Committee announced it would pay swimmers A$35,000, A$21,000, and A$9,000 for gold, silver, and bronze medals respectively at international events). In 1998, after pressure from key lobby groups and influential members of the ruling Liberal-National Party, the Prime Minister announced that tickets for the 2000 Games would be exempt from a proposed indirect tax.

Britain's recent history is similar. When the British government transferred sport policy to the Department of National Heritage in 1991, this represented a twin shift. First, its rhetoric ('Sport for All') linked access and participation to fitness, articulating democracy to industry. Second, the location marked the ideological meanings of international sport for Englishness, just when closer ties to the EU were bringing cultural autonomy into question (Houlihan, 1997: 2, 46–47). The claims that TV money revived British soccer (see Chapter 3) generally ignore the critical role of the state in utilizing public money to fund ground rebuilding, a hidden subsidy to business (Hamil, 1999).

Something similar could be said of the United States. Once the state recognized the importance of geopolitical ideology, it was quick to intervene when necessary. Following anxieties that the US team had been hampered at the 1972 Olympics by inefficient private administration, Congress restructured amateur athletics (Houlihan, 1997: 104). Today, the US has responded to the long economic crisis by withdrawing into a sheath of cultural protectionism in sport, even as it has sought to expand overseas.

Gender Equity and Government

> Gold medals are won around the boardroom table. (Sir Ronald Scott, foundation chair of the Hillary Commission for Recreation and Sport, quoted in Tew, 1994: 182)

We need to interrogate who stands for the nation in gender and racial terms. Approximately 75% of black male athletes on US college sports scholarships do not gain degrees, and many National Collegiat Athletic Association (NCAA) schools never graduate freshman-class sports scholars. Nor does sport itself lead to personal success for the students. Black men and women have much greater chances of becoming doctors, lawyers, and dentists than professional athletes. For all men and women, the prospects for upward mobility from sport in the US vary between 0.004% and 0.007%, and there appear to be shorter careers for African-American professional baseballers than for whites, who are kept on longer after their prime (Cahn, 1994: 269–71; Rowe and Brown, 1994: 101; Jiobu, 1988; Lapchick and Benedict, 1993).

Women of colour occupy a particularly ambiguous position in American sport. Whilst the Olympic triumphs of African-American women sprinters since the 1960s have given them (quadrennial) national attention, they have suffered sexist and racist depictions in the media. When women are given the mantle of national sporting symbolism, the result is always overdetermined. Consider the 1996 Olympic gymnasts, hailed by the media as 'The Face of America'. What did this mean? Supposedly, they formed 'The Face' because of diversity: the team included one Asian American (Amy Chow) and an African-American (Dominique Dawes) amidst white representatives. In the previous Olympics, Dawes had been joined by another black athlete, Betty Okino. Officials in 1992 and 1996 did not talk *that* team up in the same way. It seems that blackness did not constitute promotable diversity (Chisholm, 1999: 135).

National mythmaking through sport is common across continents. Stereotypes are ethical norms that argue for/train/generate new habits amongst the citizenry. Still, fissures do appear. In 1990, the *Los Angeles Times* ran what has become an infamous interview with British Tory politician Norman Tebbitt, who charged migration with endangering the 'special relationship' between the UK and the US. He also suggested Britain impose a 'cricket test' on immigrants. Asking 'Which side do they cheer for?' would sort out whether South Asians in England watching the local side play Pakistan or India had adequately assimilated. In the House of Commons itself, Tebbitt related this question to death threats against the author Salman Rushdie, before warming to his real intention: keeping Hong Kong Chinese (British subjects) from migrating before 1997. When South Asians flew into Heathrow for the 1999 World Cup of cricket, officials allegedly posed a 'cricket quiz' to decide whether their level of knowledge meant that they were *really* there to watch. South Africans were not subjected to this (perhaps it was assumed they were 'white'). Prior to a Euro 2000 qualifying match in London between Scotland and England, telephone booking staff were instructed in the art of detecting Scottish accents in order to prevent Scots supporters from exceeding their quota of tickets and occupying sections of the ground designated for the English.

This question of who counts as a citizen has an old and complex lineage in gender. The International Working Group on Women and Sport (IWGWS) has mounted perhaps the most impressive global campaign for gender equity in sport. In 1994, nearly 300 delegates from over 80 countries met in England for the 'Women, Sport and the Challenge of Change' conference, supported by the British Sports Council and the IOC. Some of the key outcomes of the event were the formation of the IWGWS, the launch of the International Strategy of Women in Sport, and a 10-point *Brighton Declaration* (see Appendix 4.1). Since then, over 200 organizations throughout the world have formally adopted the *Declaration*. A second world conference on women and sport, attended by about 400 delegates from over 70 countries, was held in Namibia in 1998. Those attending the latter gathering evaluated progress since Brighton. On the one hand, the representatives were optimistic:

> world wide action includes ten international government organizations, including the United Nations, five multi-sport organisations, including the International Olympic Committee and the International Paralympic Committee; six international physical education organisations including the Council of Sports Science and Physical Education and the International Council on Health, and Physical Education and Recreation and nine international women and sport groups. The number and range of national organisations

is also encouraging. Twenty-four European nations, twenty African nations, thirteen Asian nations, eight from the Americas and five from Oceania. (International Working Group on Women and Sport, 1998: 46)

However, the delegates were concerned about the slow rate of progress in some countries and organizations (including the IOC). They flagged an intention to forge links with the Beijing Platform for Action and the Convention for the Elimination of All Forms of Discrimination Against Women, and issued the *Windhoek Call for Action* (see Appendix 4.2). It is worth noting that despite the emphasis on activism, diversity, inclusiveness, and empowerment in both the Brighton and Windhoek manifestos, no mention is made of how these principles relate to heterosexism, lesbianism, and homophobia in sport.[1] As we shall see, a fragile consensual liberalism has long characterized the area, that is blind to differences between women (Hargreaves, 1999).

The most important historical advance toward addressing these pervasive gender inequalities occurred in 1972, when the US federal government passed Title IX of the Education Amendments Act, which was specifically aimed at intercollegiate and interscholastic sports.[2] Many other Western countries followed suit by implementing policies or laws designed to eliminate or mitigate discrimination against females in sport, and several national and international organizations have emerged as advocates for women's rights in sport. Under terms such as 'affirmative action', 'gender equity', and 'equal opportunity', state and advocacy organizations have promoted women's sport through special training schemes for women coaches and administrators, pressure on the media to cover more women's sport and present positive images of sportswomen, and a search for private and public funding.

In most Western countries, initiatives to enhance the status of women have emanated almost entirely from the state. However, there is a profound tension between these governments' largely rhetorical commitments to promoting the standing of women, and the mutually reinforcing régimes of masculinity, corporate-managerialism, and global competitiveness that are ascendant in both public and private spheres. Framing equal opportunity in this manner sets obdurate limits on how affirmative action is formulated, implemented, and monitored (McKay, 1997). Special programmes for women can actually dovetail with neoliberal régimes that frame women as subject-citizens who can be successful, enterprising *individuals*, if they compete on men's terms in a seemingly meritocratic system. As Anna Yeatman (1990: 16) puts it in her analysis of gender, the state, and globalization, within the current corporate-managerial régimes of Western governments: 'Equal opportunity … comes to be reframed in terms of what it can do to improve management, not what it can do to develop the conditions of social justice and democratic citizenship.' Consider, for instance, the following comments in *Enterprising Nation*, a landmark report on how the government should exploit Australia's diverse labour force:

Capitalising on the talents of diversity involves half our population – women – and we must also utilise the skills of our multicultural society. Major improvements in management skills can be effected simply by opening up equal opportunities for these under-utilised groups to attain the senior levels of corporate management. (Karpin, 1995: 11)

Similar sentiments are evident in a Canadian government report on barriers to women's advancement in Federal employment. The report stated that the ageing nature of the civil service and changing demographics of the wider workforce would compel the government to recruit more women. The authors claimed that unless barriers to women's advancement are diminished, the civil service 'will not be able to attract and retain capable, well-educated women, for whom they will have to compete with a private sector that already recognizes the challenge it faces in securing the necessary work force in the next decade' (Ministry of Supply and Services, 1991: 123).

Framing equal opportunity in this manner sets obvious limits to affirmative action (McKay, 1997). In their study of policy-making processes in Canadian NSOs, Donald Macintosh and David Whitson report that most managers perceive barriers to women's participation to lie outside of sport and that affirmative action policies impede élite performance. Despite some constructive moves by Sport Canada, the Federal body responsible for planning and funding amateur sport, its meagre financial and moral commitments to affirmative action gave executives of NSOs a justification for also assigning a low priority to it:

> the federal government's emphasis on high-performance sport, and its preoccupation with institutionalizing a performance support system capable of preparing élite Canadian athletes to compete successfully in international sport, have undercut the pursuit of equity-related objectives. (Whitson and Macintosh, 1990: 27–28)

As L. Kikulius, T. Slack, and B. Hinings (1992) argue in a more general context, NSOs have gone from *ad hoc* formations around kitchen tables to institutionalized management in the boardrooms and executive offices with consequences for gender. Virtually every study of gender and sport has shown immense gaps between males and female sports in media coverage, opportunities to participate, public and private funding, prize money, and access to representation in key decision-making positions. To take just one example from the élite level, at the summer Olympic Games men compete in nearly double the number of events as women; about 25% of all participating countries, mainly Muslim ones, send no women competitors to the Games; and only six of the 174 national Olympic associations in the world have women presidents (Hall, 1995). In a study of 600 female competitors at the 1994 Commonwealth Games, M. Talbot (1998) reported that women faced significant structural and social barriers to achievement in sport, many within sports organizations.

In Australian NSOs, women comprise 17% of the national coaching directors, 10% of the presidents, 12% of the national development officers, and 18% of the executive directors (ASC, 1998). Moreover, sports management displays patterns of horizontal and vertical segregation, with men usually located in finance, marketing, policy planning, talent identification, sports science, élite sports, the Olympics, and men's events, while women work in affirmative action, youth sports, people with disabilities, women's events, human resources, and public relations (McKay, 1997).

Research on attempts by the ASC to redress this specific gender imbalance shows that current gender-equity policies in sport are unlikely to lead to more equitable relationships between men and women. McKay (1997) found that gender initiatives had been marginalized, trivialized, or incorporated into the androcentric and neoliberal practices that pervade sporting organizations, the media, and the state. When gender equity did get on the agenda in the state sector, it either received rhetorical attention or was couched in terms of what it could do to improve efficiency, rather than as a substantive commitment to social justice. A formidable obstacle to implementing gender equity was indifference and resistance by the senior managers responsible for administering the programmes, including the few women, known as 'Queen Bees', who receive some of the material rewards that ensue from playing by men's rules.

M. Bell and L. Hayes observe that during the 1993 New Zealand Women's Suffrage Year celebrations, the Hillary Commission for Recreation and Sport focused on

> the need for 'up-skilling' women as more effective leaders, more efficient administrators, more women-oriented marketers and more visible coaches.
>
> 'Managing' women, not as a special needs group but as consumers in the leisure industry, constitutes all women as a homogeneous group with fixed and measurable choices.... It gives the already doubly burdened woman – responsible for, and often servicing, through their paid and unpaid work, others' fitness and leisure – the *unpaid* task of organising and lobbying for their own activities. The shift from programming and promotion to policy and advocacy thinly disguises a devolution of financial responsibility to people who are not trained in areas of gender equity issues, and abandons policy functions of education, research and liaison. (1994: 8, 15–16)

The rationalization, commodification, and professionalization of virtually all amateur sports on a global basis has shifted government policies away from a broad concern with recreational and high-performance sport to a narrow focus on the latter. There have been qualitative changes in the composition and operation of traditional grass-roots sporting organizations. In their analysis of how these sorts of changes have affected NSOs, Slack and Hinings discern

> a move away from their traditional design type, that is, an organization controlled by volunteers and operated relatively informally with professional help, to a new organizational design type – an organization which is highly structured along bureaucratic lines controlled by professionals with volunteer help. (1994: 808)

These hierarchical divisions of gender are evident even in Norway, which is often considered to have the most progressive gender-equity policies in the world. In her analysis of selection processes in Norwegian NSOs, J. Hovden (2000) found that the most desirable candidates for leadership positions possessed professional-managerial skills that could open corporate doors. Of course, it would be a retrograde step to dismiss affirmative-action programmes in sport by the state because they do not cater to the needs of all women – an impossible task. As R.W. Connell (1990: 6) notes, affirmative action provides some leverage for some women, in the absence of 'a more radical form of engagement with the state'. In the US, the UK, Australia, Canada, New Zealand/Aotearoa, and many

European countries, women working in the civil service have made inroads by lobbying for more equitable funds and media coverage of women's sport, and challenging homophobia, sexual harassment, and sexual violence, despite resistance both within and outside the state. Nevertheless, the constant appropriation of affirmative action for corporate-managerial ends has meant that the hegemonic masculine model of both sport and equal opportunity has remained relatively undisturbed:

> The underlying theoretical assumption in the redistributive ... liberal reform model is that male-constructed and male-dominated organisational structures and processes are the yardstick against which success or failure to provide 'equal employment opportunities' for women are measured. There is no questioning of the nature of the structures themselves and the contexts within which they are created, nor of the part they play in constructing and maintaining the very inequality we are attempting to eliminate. (Wieneke, 1992: 137)

This discourse is underpinned by orthodox liberal-feminist definitions of fairness, which assume that equality can be achieved by getting more women to the same starting-point as men (Blum and Smith, 1998; Poiner and Wills, 1991; Thornton, 1994). But increasing the numbers of women in sporting organizations will not necessarily change masculine cultures, or the stresses that women experience in combining work and family responsibilities. Therefore, if an organization attempts to recruit more women, but retains policies that are based on sameness rather than difference, it is unlikely there will be any impact on what C. Cockburn (1991: 219) calls the 'white male heterosexual and largely ablebodied ruling monoculture'. C. Cohn (1987: 714) notes that it is pleasurable and seductive for women to 'seemingly beat the boys at their own game'. But overcoming women's oppression in sport (and society) is unlikely to be achieved by the efforts of a minuscule number of white, affluent, heterosexual women who compete on men's terms (Kenway, 1995). As V. Stolcke (1981: 46) puts it: 'To propose that women have first to become like men in order to become free is almost like suggesting that class exploitation might be ended by making it possible for workers to become capitalists.' Or to borrow an apposite phrase from Judith Allen (1990: 34), this strategy merely helps to reproduce a gender order which is based on 'males judging their own value in terms of competitive performance against other males, and females judging their own value in terms of the degree to which they are valued by males'. There is also a prospect of women being co-opted:

> [Women] are playing in a game that uses men's rules on a playing field designed for men with male referees who have strong loyalty to the home team. The men have had decades more practice. Even if the women become more skilful than the men at the men's games, they might win only to find that winning has cost them their souls. (Carpenter and Acosta, 1991: 23, 27)

The corporate-feminist scenario does not democratize sport by encouraging diversity and criticism, and has little relevance to most indigenous, aged, widowed, disabled, and lesbian women, plus those with dependent children – few corporations are interested in these 'target groups'. Fortunately, rather than emulating the corporate model, certain sporting organizations and movements have promoted activities that emphasize cooperation, fun, and intrinsic outcomes, explicitly combat heterosexism, homophobia, and sexual harassment and violence, and openly celebrate gay and lesbian lifestyles (Birrell and Ritcher, 1987; Griffin, 1992; Lenskyj, 1991).

According to M. Ann Hall (1994: 54), the failure by governments in Australia, Canada, the UK, and the US to implement substantial gender-equity policies in sport has placed women in the schizoid political predicament of whether to promote *sport for women* or *women in sport*. Hall sees the former as 'a more radical feminist perspective' which 'promotes its aims through sport', while the latter is 'a distinctly liberal approach which seeks to improve the lot of women already in sport through a sports organization for women'. Referring to the Canadian situation, Hall argues that a combination of masculine domination of sport, the traditionally conservative political views of sportswomen, and neoliberal state policies have depoliticized the agency responsible for advocating gender equity in sport, gradually moving it toward a liberal-feminist orientation. She notes a tendency for women's sporting organizations to emulate the hierarchical aspects of bureaucratic organizations as professional experts skilled in marketing, business administration, and management have supplanted grass-roots volunteers:

> From a radical feminist perspective ... the problem of change for the betterment of women (and men) is how to create change so that the values of people in power are not necessarily the values of a fundamentally homogeneous group of specifically white, middle-aged men of privilege. If women who are imitation men are placed in these positions, fundamental change will not occur. (Hall et al., 1989: 42)

Governmentalizing everyday life in the interest of expanding citizen rights (and streamlining the labour force) has been equally significant on the terrain of race and ethnicity. Again, reformism has been dominant.

Ethnicity and Multiculturalism

The vast majority of states have populations comprised of varied ethnic groups. These groups divide in terms of their distance from the dominant cultural order or, more positively, in relation to their own heritage. Greek, for instance, distin-guishes *ethnos* (folk) from *kratos* (state). The 'Good Greek' can also be the 'Good Australian Citizen' because of the split between fealty to a culture of origin and fealty to a place of habitation. As the distinctions between ethnic groups are superficially so apparent, they may have the effect of marking out alliances and differences that are less significant than they are obvious. Relationships to processes of production, distribution, and reproduction are made mani*fold* but not mani*fest*. Questions around the division of labour, for example, may not be discernible because they come to be posed at the level of ethnicity.

Nevertheless, ideals of citizenship have buttressed claims that homogenizing dominant cultures fails to allow adequate expression of ethnic difference. And multiculturalism has become the response of certain liberal-capitalist states to such pressures. 'Multiculturalism' was coined in the US sixty years ago in opposition to notions of nationalism. In liberal-democratic societies, the idealized assimilable subject of the 1950s eventually gave way to an integrable one, an imagined alchemic citizen. This fully achieved subject was to be a kind of world citizen, a cosmopolitan. But it always had an underside, as Andrew Jakubowicz points out in the Australian context:

> The public representation of 'the Australian public' has in part been fashioned by images of the immigrant. She has been in turn a new settler, a new citizen, a new Australian, a refugee, a migrant: the obverse image has also shadowed this formal public representation – refo, Balt, wog, dago, slope … an unresolved dichotomy, signalling at once threat, challenge, competition and a lesser form of life: deviant, underprivileged, bizarre, unnatural. Throughout there has been the fear of the enclave, so that every element of the public discourse of settlement has sought to fragment, isolate and scatter the immigrants. (1989: 106)

Riven with different leanings and histories, the migrant citizen must be tied to the political and cultural origins of the new nation while simultaneously marked as 'other'.

Despite the arrival of 3.5 million non-English speakers since 1945, Australia remains very monolingual in terms of commerce and government. The subcultural corollary is of disorganized, impoverished workers and an overconcentration of migrant women, in particular, in secondary labour markets.

We turn now to a special event in the history of Australian sport that exemplifies these tensions, utilizing a case study of the Bicentennial Gold Cup of Soccer to examine the interplay of ethnicity, sport, and nation. We argue that the attempt to 'unmark' soccer from its perceived condition as a non-Anglo-Saxon sport is an exemplary instance of the will to form a single national subjectivity, and its limitations. The attempt reversed the process in other sites, where soccer was indubitably Anglo-Celtic and had to be domesticated as a local practice. In Australia, post-Second World War domestication was achieved, at least paradoxically, in the context of multiculturalism, itself the *dispositif* (apparatus) emerging from a growing non-Anglo first-generation migrant population. The ideal-type soccer follower and player – the soccer subject – is conceived within a range of discourses. Far from soccer being a *panes et circenses* (bread and circuses) domain, where difference may be permitted free play away from serious matters, a whole host of critics, policymakers, and managers clearly ascribe a significance to the sport that calls for it to be reformed. The ideal type must be unmarked from appearing 'other than Australian' – a term from the discourse of immigration that requires the adopted subject to be loving, loyal, and industrious in a new locale.

FIFA's 1988 Bicentennial Gold Cup was part of state-sanctioned festivities designed to celebrate 200 years of white 'settlement' of Australia. The event exhibited critical drives within policy and media discourse towards silencing difference in the name of fealty to the state. This was a crucible for identifying the contours and parameters of these questions at a special conjuncture, a moment within bicentennial celebrations of the English conquest of the Aboriginal land and people that exemplified many aspects of the 'Bicentennial party', as it was officially termed. These ranged from *étatisme*, internationalism, and nationalism to a highly disposable ephemerality and showiness. The bicentenary of invasion centred sport (Spillman, 1997: 108–9). But the Gold Cup did not derive its meanings from an account of the past, which marks it out from the diligent making of history that characterized most of the 'party'. Rather than being a remark on 200 years, the Cup was an overt attempt to produce a new context in which soccer could gain parity with its competition – a promotional strategy, not always coherently or cogently conceived and executed, and itself the site of struggle, incompetence, and discontinuity. It ran over with the formation of possibilities rather than memories, in keeping with the design of forming a new, Australianized sporting subject.

FIFA ordains Gold Cups, and they must involve at least two men's World Cup winners. Because of the virtual coincidence of the European Nations' Championships in 1988, this meant a very limited choice in the Australian instance. Of the Latin American states, Brazil and Argentina – the glamour teams – were available to join the host nation. Saudi Arabia was selected because it offered huge payments for television coverage. The series itself saw Australia fare remarkably well in the context of its international footballing history, defeating the then world champion, Argentina, 4–1, and losing a close final 2–0 to Brazil. The print media gave the competition enormous coverage, although no local commercial television network had been interested in live telecasts. Crowds were good for the final (if patchy at other moments) and headlines proclaimed the opportunity to mould soccer as the dominant local brand of football. Ten years later, critiques were still emerging of the failure to exploit this opportunity to remake and remodel the code under the sign of a nationalist transcendence of ethnic difference (Hughson, 1997; Kobe, 1999).

Before the first games of the competition, the *Australian* newspaper argued that 'Australia needs to make a strong showing to finally shrug off its country-cousin image' (Gedeon, 1988). Which constituency was in mind – the Australian populace or the world of international soccer administration – was left unstated. After the Cup, Brisbane's *Sunday Mail* announced that the 'sleeping giant of Australian soccer had finally stirred' (Stead, 1988). The *Sydney Morning Herald* also anthropomorphized the sport, pronouncing an end to 'the inferiority complex which had plagued Australian soccer throughout its history' thanks to 'the enormous potential of our national soccer team … a promotable commodity' (Cockerill, 1988a). Team captain Charlie Yankos claimed after the victory over Argentina that: 'People are now starting to appreciate what we're doing for Australia' (quoted in Cockerill, 1988b).

Soccer is played all over Australia, but is very much the province of ethnically differentiated clubs. Unlike league and union, its organizational strength lies outside Anglo-Celts. Clubs are frequently known by titles derived from Croatian, Macedonian, Serbian, Greek, or Italian origins. The formation of the National Soccer League (NSL) in 1977 anticipated similar developments in other codes by almost a decade, but the League's history has been ruptured and non-linear. In 1998, there were 287,000 registered soccer players in Australia as opposed to 142,000 in rugby league and 428,000 for Australian Rules (all were dwarfed by basketball's 600,000) (Kobe, 1999). It is apparently insufficient to be numerically powerful as a participant sport to qualify as properly local. Rather, a structure of feeling amongst spectators must be invented that interpellates the game within the mythic universal Australian subject and vice versa so that it can be deployed as an agent of nation-building/*Bildung* and sport-building/*Bildung*.

Local soccer began in 1880. Twelve hundred clubs were in existence by 1939, with financial support from the English Football Association (Mason, 1986: 78). Many Australian firms paid for their employees to form soccer teams in the 1920s and 1930s, in the hope that the state's labour relations apparatus would regard this as part of a social wage (Goldlust, 1987: 57 n. 50). By the 1950s and 1960s, international games occasionally attracted crowds in excess of 50,000. From 1974, soccer was the fastest-growing school sport. What started as a game played by expatriate labourers and miners from the UK had by that time been strengthened and ordered by the influx of Italians, Greeks, and Yugoslavs after the Second World War, to the point where it became a sport marked by its subjectivity: a composite migrant came to stand for it. When Australia qualified for the 1974 men's World Cup:

> It seemed there would be no stopping soccer from shedding its Cinderella tag and becoming a major football force in this country … [but] the game slipped backwards for a while. Its European roots, its infighting and its administration threw up barriers too steep to hurdle. (Mossop, 1988: 34)

Explanations for this stressed management structure, personality conflict, and ethnic loyalty. The supposed lack of exemplary nation-sentiment in the game – its ethnicity – has been recuperated as aetiology again and again by critics, commentators, and administrators (Department of Sport, 1985: 175, 184–85). We shall read more of this below. Women's soccer, meanwhile, had seen its first inter-state game in 1921, with a crowd attendance figure of 10,000. By 1988, it had 21,000 registered players and was also evidencing a divisive internecine politics (*Australian Soccer Weekly*, 1988: 45, 68).

Whereas crowds of over 5,000 were common in 1980, the average NSL attendance in 1988 was half that. And the *Australian Soccer Weekly* (*ASW*) was arguing that the standard of professionalism at all levels – play, administration, and promotion – was not commensurate with a century of history ('Editor', 1988). Over the previous decade, the code had garnered about A$30 million in sponsorship funds, which might have ensured it some prominence within Australian sport.

Instead, soccer was known primarily for internal politicking. In particular, the NSL's relationship with the sport's ruling body Soccer Australia (then the Australian Soccer Federation [ASF]) has often been poor. Sponsors have come and gone, commercial television has shown cursory interest, and the national team has stumbled. Club bankruptcies, personal fiefdoms, aberrant appointment procedures, and arcane/archaic management practices have all been pointed to as explanations. But, to repeat, the key significatory element – vital because of its location within a realm of wider discourses about the hetero/homogeneity of Australia – has been ethnicity. Soccer in Australia is often called 'Wogball', for all the mutually British origins of the game and those who label it that. Unlike almost all other sports, the soccer subject is formed as multicultural as well as gendered: this becomes both its strength and its vulnerability. For some, the principal requirement for future growth of the code is 'Australianization'. The soccer subject's self-image and status of perception by others are to be redisciplined.

Attempts to market the sport homogeneously – in other words, in a way that can unselfconsciously address Anglo-Celtic males – have floundered, but continue remorselessly (and this at a time when rugby league has promoted itself across the social spectrum). Innovations of summer soccer, team franchising, and management audits are secondary to this massively powerful sense that the signified of soccer is 'new Australian'. Internal to the soccer world, debates proceed *ad nauseam* between poles emphasizing, respectively, the need to maintain an existing base in ethnic identity and the desirability of integration into the norms of mainstream sporting businesses.

Ethnic marking has been stigmatized as a failure to appeal to 'Australian' culture, a concept that invokes such terms as dominant, male, white, and Anglo. One could easily argue that this perception applies nowhere but in the offices of television sporting departments, whose 'policies' on equitable coverage could best be described as unreconstructed (or, in another register, as dedicated to a remorseless narcissism of their own demographic and somatic cohort). The ramifications of the problem are, of course, material, in that sponsorship becomes difficult to obtain in the absence of significant commercial coverage.

In 1989, the company chosen to market the League stated: 'The NSL must create a new image and change its name and logo so it can be identified as Australian, modern-go-ahead and exciting ... CLUB names should be amended where necessary to prevent ethnic recognition.' Leaving aside the symptomatic association of Australia with modernity and titillation, we could turn to the presentation by the state-funded multicultural Special Broadcasting Service (SBS) of the 1988 Medal for NSL Player of the Year and the comments of comic Vince Sorrenti: 'Who's ethnic here? I hope I wasn't invited here as the token ethnic ... I'm no ethnic. Let's face it, I'm a wog. [*Laughter*] You wouldn't have said that ten years ago, would you?'

This joke rehearses debates over the merits and demerits of ethnically administered and identified clubs, which activists within the sport see as related to a 'lack of professionalism and ability to address the Australian way of life' (Santina, 1988). For the *ASW*, the problem is summed up in the expression 'nationalistic clubs' and 'Nationalism must go' (Gilmour, 1988). This is not Australian nationalism. It is about identifications by officials, players, and supporters with their places of origin. The soccer citizen is split, divided not only in terms of sporting affiliation or affinity, but as a trace of difference from the ideal-type migrant subject.

The Australian government's publication *Australian Sport: A Profile* contains an essay which specifically attributes soccer's problems to these, most externally identifiable and unruly, points of signification. It argues that:

> since those first waves of southern European migrants in the 1950s, soccer authorities have been talking of their game as Australia's sport of the future.... Ethnic divisiveness lingered, making soccer most politically tangled of Australian sports and keeping its potential for furthering national unity just that – potential. Soccer in the 1980s is still waiting for its future. (Jenkinson, 1985: 27)

It was even alleged that 'the ethnic base of the game' has produced crowd violence (Gatt, 1990; Taylor, 1988). A survey of television executives, government officials, and sports marketers found that terrace disturbances tied in with 'ethnic affiliations and "funny" names' to hold the code back (Kamasz, 1989a). In short, the sport was being decried as 'unAustralian' (Hughson, 1997). The search for Anglicization fits into the same system of knowing the soccer subject as the system which stresses that many second-generation Mediterranean migrants have mocked arrivals who continue to follow soccer (Price, 1968: 11).

How realistic is it for the NSL to expect clubs to make public-address announcements in English? This has been resisted at several sites. Similarly, when multicultural public network SBS had its soccer commentator Andy Paschalidis say of an all-Greek NSL game, 'I'll be there with about a thousand relatives' (SBS TV *Sport Report*, 1 July 1988), he was entering the self-parodic ethnicity exemplified above by Sorrenti. But this self-parody asks the audience to deal with a very significant material base which problematizes shibboleths about Australia whilst insisting on the legitimacy of the marked soccer subject. Many ethnic groups have given huge amounts of money to 'their' clubs because they 'see a soccer team as an essential vehicle for establishing a community identity' (Cockerill, 1989). Whilst it continues to be argued that the mark of un-Australianism is upon soccer, such critiques deny the special meanings and strengths that ethnicity gives the game, assuming an essential local quality attached to other sports that are just as fractured, but along lines that do not describe a topography of anxiety in the face of non-Anglo origins. Nevertheless, Soccer Australia announced that from 1995–96, ethnic identification had to go from both team names and logos. This applied equally to powerful pro-Italian and pro-Croatian clubs and small indigenous clubs that flew the Aboriginal flag. The national team coach was also pressured to select 'Anglo' men ('Footy Team', 1996; Culley, 1997). In 1998–99, the spectacular success of an expansion franchise, the Perth Glory, which drew huge crowds and portrayed itself as Anglo-Celtic, was held up as a (frankly regressive) way forward. As the team's marketing consultant boasted: 'We were never intending to be an ethnic club. All our literature, our name, our positioning has been as an Australian club' (quoted in Ruffini, 1999). By late 1999, Soccer Australia had announced a plan to reduce the number of clubs in its national competition, with veiled threats that the selection would be made on the basis of 'Australianism'. Echoes of rugby league's Super League dispute reverberated.

Coda

But something may have happened to lift soccer, part of a grass-roots challenge to Murdoch's attempts to commodify each object and relation he discerns. As we saw in the previous chapter, his big moneyspinner in Australia was supposed to be rugby league. But the *Los Angeles Times* called the purchase of league 'one of News Corp's bigger blunders' (quoted in Kidman and Sexton, 1997: 89). Crowd numbers went down, with big increases in attendances, ratings, and profits for the other three kinds of football (Kidman and Sexton, 1997: 93). The deracination of organic ties between regions, cities, or suburbs and their supposed sports representatives, plus the sense that league was purchased like any other private good by no friend of Australian workers, sent spectators away. One weekend in 1997, attendance at a single soccer game exceeded the combined numbers for all league fixtures. That year, 85,000 attended the men's World Cup play-off against Iran in Melbourne, and the NSL's Grand Final attracted an unprecedented 40,000 spectators. This achievement is still not reflected in column inches or network schedules, although a major commercial deal was finally signed with a TV network in 1998 (Kobe, 1999). But what a truly heartening moment in our seemingly unstoppable motion towards sporting commodification. An irony here, too: Newcastle, a working-class part of New South Wales dogged by deindustrialization and job losses in iron and steel ('restructuring') won the last traditional, non-Murdoch rugby league competition. Fifty thousand previously disgruntled Novocastrians lined the streets in celebration – a farewell to manufacturing greatness and rugby league?

Meanwhile, the most successful sporting franchise of the 1990s was withdrawing from the most prestigious domestic competition in the world. As we saw in Chapter 3, Manchester United elected not to contest the FA Cup in the 1999–2000 season in order to participate (disgracefully, as it turned out) in the first World Club Championship. At first blush this reads like a straightforward decision to place commercial advancement over national fealty. But as noted earlier, it emerged that the club was acting with the encouragement/under the instruction of the British government, which vainly hoped to attract the 2006 World Cup as part of its 2002 re-election strategy, and saw participation in the Club Championship as a sop to the ruling class of FIFA (Sugden and Tomlinson, 1999: 180–83). It was a beautiful irony that United performed like a truly 'English' team at the event – losing poorly and behaving badly! Government was as critical to the top sports commodity as was business, an echo of the Foreign Office essentially instructing the English national team to offer a Hitler salute prior to the 1938 game between the two countries in Germany and pushing British Olympic officials to support Japan's bid for the 1940 Olympics as part of appeasement (Beck, 1999: 1, 5; Birley, 1995: 288). Sport is clearly part of the base and the symbolism of government, providing fit bodies and spectacular icons and a populist notion of citizenship. But this is a contradictory relationship: for every critique of women's access based on universal rights, there is a denial of ethnic difference in favour of corporate interests.

The cleavages of gender and race/ethnicity reference critical aspects of modernity – the opening-out of citizen rights and claims beyond the confines of Derrida's 'scriptors'. This does not mean that there has been an unstoppable push expanding citizen rights – the figure of the consumer is frequently privileged as an excuse for corporate expansion – but it does represent a complex counter-force. In our Conclusion, we look at the prospects for resistance to global neoliberalism, sporting style.

Notes

1. Some international organizations that have adopted a more radical stance toward heterosexism, lesbianism, homophobia, human rights, and violence against women in

sport are Atlanta Plus, which tried to pressure the IOC to ban teams from Muslim countries unless they included women, the Gay Games (Jefferson Lenskyj, 1999), and the International Association for the Study of Men (Burstyn, 1999).

2. In her study of the Women's National Basketball Association, McDonald (2000) shows how Title IX discourse, which was basically reformist to begin with, has been appropriated for corporate ends.

Appendix 4.1:   *Brighton Declaration on Women and Sport*

Scope and Aims of the Declaration

This Declaration is addressed to all those governments, public authorities, organisations, businesses, educational and research establishments, women's organisations and individuals who are responsible for, or who directly or indirectly influence, the conduct, development or promotion of sport or who are in any way involved in the employment, education, management, training, development or care of women in sport. This Declaration is meant to complement all sporting, local, national and international charters, laws, codes, rules and regulations relating to women or sport.

The overriding aim is to develop a sporting culture that enables and values the full involvement of women in every aspect of sport.

It is in the interests of equality, development and peace that a commitment is made by governmental, non-governmental organisations and all those institutions involved in sport to apply the Principles set out in this Declaration by developing appropriate policies, structures and mechanisms which:

- ensure that all women and girls have the opportunity to participate in sport in a safe and supportive environment which preserves the rights, dignity and respect of the individual;
- increase the involvement of women in sport at all levels and in all functions and roles;
- ensure that the knowledge, experiences and values of women contribute to the development of sport
- promote the recognition by women of the instrinsic value of sport and its contribution to personal development and healthy lifestyle.

The Principles

1.   Equity and Equality in Society and Sport

Every effort should be made by state and government machineries to ensure that institutions and organisations responsible for sport comply with the equality provisions of the Charter of the United Nations, the Universal Declaration of Human Rights and the UN Convention on the Elimination of all Forms of Discrimination Against Women.

Equal opportunity to participate and be involved in sport whether for the purpose of leisure and recreation, health promotion or high performance, is the right of every woman, regardless of race, colour, language, religion, creed, sexual orientation, age, marital status, disability, political belief or affiliation, national or social origin.

Resources, power and responsibility should be allocated fairly and without discrimination on the basis of sex, but such allocation should redress any inequitable balance in the benefits available to women and men.

2.   Facilities

Women's participation in sport is influenced by the extent, variety and accessibility of facilities. The planning, design and management of these should appropriately and equitably meet the particular needs of women in the community, with special attention given to the need for childcare provision and safety.

3. School and Junior Sport

Research demonstrates that girls and boys approach sport from markedly different perspectives. Those responsible for sport, education, recreation and physical education of young people should ensure that an equitable range of opportunities and learning experience, which accommodate the values, attitudes and aspirations of girls, is incorporated in programmes to develop physical fitness and basic sport skills of young people.

4. Developing Participation

Women's participation in sport is influenced by the range of activities available. Those responsible for delivering sporting opportunities and programmes should provide and promote activities which meet women's needs and aspirations.

5. High Performance Sport

Governments and sports organisations should provide equal opportunities to women to reach their sports performance potential by ensuring that all activities and programmes relating to performance improvements take account of the specific needs of female athletes.

Those supporting elite and/or professional athletes should ensure that competition opportunities, rewards, incentives, recognition, sponsorship, promotion and other forms of support are provided fairly and equitably to both women and men.

6. Leadership in Sport

Women are under-represented in the leadership and decision-making in all sport and sport-related organisations. Those responsible for these areas should develop policies and programmes and design structures which increase the number of women coaches, advisers, decision makers, officials, administrators and sports personnel at all levels with special attention given to recruitment, development and retention.

7. Education, Training and Development

Those responsible for the education, training and development of coaches and other sports personnel should ensure that education processes and experiences address issues relating to gender equity and the needs of female athletes, equitably reflect women's role in sport and take account of women's leadership experiences, values and attitudes.

8. Sports Information and Research

Those responsible for research and providing information on sport should develop policies and programmes to increase knowledge and understanding about women and sport and ensure that research norms and standards are based on research on women and men.

9. Resources

Those responsible for the allocation of resources should ensure that support is available for sportswomen, women's programmes and special measures to advance this Declaration of Principles.

10. Domestic and International Cooperation

Government and non-government organisations should incorporate the promotion of issues of gender equity and the sharing of examples of good practice in women and sport policies and programmes in their associations with other organisations, within both domestic and international arenas.

Strategy

International Women and Sport Strategy

Governments and organisations committing to be a part of an International Women and Sport Strategy will:

- endorse and commit to the application of the Declaration of Principles, to be known as the 'Brighton Declaration on Women and Sport';
- develop and execute an implementation plan which reflects full and practical fulfilment of the principles contained in the Brighton Declaration;
- nominate a representative for the purposes of communications with the International Working Group on Women and Sport;
- support international cooperation by striving to send qualified representatives to future international conferences conducted to discuss issues, share exemplary practices and model programmes, network and monitor progress in aplication of the principles;
- provide feedback to the working group on the effectiveness of their actions taken to advance the principles.

Source: WomenSport International: <http://www.de.psu.edu/wsi/brighton.htm>

Appendix 4.2: *The Windhoek Call for Action*

(Emanating from the Second World Conference on Women and Sport, Windhoek, Namibia, 19–22 May 1998)

The Conference focused on the successes which have been achieved during the last four years following the first World Conference and the endorsement of the Brighton Declaration. Following the Conference delegates endorsed the 'Windhoek Call for Action' which aims to build on the Brighton Declaration, bringing about more positive action to address inequalities and enhance women's development through sport and physical activity.

The Call for Action is addressed to all men and women in those national and international sport organisations, governments, public authorities, development agencies, schools, businesses, educational research institutions, women's organisations, who are responsible for, or who directly influence the conduct, development or promotion of sport, or who are in any way involved in the employment, education, management, training, development or care of girls and women in sport.

In addition to re-affirming the principles of the Brighton Declaration, the Conference delegates called for action in the following areas:

1. Develop action plans with objectives and targets to implement the principles of the Brighton Declaration, and monitor and report upon their implementation.
2. Reach out beyond the current boundaries of the sport sector to the global women's equality movement and develop closer partnerships between sport and women's organisations on the one side, and representatives from sectors such as education, youth, health, human rights and employment on the other. Develop strategies that help other sectors obtain their objectives through the medium of sport and at the same time further sport objectives.
3. Promote and share information about the positive contribution that girls' and women's involvement in sport makes, *inter alia*, to social, health and economic issues.
4. Build the capacity of women as leaders and decision-makers and ensure that women play meaningful and visible roles in sport at all levels. Create mechanisms that ensure that young women have a voice in the development of policies and programmes that affect them.
5. Avert the 'world crisis in physical education' by establishing and strengthening quality physical education programmes as key means for the positive introduction to young girls of the skills and other benefits they can acquire through sport. Further, create policies and mechanisms that ensure progression from school to community-based activity.

6. Encourage the media to positively portray and significantly cover the breadth, depth, quality and benefits of girls' and women's involvement in sport.
7. Ensure a safe and supportive environment for girls and women participating in sport at all levels by taking steps to eliminate all forms of harassment and abuse, violence and exploitation, and gender testing.
8. Ensure that policies and programmes provide opportunities for all girls and women in full recognition of the differences and diversity among them – including such factors as race, ability, age, religion, sexual orientation, ethnicity, language, culture or their status as an indigenous person.
9. Recognise the importance of governments to sport development and urge them to conduct gender impact analyses and to develop appropriate legislation, public policy and funding that ensures gender equality in all aspects of sport.
10. Ensure that Official Development Assistance programmes provide equal opportunities for girls' and women's development and recognise the potential of sport to achieve development objectives.
11. Encourage more women to become researchers in sport, and more research to be undertaken on critical issues relating to women in sport.

Adoption of the Brighton Declaration

Over 200 organisations have notified the International Working Group on Women and Sport that they have adopted or endorsed the Brighton Declaration, including nation-states from all over the globe.

Source: Women's Sport Foundation <http://www.wsf.org.uk/namibia.htm>

Conclusion – Global Sport and Cultural Labour

Holland *vs.* Germany. Good *vs.* Evil. Our shirts were bright, if unfortunately striped; the Germans wore black and white. We had several coloured players, including our captain, and our fans wore Gullit-hats with rasta hair; their players were all white and their fans made monkey noises. Our players were funny and natural; *A Thousand Years of German Humour* is the shortest book in the world. (Simon Kuper, 1998: 9)

If chauvinism is ugly, so is globalization. It stands for something real, a sense from across time, space, and nation, that those very categories are in peril. Our sense of the temporal is questioned – think of the panic generated by computers dealing with the difference between 1900 and 2000. Space is problematized by the NICL, as jobs are undertaken by folks on the basis of price and docility rather than locale. And nations are threatened by corporate control, as unelected, far-distant élites displace locally accountable politicians. In each category, the sporting corollary is clear. Time is manipulated in concert with the interests of global capital – hence NBC's 'plausibly live' policy of editing Olympic events to suit narrative drive, audience targeting, and commercial spacing, rather than the live-ness ontology of sport. Space is torn asunder, as traditional social bonds are compromised by ownership based on profit rather than township. Democracies seem unable to deal with economic forces.

Two Olympic stories encapsulate this dynamic. After winning the gold medal for basketball at the 1992 Olympics in Barcelona, Jordan and his colleagues on the American 'Dream Team' staged a protest on the victory podium (Wenner, 1994). Reebok, an official Olympic sponsor, had supplied the American team with warm-up suits that displayed its logo. Jordan, a Nike client, threatened to boycott the proceedings because he did not believe in supporting a rival corpora-tion: 'I feel very strongly about loyalty to my own company.' His teammate Barkley stated: 'Us Nike guys are loyal to Nike because they pay us a lot of money. I have two million reasons not to wear Reebok.' At the ceremony, Barkley and Jordan wrapped themselves in an American flag to cover the Reebok emblem, while the other players unzipped their jackets to obscure it. As we saw in Chapter 3, Mexico City in 1968 had found Smith and Carlos on the podium, using their bodies to protest the oppression of African-Americans in front of a global TV audience; in Barcelona two decades on, Barkley and Jordan used *their* bodies to show the world they were good company men. At the Sydney Olympics, the celebrations of the African-American 100-metre relay track team, wrapping themselves in the stars and stripes, were deemed disrespectful to the flag.

But counter-power is always at work. The 1999 Seattle action in opposition to neoliberalism's World Trade Organization hacks illustrated as much, as environmentalists, trade unions, and consumer groups problematized globalization as defined by *laissez-faire* nostrums. Textiles, shipping, and agriculture remain massively subsidized across the world. The US, supposedly the poster-child for free trade and true competition, has hundreds of anti-dumping measures aimed at blocking imports where prices have been 'unfairly' set, and even has a semi-secret deal with Japan to restrict steel sales, while the EU remains firm on refusing to import bananas and genetically modified beef. All of this leads *The Economist*, a key neoliberal business advocacy voice, to admit that 'Globalisation is not irreversible' ('Storm Over Globalisation', 1999).

The modernizing impulse announced for the 1994 Winter Olympics, heralded by the Norwegian media and government as 'good' for Lillehammer, was met with serious retorts from conservation and environmental movements, coupled in a contingent alliance with neoclassical economists' appropriate questioning of the actual multiplier effects of state investment in expensive sporting arenas and allied facilities. This coalition did not stop the Games, but it did persuade the IOC and its local apparatchiks to include environmental considerations in their plans. And not just for the 1994 Games, but as a permanent, codified item, alongside culture and sport itself. When the son of an IOC official was appointed without consultation to produce the Games mascot, a Disney-style figure, local outrage saw the decision overturned and the mascot altered in concert with local cultural workers (Klausen, 1999b: 34–35, 39). Similarly, for all its neoliberal *frottage*, the Labour government in Britain commissioned a 1997 report on soccer that proposed fan fora to monitor clubs' commitment to their supporters and regular low-admission games ('Chairman Slams', 1997). It went on to establish a unit to help fans set up supporter–shareholder trusts (Hamil, 1999).

Bourdieu postulates a model of world culture that continues the bipolarity of the Cold War, but without its political ramifications, military corollaries, and economic isolations. His vision of the struggle for world culture puts the United States against France – *laissez-faire* dogma juxtaposed with nationalism. This Enlightenment conflict, between anomic monads and collective identities, sets bourgeois individualism and collaborative unity against each other, with the incarnation of the Depression and Sovietism hanging over each model. Bourdieu calls for a pre-Marxist, Hegelian way through the debate, a democratic mode that favours the state not as totalitarian or an aid to capital accumulation, but as the expression of a popular will that acts under the sign of general interest rather than singular egotism (1999: 20). French sport in the 1990s resembled the ethos of imperial Britain, as a metaphor for the good life – but with integration displacing war as the crucible, and multiculturalism rather than chauvinism as the problematic (Marks, 1999: 54).

This is equally relevant for the grass roots. Glancing at soccer fans, we might casually note the *ultràs* model of Southern European play, with its connotations of carnival or hooliganism, depending on where you sit; the *barras bravas* of Argentina, with their spectacular arena conduct and its global intertexts for Spanish speakers; the uptake of Latin American chants on British terraces in the 1990s; and the 1999 Liverpool fans who paraded a banner reading 'Cosmopolitanisme Vaincra' (Cosmopolitanism will Triumph) (Giulianotti, 1999: 64; J. Williams,

1999). Whilst these groups may be queried for their maleness and violence, they are significant counters to the deracinated domain of corporatized sports.

In New York City projects, African-American youth responded to 1998 disclosures of Asian sweatshops making Nike shoes by returning their sneakers to the corporation's Manhattan Niketown, all too aware that these essentially unwaged jobs were at the expense of their own class prospects (LaFeber, 1999: 154–55). We do not wish to get too romantic about this, for the right wing is alive to worker rejection of neoliberalism and seeks to exploit this disaffection. The Nazi fellow-travellers of the British National Party recruit at soccer games in the name of 'the British working classes ... angry young men' who have seen their country 'sold off by those who want the fast buck' (Brimson and Brimson, 1996: 97–99). Clearly, this opportunistic exploitation by racist violence is not a desirable alternative – but it manifests the disaffection of ordinary people with the powerlessness handed down to them by the high priests of neoliberalism. The deterritorialization brought on by economic exigencies and political fractures has also produced a vast array of stateless European soccer fans, represented by teams whose locale has no sovereign referent (Giulianotti and Armstrong, 1997: 240). This has long been the case for Palestinians. The famous al-Wihdat soccer club in Jordan's refugee camp is both a symbol of the many defeats in military action that have led to dispossession, and a sign that they will not be totally suppressed (Tuastad, 1997: 105).

Criticisms that neoliberal true believers are faceless, unrepresentative, and gormless have hit home. Consider our friends over at the World Bank (the words that follow in quotation marks are theirs). Concerned as the century drew to a close that its name conjured up images of 'overpaid and underworked bureaucrats' in a 'beehive of corruption', who 'value economic theories' over 'human beings', the Bank's staff association promulgated personal anecdotes recounting small acts of kindness perpetrated by its functionaries in the course of their office duties. As a more public part of improving staff morale, Jim Wolfensohn, who runs the Bank, encouraged employees to wear badges in the shape of a soccer ball. What a neat way of humanizing World Bank executives! No doubt it will be easier now for the rest of us to identify them as organic intellectuals of the working class ('Kick and Tell', 1999).

Such attempts to paper over the exercise of power through sport are all too common. We recall the ecstasy when a multiracial French team won the '98 World Cup, a pleasure all the greater for the grip of racism that has long characterized that country. Here, some of us thought, might be a moment when Zinedine Zidane and his colleagues symbolically trumped the banality and brutality of white racism. But a few months later, the comedian Guy Bedos referred to the North African Zidane's goals in the Final like this: 'two head shots from an Arab and France starts going around like it's in some kind of Benetton one-world commercial. What is this?' (quoted in Vinocur, 1999: 34). Just as Benetton has a paper-thin commitment to multiculturalism and the environment, so the suggestion that myths of nationhood can be transformed by a new racial makeup of a football team is wish-fulfilment in the extreme. Here, liberal and radical thought was caught in a mirror-image of right-wing mythification. Oh, we almost forgot: when the World Bank's soccer-badge campaign was formally inaugurated in December 1998, a net and posts were erected at HQ. Executives lined up to demonstrate their prowess. But the Bank's principal neoclassical economics maven missed his shot on-goal ('Kick and Tell', 1999).

This cosmic ambivalence has become part of capital's own, ironized delivery. Consider a 1999 US television commercial for Adidas. It shows a white business-man in the back of a New York cab, whingeing and whining about Yankees base-ball and how much he loathes the Bronx Bombers. The driver is not identified, but it is Sunil Gavaskar – illegible to the majority of the TV audience, but read-able by South Asian taxi workers and audiences as the most storied batsman in Indian cricket history. He deposits the business leech in a derelict neighbourhood for an assignation with someone coded as a transsexual prostitute. As Gavaskar drives off laughing, the final shot of the sequence discloses that his cab bears a Yankee licence plate, and we are drawn to the US network Home Box Office's candid documentaries on taxis and their late-night denizens. In its latent and mani-fest levels of address and content, this commercial bears witness to the complex intermeshing of global and local, and their conflicts, that we have sought to trace in this book, as sport makes its contradictory way somewhere between civil society, the marketplace, and unrepresentative demagoguery – always collective, however commodified it may become (Dietrich et al., 1999).

Sport is assuredly a source of pleasure to many of us, including the authors of this book. Contemporary technology increases the availability of this pleasure in ways that we can all enjoy, and it is possible to see commodification and govern-mentalization as adding to the quality of athletic performance and its artistry, not to mention breaking down pre-existing social relations (Burbach et al., 1997: 52). Our message is, however, a cautionary one – before you buy the sneaker, or sign on for the TV package, follow the life of the commodity sign through its history, keeping citizenship and labour at the forefront of your thoughts.

Glossary

Americanization: the export of products, symbols, ideologies, and organizational practices of the US, producing an Americo-centric view of how the world should be, including the ways people should act, and the icons and symbols they should admire.

Autotelic: a term derived from philosophy describing a situation in which the self achieves its own ends.

Capitalism: the form of social and economic organization most consistently associated with the pursuit of private wealth; the defence of private property; the creation and exchange of commodities for profit; and the direct sale by workers (the working class) of their labour power to employers (the ruling class). Over the last two or three centuries of its existence, capitalism has gone through various stages. The current phase of capitalism is characterized by shifts in class relations and identities, linked to changes in the organization both of paid work in the public world (such as the shift from manual to non-manual labour) and of unpaid work in the private world (like the large-scale movement of women into the workplace and pressures for gender equality at home and at work).

Commodification: the making into a commodity for sale on the marketplace of items or services which were previously not part of market logic. The sale of the sporting body, Olympic rings, or sporting personae as part of a process in which private firms can derive income from the development of new products.
Or the process by which people and things acquire value, which enables them to be exchanged for profit. In sport, for example, amateur play and players have been turned into exchangeable services and products.

Corporatization: the growth in the number, importance, and influence of private corporations, as capitalism, especially in its global form, provides opportunities for private entities to invest in new areas.

Cultural economy: a term used to describe both the cultural industries (such as publishers, music companies, and art galleries) and the manner in which forms of culture (like films, books, music, and even ideas and values) take on the appearance of ordinary commodities, with their value rising and falling according to critical reception, status, scarcity, public demand, and so on.

Decolonization: the movement within older, colonized nations, toward nation-statehood. While political domination from the centre may be formally ended, there is often a significant economic tie to the old, or to new, nations or bodies for the financing of development. When this results in increasing debt and the need for internal policies which act, ultimately, to disadvantage the local population, this economic dependence can be viewed as imperialism.

Deindustrialization: a process in which industrialized nations lose their so-called comparative advantage in manufacturing, as the withdrawal of private capital leads to such rust-belt outcomes as idle plant and equipment, increased unemployment, and regional economic decline.

Deterritorialization: the loss of the bonds of time and space, as people and texts move from one place to another in concert with capitalist mobility, delocalizing processes and practices as they move.

Developmentalization: a prevailing ideology and practice from the Second World War to the mid-1970s which justified the application of science and technology to underpin the economic progress of both developed and developing nations. In the capitalist nations and the colonies, it was characterized by faith in science (such as the green revolution), state–capital relations (regulated national markets to assist profit-making), and the view that economic growth would provide the best outcomes for society.

Diaspora: derived from the Greek word for scattering, it refers to the dispersion of people of common nationality or beliefs from one home location to other sites throughout the world.

Discourse: the social and cultural framework of institutions and (often unacknowledged) assumptions that organize everyday language, thought, and behaviour. Because multiple discourses exist and are connected to structures of power, social life is characterized by competition between discourses for legitimacy (for example, monarchism versus republicanism) and, consequently, sovereignty over groups in society.

GGATaC (Globalization, Governmentalization, Americanization, Televisualization, and Commodification): the combination of processes leading to the contours of modern social existence. Sport is fashioned in particular ways under the influence of these five factors, such that it becomes yet another product within capitalism – but one, importantly, which can be made spectacular, can be used for profit-making, and carries with it older meanings (of tradition, history, and dedication) that allow it to be harnessed for ideological purposes.

Globalization: a process through which space and time are compressed by technology, information flows, and trade and power relations, allowing distant actions to have increased significance at the local level.

Governmentality: coined by Roland Barthes and applied, later, by Michel Foucault to describe the management and regulation of citizens both through the formal organs of the state, and the informal interpersonal interactions which are subject not to external but to internal sanction.

Media: all the organizations, large and small, through which pass various types of message in the process of communication (by which meaning is exchanged). The term is increasingly restricted to specialist organizations with the substantial technology, knowledge, and capital at their disposal to enable large scale or mass communication. The term **mediatization** refers to the extension of the influence of media into all spheres of social life.

Media–Sports–Culture complex: a concept which embraces all the media and sports organizations, processes, personnel, services, products, and texts which combine in the creation of the broad, dynamic field of contemporary sports culture.

Multinational corporation (MNC): a capitalist firm with a main office in one nation-state, but which has created similar firms in other nations. MNCs aim to maximize profits by producing, or selling, similar products in each location where they are based. The idea here is the production of similar products in similar countries, rather than trading components between branches of the firm on a world scale. Such firms may organize their economic activities on a global, rather than a national, scale. Production is for the world system, rather than for domestic distribution, and sites of production are coordinated through a web of exchange by companies that often owe loyalty to no one nation.

Myths: wide-ranging cultural beliefs and meanings, usually so familiar that they appear to be natural, universal and eternal elements of society. Sport, which generates strong emotions, antagonisms, hierarchies, and romantic ideals, is particularly prone to mythologization.

Neoliberalism: describes a belief system in which the individual pursuit of self-gain is understood to provide maximum benefits to the individual and society. Once such an ideology is accepted, other things fall into place. It is considered inappropriate for governments to undertake activities for the good of citizens. Governments should, in contrast, not hamper individual decision-making. Market liberalization, restrictive monetary policy, reduction in tariff levels, removal of the welfare net, privatization of government utilities and outsourcing are all components of the policies of neoliberalism.

New International Division of Cultural Labour (NICL): as per the NIDL (see below) but with reference to cultural industries.

New International Division of Labour (NIDL): the division of the world into areas of specialized economic activity, including enclaves of cheap labour (particularly areas in the Third World), state-subsidized production (free trade zones), and centres of finance capital (capital cities such as London, New York, and Tokyo) and raw-material extraction.

Political economy: an analytical approach which links socioeconomic power (for example ownership of a major newspaper chain) with politico-cultural power (such as the promotion of conservative values through the owner's newspapers or the shaping of newspaper stories by commercial rather than cultural or ethical considerations). The master concepts in political economy are class and class conflict, although there is often substantial departure from elements of Marxism that have traditionally underpinned these (such as the inevitability of a proletarian revolution).

Spectacularization: in sport, this refers to the ways in which sporting activities have been reorganized, often by the media, to focus spectator attention upon the more dramatic, controversial, emotional, and confrontational aspects of display.

Sport: recreational and professional competitive, rule-governed physical activity. While physical play and game contests have clearly existed in many societies and epochs, sport of a regular and organized kind is the product of a social institution with its origins in Victorian England.

Technologization: the embedding of technology into all major components of life, together with the celebration and endorsement of technology as a major force for good in society.

References

'Advertisement' (1997) *Variety* 15–21 September: 27.

'Asia in the Rough' (1997) *The Economist* 20 December.

'Aussie Rules the World' (1999) <www.iafc.org.au>

'Australia: Olympus with an Ocean View' (1999) *New York Times* 12 December: 1.

'Australians Plan Track in China' (1999) *New York Times* 1 January: D6.

'Batson Calls for End to Foreign Influx' (1999) *Guardian* 23 June: 24.

'Chairman Slams "Joke" Task Force Report' (1997) 15 September: <www.fa-carling.com>

'Country-by-Country Schedule: WORLD' (1999) <http://nhl.com/hockeyu/international>

'Diary' (1999) *When Saturday Comes* 155: 6–9.

'Dream "Signing" Leaves Liverpool the Laughing Stock: Payments Go Through the Roof' (1999) *Newcastle Herald* 27 November: 120.

'Dupont Victory Would Damage Game Warns Taylor' (1999) 22 July: <www.fa-carling.com>

'Editor' (1988) *Australian Soccer Weekly* 9, no. 347: 10.

'European Union and Football: The Beginning of a New Era' (1999) 10 November: <www.fifa.com>

'FIFA and UEFA Welcome Helsinki Report on Sport from the European Commission' (1999) 4 December: <www.fifa.com>

'Flirtation and Frustration' (1999) *The Economist* 11 December: 61–63.

'Footy Team to Lose Colours!' (1996) *Farr Post* October: <sportsprint.com.au/SWF01.htm>

'German Team Takes on a Cuban Flavor' (1999) *New York Times* 1 January: D4.

'Global Basketball' (1999) <www.nba.com/global>

'Global Finance: Time for a Redesign?' (1999) *The Economist* 30 January: 4–8 Survey Global Finance.

'Global Player List Grows' (1999) <www.nba.com>

'Global Sports, Inc. to Hold Press Conference to Discuss Global Sports Interactive' (1999) *Business Wire* 5 October.

'Grace v. Power: An Eternal Struggle' (1999) *Sydney Morning Herald* 30 January: 50.

'The G-Word' (1997) *Financial Times* 30 July: 15.

'Hingis, Mauresmo to Meet in Final' (1999) *Washington Times* 28 January: B2.

'Implications of the BSkyB/Manchester United Case' (2000) *Football in the Digital Age: Whose Game is it Anyway?* Ed. S. Hamil, J. Michie, C. Oughton, and S. Warby. Edinburgh: Mainstream. 64–92.

'International Broadcasters' (1999) <www.majorleaguebaseball.com/u/baseball/mlb-com/int>

'Kick and Tell' (1999) *The Economist* 13 February: 72.

'Lazio Likes a London Listing' (1997) *Sun-Herald* 26 October: 97.

'Leading Off' (2000) *Sports Illustrated* 14 February: 4–9.

'Market Development' (1999) <www.majorleaguebaseball.com>

'Mauresmo, to Cheers, Hammers Hingis' (1999) *New York Times* 27 February: D7.

'Media Release' (1998) 19 August: <www-usa5.cricket.org/link_to_database/NATIONAL/ICC>

'MLB Honors Latin Impact in 2000 with "Month of the Americas"' (1999) 10 November: <www.majorleaguebaseball.com>

'NBA Renews Coca-Cola Deal' (1999) 9 June: <www.nba.com>

'New Television Deals Mean More NBA Worldwide' (1999) <www.nba.com/ON THE AIR>

'NFL Full of Foreign-Born Players' (1999) <www.nfl.com/international>

'NFL International' (1999) <www.nfl.com/international>

'Obituary: Death of the Right Honourable Game Football' (1992) *The Faber Book of Soccer* Ed. I. Hamilton. London: Faber & Faber. 5–6.

'Old Glory Gets a Cheer as US Team Plays in Iran' (1998) *New York Times* 18 February: A3.

'Out in the Open' (1999) *Village Voice* 9 February: 174.

'Payments Go through the Roof' (1999) *Newcastle Herald* 1 May: 109.

'President Offers Athletes Rewards' (1999) *New York Times* 25 December: D7.

'Sport and Television: Swifter, Higher, Stronger, Dearer' (1996) *The Economist* 20 July: 17–19.

'Sports is Global Entertainment' (1998) *Interactive Sports Wire* 22 September.

'SportsLine USA and CricInfo Launch 1999 World Cup Site' (1999) *Business Wire* 13 May.

'Steps in the Right Direction?' (1999) *Sports Illustrated* 20 December.

'Storm over Globalisation' (1999) *The Economist* 27 November: 15–16.

'Teenager Stuns World's Best Player' (1999) *The Daily Telegraph* 29 January: 3, 116.

'Trade Barriers, Erected in Fear, Hurt US Workers' (1997) *USA Today* 16 October: 10A.

'TV Times' (1999) <www.afl.com.au>

'The World Bids Farewell to Michael' (1999) <http://nba.com/mjretirement/world-farewell.html>

'Zia Declares Cricket Diplomacy a Success' (1987) *Sydney Morning Herald* 24 February: 31.

Adalian, J. (1998) 'ABC Pigskin Pickle: "Monday Night Football" Ratings Tackled by Viewer Decline.' *Variety* 30 December: 1, 17.

Adorno, T.W. and M. Horkheimer (1977) 'The Culture Industry: Enlightenment as Mass Deception.' *Mass Communication and Society*. Ed. J. Curran, M. Gurevitch, and J. Woollacott. London: Edward Arnold. 349–83.

Aggrey, J. (1999) 'Great Expectations.' *African Soccer* 50: 32–35.

Agnew, R. and D.M. Petersen (1989) 'Leisure and Delinquency.' *Social Problems* 36, no. 4: 332–50.

Allen, J. (1990) 'The Wild Ones: The Disavowal of Men in Criminology.' *Dissenting Opinions: Feminist Explorations in Law and Society*. Ed. R. Graycar. Sydney: Allen & Unwin. 21–39.

Allison, S. (1999) 'You Plank, Banks: Tony Pulls Strings behind United Cup Pull-Out.' *Daily Sport* 1 July: 29.

Althusser, L. (1977) *Politics and History: Montesquieu, Rousseau, Hegel, Marx*. Trans. B. Brewster. London: New Left Books.

Amin, S. (1997) *Capitalism in the Age of Globalization*. London: Zed.

Amsden, A.H. and T. Hikino (1999) 'The Left and Globalization.' *Dissent* 46, no. 2: 7–9.

Anders, G. (1999) 'A Dream Team Online – Elway, Gretzky, Jordan.' *Wall Street Journal* 21 December: B1, B4.

Anderson, B. (1983) *Imagined Communities: Reflections on the Origin and Spread of Nationalism*. London: Verso.

Andrews, D.L. (ed.) (1996a) 'Deconstructing Michael Jordan: Reconstructing Post-industrial America.' *Sociology of Sport Journal* 13, no. 4: 315–467.

Andrews, D.L. (1996b) 'The Fact(s) of Michael Jordan's Blackness: Excavating a Floating Racial Signifier.' *Sociology of Sport Journal* 13, no. 4: 325–58.

Andrews, D.L. (1999) 'Whither the NBA, Whither America?' *Peace Review* 11, no. 4: 505–10.

Andrews, D.L. and C.L. Cole (2000) 'Tiger Woods: America's New Son.' *Cultural Studies: A Research Annual* 5.

Andrews, D.L., B. Carrington, Z. Mazur, and S.J. Jackson (1996) 'Jordanscapes: A Preliminary Analysis of the Global Popular.' *Sociology of Sport Journal* 13, no. 4: 428–57.

Andrews, E.M. (1998) 'World Bowl Ends Season of Hard Sell for N. F. L.' *New York Times* 14 June: L5.

Appadurai, A. (1990) 'Disjuncture and Difference in the Global Cultural Economy.' *Global Culture: Nationalism, Globalization and Modernity.* Ed. M. Featherstone. London: Sage. 295–310.

Araton, H. (1999) 'King says Hingis Needs a Talking-to.' *New York Times* 9 February: D1.

Arbena, J.L. (1993) 'Sport and Social Change in Latin America.' *Sport in Social Development: Traditions, Transitions, and Transformations.* Ed. A.G. Ingham and J.W. Loy. Champaign, IL: Human Kinetics. 97–117.

Arnedt, R.B. (1998) 'European Union Law and Football Nationality Restrictions: The Economics and Politics of the Bosman Decision.' *Emory International Law Review* 12: 1091–130.

ASC (Australian Sports Commission) (1998) *Facts Sheets.* <http://www.ausport.gov.au/wofamenu.html>

Atkin, R. (1999) 'The Pride after the Prejudice.' *Independent on Sunday* 7 February: 17.

Atkinson, G. (1997) 'Capital and Labor in the Emerging Global Economy.' *Journal of Economic Issues* 31, no. 2: 385–91.

Australian Soccer Weekly (1988) *Australian Soccer Annual.*

Authers, J. (1997) 'Foreigner Strikes Out NY Yankees.' *Financial Times* 30 July: 7.

Avery, B. (1996) 'The Anti-Golf.' *Golf Journal* August: 38–43.

Avery, J. and J. Stevens (1997) *Too Many Men on the Ice: Women's Hockey in North America.* Victoria: Polestar Publishers.

Ayoub, L. (1999) 'Nike Just Does it – and Why the United States Shouldn't: The United States' International Obligation to Hold MNCs Accountable for Their Labor Rights Violations Abroad.' *DePaul Business Law Journal* 11: 395–441.

Bains, J. and S. Johal (1999) *Corner Flags and Corner Shops: The Asian Football Experience.* London: Phoenix.

Bairner, A. and J. Sugden (1999) 'Sport in Divided Societies.' *Sport in Divided Societies.* Ed. J. Sugden and A. Bariner. Aachen: Meyer & Meyer. 1–11.

Bale, J. (1991) *The Brawn Drain: Foreign Student-Athletes in American Universities.* Urbana: University of Illinois Press.

Bale, J. and J. Maguire (eds) (1994) *The Global Sports Arena: Athletic Talent Migration in an Interdependent World.* London: Frank Cass.

Barber, B. (1996) *Jihad vs. McWorld: How Globalism and Tribalism are Reshaping the World.* New York: Ballantine.

Barber, B. (1998) 'Democracy at Risk: American Culture in a Global Culture.' *World Policy Journal* 15, no. 2: 29–41.

Barker, E. (1927) *National Character and the Factors in its Formation.* London: Methuen.

Barnett, S. (1990) *Games and Sets: The Changing Face of Sport on Television.* London: British Film Institute.

Barroso, C. and S. Corrêa (1995) 'Public Servants, Professionals, and Feminists: The Politics of Contraceptive Research in Brazil.' *Conceiving the New World Order: The Global Politics of Reproduction.* Ed. F.D. Ginsburg and R. Rapp. Berkeley: University of California Press. 292–306.

Barthes, R. (1973) *Mythologies.* Trans. A. Lavers. London: Paladin.

Barthes, R. (1977) *Image-Music-Text.* Trans. S. Heath. London: Fontana.

Barthes, R. (1997) 'Of Sport and Men.' Trans. S. MacKenzie. *Canadian Journal of Film Studies/Revue canadienne d'études cinématographiques* 6, no. 2: 75–83.

Bauman, Z. (1998) *Globalization: The Human Consequences.* New York: Columbia University Press.

Beaverstock, J.V. (1996) 'Subcontracting the Accountant! Professional Labour Markets, Migration, and Organisational Networks in the Global Accountancy Industry.' *Environment and Planning A* 28, no. 2: 303–26.

Beck, P.J. (1999) *Scoring for Britain: International Football and International Politics 1900–1939*. London: Frank Cass.

Beeson, M. and A. Frith (1998) 'Neoliberalism as a Political Rationality: Australian Public Policy in the 1980s.' *Journal of Sociology* 34: 215–31.

Beh, M. and J. Leow (1999) 'Sports: Asia's Traditional Games Bid for Olympic Status.' *Inter Press Service English News Wire* 15 January: n. p.

Belanger, A. (1999) 'The Last Game? Hockey and the Experience of Masculinity in Quebec.' *Sport and Gender in Canada*. Ed. P. White and K. Young. Toronto: Oxford University Press. 209–300.

Bell, M. and L. Hayes (1994) 'From Programming to Partnership: "Managing" Active Women? National Policy Shifts in the Women in Sport Programmes in Aotearoa/New Zealand.' Paper presented at the 10th Commonwealth and International Scientific Congress, Victoria.

Bell, P. and R. Bell (1996) '"Americanization": Political and Cultural Examples from the Perspective of "Americanized" Australia.' *American Studies* 37, no. 1: 5–21.

Bellamy, R. (1998) 'The Evolving Television Sports Marketplace' *MediaSport: Cultural Sensibilities and Sport in the Media Age*. Ed. Lawrence A. Wenner. New York: Routledge. 73–87.

Beloff, M.J., T. Kerr, and M. Demetriou (1999) *Sports Law*. Oxford: Hart.

Beltrame, J. (1999) 'Pay Dispute Keeps Canadian Hockey on Thin Ice.' *Wall Street Journal* 16 December: B1, B4.

Benhabib, S. (1999) 'Citizens, Residents, and Aliens in a Changing World: Political Membership in the Global Era.' *Social Research* 66, no. 3: 709–44.

Berkaak, O.A. (1999a) 'A Place in the Sun: The Vernacular Landscape as Olympic Venue.' *Olympic Games as Performance and Public Event: The Case of the XVII Winter Olympic Games in Norway*. Ed. A.M. Klausen. New York: Berghahn. 137–72.

Berkaak, O.A. (1999b) 'Introduction.' *Olympic Games as Performance and Public Event: The Case of the XVII Winter Olympic Games in Norway*. Ed. A.M. Klausen. New York: Berghahn. 1–8.

Berkow, I. (1999) 'Looking over Jordan: David Halberstam Examines the Life and Times of the World's Greatest Athlete.' *New York Times Book Review* 31 January: 11.

Birley, D. (1995) *Playing the Game: Sport and British Society, 1910–45*. Manchester: Manchester University Press.

Birrell, S. and D. Ritcher (1987) 'Is a Diamond Forever? Feminist Transformations of Sport.' *Women's Studies International Forum* 10, no. 4: 395–409.

Bita, N. (1999) 'Freeze Athletes' Blood and Urine: US.' *Australian* 14 October: 3.

Black, M. and D. Hebdige (1999) 'Women's Soccer and the Irish Diaspora.' *Peace Review* 11, no. 4: 531–37.

Blain, N. and R. Boyle (1998) 'Sport.' *The Media: An Introduction*. Ed. A. Briggs and P. Cobley. Harlow: Addison Wesley Longman. 365–76.

Blain, N. and H. O'Donnell (1998) 'European Sports Journalism and its Readers during Euro 96: "Living without the *Sun*".' *Sport, Popular Culture and Identity*. Ed. M. Roche. Aachen: Meyer and Meyer Verlag. 37–56.

Blake, A. (1995) 'Sport and the Global Media: Unofficial Citizens.' *New Statesman & Society* 2 June: 47–48.

Bloom, M. (1998) 'Kenyan Runners in the U.S. Find Bitter Taste of Success.' *New York Times* 16 April: A1, C2.

Bloomberg News (1997) 'NBA Out to Conquer the World.' *Sunday Age* 16 November: 16.

Blount, J. (1997) 'Sporting Life.' *Latin Trade* May: 29–37.

Blum, L. and V. Smith (1998) 'Women's Mobility in the Corporation: A Critique of the Politics of Optimism.' *Signs: Journal of Women in Culture and Society* 13: 528–45.

Boardman, A.E. and S.P. Hargreaves-Heap (1999) 'Network Externalities and Government Restrictions on Satellite Broadcasting of Key Sporting Events.' *Journal of Cultural Economics* 23, no. 3: 167–81.

Boehm, E. (1998a) 'Jocks Itchy Over Costly Cup.' *Variety* 8–14 June: 1, 85.

Boehm, E. (1998b) 'A Whole New Ballgame: Murdoch Deal Kicks Off Match for Global Soccer Rights Biz.' *Variety* 14–20 September: 28.

Boehm, E. (1999) 'Mergers Alter Euro Dynamics.' *Variety* 13–19 December: 68.

Booth, D. (1998) *The Race Game: Sport and Politics in South Africa*. London: Frank Cass.

Bose, M. (1999) *Manchester Unlimited: The Rise and Rise of the World's Premier Football Club*. London: Orion Business.

Bourdieu, P. (1998) *On Television*. Trans. P. Parkhurst Ferguson. New York: New Press.

Bourdieu, P. (1999) 'The State, Economics and Sport.' Trans. H. Dauncey and G. Hare. *France and the 1998 World Cup: The National Impact of a World Sporting Event*. Ed. H. Dauncey and G. Hare. London: Frank Cass. 15–21.

Boyd, T. (1997) 'The Day the Niggaz Took Over: Basketball, Commodity Culture, and Black Masculinity.' *Out of Bounds: Sports, Media, and the Politics of Identity*. Ed. A. Baker and T. Boyd. Bloomington: Indiana University Press. 123–42.

Boyle, R. and R. Haynes (1996) '"The Grand Old Game": Football, Media and Identity in Scotland.' *Media, Culture & Society* 18, no. 4: 549–64.

Boyle, R. and R. Haynes (2000) *Power Play: Sport, the Media and Popular Culture*. London: Longman.

Branch, S. (1999) 'Ad Notes.' *Wall Street Journal* 14 December: B8.

Brearley, D. (1998) 'Say it Ain't So.' *Weekend Australian* 12–13 December: 19, 25.

Brewster, D. (1997) 'BSkyB Faces Soccer Red Card.' *Australian* 25 June: 21.

Brimson, D. and E. Brimson (1996) *England, My England: The Trouble with the National Football Team*. London: Headline.

Broomhill, R. (1995) 'Globalization, Neo-liberalism and the Local State.' *Altered States: The Regional Impact of Free Market Policies on the Australian States*. Ed. J. Spoehr and R. Broomhill. Adelaide: Centre for Labour Studies. 26–40.

Browett, J. and R. Leaver (1989) 'Shifts in the Global Capitalist Economy and the National Economic Domain.' *Australian Geographical Studies* 27, no. 1: 31–46.

Brown, P. (1996) 'Gender, Sport and the Media: An Investigation into Coverage of Women's Sport in the *Newcastle Herald* and *Sydney Morning Herald* 1890–1990'. Unpublished PhD Thesis, University of Newcastle, Australia.

Brunt, S. (1996) 'Why US Has Replaced Russia as Canada's Most Wanted.' *Globe and Mail* 12 September: 23.

Buckley, James, Jr (1999) 'Football is Booming around the World.' <www.nfl.com/international>

Burbach, R., O. Núñez, and B. Kagarlitsky (1997) *Globalization and its Discontents: The Rise of Postmodern Socialisms*. London: Pluto.

Burke, F. (1998) 'PBL Moves on Foxtel: Revived PMT Consortium a Threat to Optus.' *Australian Financial Review* 30 October: 1, 40.

Burroughs, A., L. Seebohm, and L. Ashburn (1995) '"Add Sex and Stir": Homophobic Coverage of Women's Cricket in Australia.' *Journal of Sport & Social Issues* 19, no. 3: 266–84.

Burstyn, V. (1999) 'The Rites of Men.' *International Association for the Study of Men Newsletter* 6, no. 2: 10–15.

Burton, R. (1999) 'From Hearst to Stern: The Shaping of an Industry over a Century.' *New York Times* 19 December: 11.

Cahn, S.K. (1994) *Coming on Strong: Gender and Sexuality in Twentieth-Century Women's Sport*. Cambridge, Mass.: Harvard University Press.

Calkins, P. and M. Vézina (1996) 'Transitional Paradigms to a New World Economic Order.' *International Journal of Social Economics* 23, nos 10–11: 311–28.

Carpenter, L. and V. Acosta (1991) 'Back to the Future: Reform with a Woman's Voice.' *Bulletin of the American Association of University Professors* January/February: 23, 27.

Carrington, B. (1998) '"Football's Coming Home." But Whose Home? And Do We Want It? Nation, Football and the Politics of Exclusion.' *Fanatics! Power, Identity and Fandom in Football*. Ed. A. Brown. London: Routledge. 101–23.

Carter, T. (1999) 'The Political Fallacy of Baseball Diplomacy.' *Peace Review* 11, no. 4: 579–84.

Cashman, R. (1995) *Paradise of Sport: The Rise of Organised Sport in Australia*. Melbourne: Oxford University Press.

Cashman, R. and A. Hughes (1998) 'Sydney 2000: Cargo Cult of Australian Sport?' *Tourism, Leisure, Sport: Critical Perspectives*. Ed. D. Rowe and G. Lawrence. Melbourne: Cambridge University Press. 216–25.

Cashmore, E. (1996) *Making Sense of Sport*, 2nd edn. London: Routledge.

Chass, M. (1998a) 'A New Baseball Strategy: Latin-American Bargains.' *New York Times* 22 March: 1, 26.

Chass, M. (1998b) 'Baseball's Game of Deception in the Search for Latin Talent.' *New York Times* 23 March: A1, C6.

Chass, M. (1999) 'Major Leagues Have Security Concerns over Orioles' Proposal to Play Cuba.' *New York Times* 5 March: D8.

Chatterjee, P. (1993) 'Clubbing Southeast Asia: The Impact of Golf Course Development.' <http://www.essential.org/monitor/hyper/issues/1993/11/mm1993_13.html>

Chaudhary, V. (1999) 'Work Permit Plan Stirs Up Fresh Controversy.' *Guardian* 3 July: 7.

Chisholm, A. (1999) 'Defending the Nation: National Bodies, U.S. Borders, and the 1996 U.S. Olympic Women's Gymnastic Team.' *Journal of Sport & Social Issues* 23, no. 2: 126–39.

Clarey, C. (1998) 'Just Who Are the Members of the Arcane IOC? Bribery Allegations Suddenly Raise International Olympic Committee's Visibility.' *International Herald Tribune* 22 December.

Clarey, C. (1999a) 'Unseeded Wonder Serves Davenport a Defeat.' *International Herald Tribune* 29 January.

Clarey, C. (1999b) 'Runner-up's Revelation Likely to Test the Waters.' *New York Times* 31 January: 10.

Clark, J. (1994) 'Let the Games Begin.' *Village Voice* 21 June: 12.

Clarke, J. and C. Critcher (1986) '1966 and All That: England's World Cup Victory.' *Off the Ball: The Football World Cup*. Ed. A. Tomlinson and G. Whannel. London: Pluto. 112–26.

Clarke, N. (1999) 'No Defence for Houllier Flops.' *Soccernet England: News* 14 October: <http://www.soccernet.com/english/news/151099lfcflops.html>

Closson, P. (1998) 'Penalty Shot: The European Union's Application of Competition Law to the Bosman Ruling.' *Boston College International and Comparative Law Review* 21: 167ff.

CNN/Reuters (1999) 'Just (Get Paid to) Do It: Fake Fans Swooshing with Pride, Keeping Nike Happy.' 25 January: <http://www.cnnsi.com/tennis/1999/australian_open/news/1999/01/25/nike_fans/>

Cockburn, C. (1991) *In the Way of Women: Men's Resistance to Sex Equality in Organizations*. London: Macmillan.

Cockerill, M. (1988a) 'Why 28,000 Fans Can't be Wrong about Soccer's Future.' *Sydney Morning Herald* 19 July: 45.

Cockerill, M. (1988b) 'A Special Bond of Brotherhood at the Heart of Socceroos' Spirited Success.' *Sydney Morning Herald* 16 July: 67.

Cockerill, M. (1989) 'Australian Soccer Still Rides the Financial Rollercoaster.' *Sydney Morning Herald* 11 February: 70.

Cohen, R. (1991) *Contested Domains: Debates in International Labor Studies*. London: Zed Books.

Cohen, R. (1997) *Global Diasporas: An Introduction*. Seattle: University of Washington Press.

Cohen, R. and J. Longman (1999) 'Olympic Chief's Expansion Goals Left Little Zeal to Pursue Abuses.' *New York Times* 7 February: 1, 26.

Cohn, C. (1987) 'Sex and Death in the Rational World of Defense Intellectuals.' *Signs* 12: 687–718.

Cole, C.L. (1998) 'Addiction, Exercise, and Cyborgs: Technologies of Deviant Bodies.' *Sport and Postmodern Times*. Ed. Geneviève Rail. Albany: State University of New York Press. 261–75.

Cole, C. and D. Andrews (1996) '"Look it's NBA *Showtime!*" Visions of Race in the Popular Imaginary.' *Cultural Studies Annual* 1: 141–81.

Cole, C.L. and A. Hribar (1995) 'Celebrity Feminism: Nike Style, PostFordism, Transcendence, and Consumer Power.' *Sociology of Sport Journal* 12, no. 4: 347–69.

Collins, T. (1998) *Rugby's Great Split: Class, Culture and the Origins of Rugby League Football*. London: Frank Cass.

Colman, M. (1996) *Super League: The Inside Story*. Sydney: Ironbark.

Coman, J., C. Endean, and E. Coron (1998) 'Fight to Control the Game that Turned to Gold.' *European* 8 June.

Connell, R.W. (1990) 'The State, Gender and Sexual Politics: Theory and Appraisal.' *Theory and Society* 19: 507–44.

Cooper, J. (1998) 'American League Far East: Playing Baseball in Japan is a World Series of Mysteries.' *Village Voice* 21 April: 142.

Cooper, K.J. (1998) 'Wrestlers Win Matches – and Friends.' *Washington Post* 21 February: A13.

Cooper, M. (1999) '2-TV Béisbol: Ramirez and Sosa.' *New York Times* 18 September: B1, B6.

Copetas, A.C., C. Vitzthum, and R. Thurow (1999) 'Franco's Ghosts.' *Wall Street Journal* 7 December: A1, A6.

Croci, O. and J. Ammirante (1999) 'Soccer in the Age of Globalization.' *Peace Review* 11, no. 4: 499–504.

Cronin, M. (1999) *Sport and Nationalism in Ireland: Gaelic Games, Soccer and Irish Identity since 1884*. Dublin: Four Courts Press.

Crook, S., J. Pakulski, and M. Waters (1992) *Postmodernization: Change in Advanced Society*. London: Sage.

Crook, T. (1998) *International Radio Journalism: History, Theory and Practice*. London: Routledge.

Cross, J. (1999) 'Where Have All the Bloody English Heroes Gone?' *Daily Mirror* 12 June: 54–55.

Culley, J. (1997) 'That Was the Weekend That Was.' *Independent* 17 February: S7.

Cunneen, C. (1992) 'Rugby League.' *Oxford Companion to Australian Sport*. Ed. W. Vamplew, K. Moore, K.J. O'Hara, R. Cashman, and I. Jobling. Melbourne: Oxford University Press. 296–302.

Cunningham, S. and T. Miller (with D. Rowe) (1994) *Contemporary Australian Television*. Sydney: University of New South Wales Press.

Davis, L. (1997) *The Swimsuit Issue and Sport: Hegemonic Masculinity in Sports Illustrated*. Albany: State University of New York Press.

Dawtrey, A. (1997) 'Brit Soccer Team Kicks Off Sat Outlet.' *Variety* 6–12 October: 46.

de Carvalho, J. (1997) 'Premier League Battens Down for Foreign Invasion.' *Newcastle Herald* 9 August: 20.

Delannoi, G. and E. Morin (1987) 'Avant-Propos.' *Communications* 45: 5–6.

de Moragas Spà, M., N.K. Rivenburgh, and J.F. Larson (1995) *Television in the Olympics*. London: John Libbey.

Dempsey, J. (1999a) 'WNBA Games Going Global.' *Variety* 14–20 June: 22.

Dempsey, J. (1999b) 'NFL Kicks Off Online in 3 O'seas Markets.' *Variety* 27 September: 6.

Dempsey, J. (1999c) 'Sports-Crazy Showbiz Finds Score Still Iffy.' *Variety* 20–26 September: 1, 103.

Denham, D. (1998) 'From a Local to a Global Sport: The Commodification of Rugby League in Britain.' Paper delivered to the 14th World Congress of Sociology, Montréal.

Department of Sport, Recreation and Tourism and Australian Sports Commission (1985) *Australian Sport: A Profile*. Canberra: Australian Government Publishing Service.

Derrida, J. (1987) 'Women in the Beehive: A Seminar with Jacques Derrida.' *Men in Feminism*. Ed. Alice Jardine and Paul Smith. New York: Methuen. 189–203.

Dietrich, M., G. Wright, B. Gerrard, J. Edwards, and I.P. Henry (1999) 'The Political Economy of Sport: Introduction.' *New Political Economy* 4, no. 2: 267.

Dillman, L. (1999a) 'Davenport Finally Meets Her Match.' *Los Angeles Times* 28 January: 1.

Dillman, L. (1999b) 'Hingis Fires the First Volley.' *Los Angeles Times* 29 January: 3.

Donnelly, P. (1996) 'The Local and the Global: Globalization in the Sociology of Sport.' *Journal of Sport & Social Issues* 20, no. 3: 239–57.

Dunning, E. and K. Sheard (1979) *Barbarians, Gentlemen and Players*. Oxford: Martin Robertson.

Dutter, B. and J. Parsons (1999) 'Muscular Lesbian is a Very Nice Girl, Says Tennis No 1.' *The Daily Telegraph* 30 January: 4.

Dworkin, S.L. and M. Messner (1999) 'Just Do ... What? Sport, Bodies, Gender.' *Revisioning Gender*. Ed. J. Lorber, M. Marx Ferree, and B. Hess. Thousand Oaks: Sage. 341–61.

Earle, N. (1995) 'Hockey as Canadian Popular Culture: Team Canada 1972, Television and the Canadian Identity.' *Journal of Canadian Studies* 30: 107–23.

Echikson, W. (1998) 'The Olympics: Governance: Making the Games Run on Time.' *Business Week* 9 February.

Egan, T. (1998) 'The Swoon of Swoosh.' *New York Times Magazine* 12 September: 66–70.

El-Bashir, T. (1999) 'N.H.L. Seeks Aid to Keep Canada's Sport in Canada.' *New York Times* 25 September: A1, D2.

Elias, N. (1986) 'The Genesis of Sport as a Sociological Problem.' *Quest for Excitement: Sport and Leisure in the Civilizing Process*. N. Elias and E. Dunning. Oxford: Basil Blackwell. 126–49.

Ellul, J. (1964) T*he Technological Society*. Trans J. Wilkinson. New York: Knopf.

Endean, C. (1998) 'Planet Soccer.' *Hemispheres* July: 86–91.

Enloe, C. (1995) 'The Globetrotting Sneaker.' *Ms*. March–April: 10–15.

Etue, E. and M. Williams (1996) *On the Edge: Women Making Hockey History*. Toronto: Second Story Press.

Evans, P. (1979) *Dependent Development: The Alliance of Local Capital in Brazil*. Princeton: Princeton University Press.

Falk, P. (1994) *The Consuming Body*. London: Sage.

Falk, R. (1997) 'State of Siege: Will Globalization Win Out?' *International Affairs* 73, no. 1: 123–36.

Farber, M. (1999) 'Soul on Ice.' *Sports Illustrated* 4 October: 63–71.

FIFA (1997) 'Major Contributors to the Football Cause.' *FIFA Magazine* April.

FIFA (n. d.) <http://www.fifa.com>

Finn, G. and R. Giulianotti (1998) 'Scottish Fans, Not English Hooligans! Scots, Scottishness and Scottish Football.' *Fanatics! Power, Identity and Fandom in Football*. Ed. A. Brown. London: Routledge. 189–202.

Fitzsimons, P. (1996) *The Rugby War*. Sydney: HarperCollins.

Fogel, A. (1993) 'The Prose of Populations and the Magic of Demography.' *Western Humanities Review* 47, no. 4: 312–37.

Fordham University (1999) 'Are You Prepared for the Global Business Game?' *Wall Street Journal* 25 August: A4.

Foucault, M. (1977) *Discipline and Punish: The Birth of the Prison*. Trans. A. Sheridan. London: Penguin.

Foucault, M. (1978) 'Politics and the Study of Discourse.' Trans. A.M. Nazzaro. Revised C. Gordon. *Ideology and Consciousness* 3: 7–26.

Foucault, M. (1984) *The History of Sexuality: An Introduction*. Trans. R. Hurley. Harmondsworth: Penguin.

Foucault, M. (1991a) 'Governmentality.' Trans. P. Pasquino. *The Foucault Effect: Studies in Governmentality*. Ed. G. Burchell, C. Gordon, and P. Miller. London: Harvester Wheatsheaf. 87–104.

Foucault, M. (1991b) *Remarks on Marx: Conversations with Duccio Trombadori*. Trans. J.R. Goldstein and J. Cascaito. New York: Semiotext(e).

Foucault, M. (1994) 'Problematics: Excerpts from Conversations.' *Crash: Nostalgia for the Absence of Cyberspace*. Ed. R. Reynolds and T. Zummer. New York: Third Waxing Space. 121–27.

Frank, T. (1999) 'Brand You. Better Selling through Anthropology.' *Harper's Magazine* July: 74–79.

Frayne, T. (1990) *The Tales of an Athletic Supporter*. Toronto: McClelland & Stewart.

Freddi, C. (1999) 'Hope for 2000.' *When Saturday Comes* 155: 24.

Fröbel, F., J. Heinrichs, and O. Kreye (1980) *The New International Division of Labor: Structural Unemployment in Industrialised Countries and Industrialisation in Developing Countries*. Trans. P. Burgess. Cambridge: Cambridge University Press; Paris: Éditions de la Maison des Sciences de l'Homme.

Fry, A. (1998a) 'On Top of Their Game: Sports Cabler Casts Net on Four Corners of the Globe and Scores.' *Variety* 19–25 January: A1, A11.

Fry, A. (1998b) 'Savvy Dealmaking Woos Worldly Auds and Coin.' *Variety* 19–25 January: A4, A9.

Galbraith, J.K. (1999) 'The Crisis of Globalization.' *Dissent* 46, no. 3: 13–16.

Galtung, J. (1984) 'Sport and International Understanding: Sport as a Carrier of Deep Structure and Culture.' *Sport and International Understanding*. Ed. M. Ilmarinen. Berlin: Springer-Verlag. 12–19.

Garfield, A. (1998) 'ENIC Shoots at Premiership Goal.' *Independent* 9 September: 15.

Gatt, R. (1990) 'Segregation Sickness Reaches Australia.' *Australian* 21 March: 39.

Gedeon, D. (1988) 'If Krncevic Gets a Chance, So Will Socceroos.' *Australian* 7 June: 26.

Gellner, E. (1981) 'Nationalism.' *Theory and Society* 10, no. 6: 753–76.

Gibson, R. (1992) *South of the West: Postcolonialism and the Narrative Construction of Australia*. Bloomington: Indiana University Press.

Gibson-Graham, J.K. (1996–97) 'Querying Globalization.' *Rethinking Marxism* 9, no. 1: 1–27.

Giddens, A. (1985) *The Nation-State and Violence (A Contemporary Critique of Historical Materialism, Volume 2)*. Cambridge: Polity.

Gillet, J., P. White, and K. Young (1996) 'The Prime Minister of Saturday Night: Don Cherry, the CBC, and the Cultural Production of Intolerance.' *Seeing Ourselves: Power and Policy in Canada*. Ed. H. Holes and D. Taras. Toronto: Harcourt, Brace and Javanavich. 59–72.

Gilmour, K. (1988) 'Franchise the Clubs!' *Australian Soccer Weekly* 9, no. 348: 3.

Ginsburg, F.D. and R. Rapp (1995) 'Introduction: Conceiving the New World Order.' *Conceiving the New World Order: The Global Politics of Reproduction*. Ed. F.D. Ginsburg and R. Rapp. Berkeley: University of California Press. 1–17.

Giulianotti, R. (1991) 'Scotland's Tartan Army in Italy: The Case for the Carnivalesque.' *Sociological Review* 39, no. 3: 503–27.

Giulianotti, R. (1999) *Football: A Sociology of the Global Game*. Cambridge: Polity.

Giulianotti, R. and G. Armstrong (1997) 'Introduction: Reclaiming the Game – An Introduction to the Anthropology of Football.' *Entering the Field: New Perspectives on World Football*. Ed. G. Armstrong and R. Giulianotti. Oxford: Berg. 1–30.

Given, J. (1995) 'Red, Black, Gold to Australia: Cathy Freeman & the Flags.' *Media Information Australia* 75: 46–56.

Glasgow Celtic (1999) *Classic Match Reports*. <http://www.celticfc.co.uk/>

Goldlust, J. (1987) *Playing for Keeps: Sport, the Media and Society*. Melbourne: Longman.

Goldman, R. and S. Papson (1998) *Nike Culture: The Sign of the Swoosh*. London: Sage.

Gordon, S. and R. Sibson (1998) 'Global Television: The Atlanta Olympics Opening Ceremony.' *Tourism, Leisure, Sport: Critical Perspectives*. Ed. D. Rowe and G. Lawrence. Melbourne: Cambridge University Press. 204–15.

Gray, W. (1998) 'New Zealand's Silver Fern the Key to a Rugby Gold Mine.' *Worldpaper* 5 August.

Green, G. (1992) 'The Match of the Century – 1.' *The Faber Book of Soccer*. Ed. I. Hamilton. London: Faber & Faber. 65–68.

Greenfield, S. and G. Osborn (1998) 'From Feudal Serf to Big Spender: The Influence of Legal Intervention on the Status of English Professional Footballers.' *Culture, Sport, Society* 1, no. 1: 1–23.

Griffin, C. (1993) *Representations of Youth: The Study of Youth and Adolescence in Britain and America*. Cambridge: Polity.

Griffin, P. (1992) 'Changing the Game: Homophobia, Sexism, and Lesbians in Sport.' *Quest* 44: 251–65.

Grove, C. (1998) 'Tapping into Culture to Find the Right Program.' *Variety* 19–25 January: A6, A16.

Gruneau, R. (1999) *Class, Sports, and Social Development*. Champaign, IL: Human Kinetics.

Gruneau, R. and D. Whitson (1993) *Hockey Night in Canada: Sport, Identities and Cultural Politics*. Toronto: Garamond Press.

Gunther, M. (1997) 'They All Want to be Like Mike: Led by the NBA and Global Superstar Michael Jordan, U.S. Pro Sports Leagues are Extending their Worldwide TV Presence All the Way from Chile to China.' *Fortune* 21 July: 51+.

Guttmann, A. (1994) *Games and Empires: Modern Sports and Cultural Imperialism*. New York: Columbia University Press.

Habermas, J. (1989) *The New Conservatism: Cultural Criticism and the Historians' Debate*. Trans. and Ed. S.W. Nicholsen. Cambridge, Mass.: MIT Press.

Hackel, S. (1999) 'On Thin Ice.' *Village Voice* 2 November: 205.

Hall, M.A. (1994) 'Women's Sport Advocacy Organizations: Comparing Feminist Activism in Sport.' *Journal of Comparative Physical Education and Sport* 16: 50–59.

Hall, M.A. (1995) 'Women in Sport: From Liberal Activism to Radical Cultural Struggle.' *Changing Methods: Feminists Transforming Practice*. Ed. L. Code and S. Burt. Toronto: Broadview Press. 265–99.

Hall, M.A., D. Cullen, and T. Slack (1989) 'Organizational Elites Recreating Themselves: The Gender Structure of National Sports Organizations.' *Quest* 41, no. 1: 28–45.

Hamil, S. (1999) Letter. *When Saturday Comes* 155: 44.

Hamilton, C. (1996) 'Globalization and the Working People: The End of Post-War Consensus.' Paper delivered at the Australian and New Zealand Association for the Advancement of Science, Canberra.

Hare, G. (1999) 'Buying and Selling the World Cup.' *France and the 1998 World Cup: The National Impact of a World Sporting Event*. Ed. H. Dauncey and G. Hare. London: Frank Cass. 121–44.

Hargreaves, Jennifer (1999) 'The "Women's International Sports Movement": Local–Global Strategies and Empowerment.' *Women's Studies International Forum* 22, no. 5: 461–71.

Hargreaves, John (1986) *Sport, Power and Culture*. Cambridge: Polity.

Harper, P. (1999) 'Future of Sports: Big Money, Big Media Rob Games of their Innocence.' <www.msnbc.com>

Hart, J. (1997) 'Introduction.' *Change of Hart*. P. Thomas. Auckland: Hodder Moa Beckett. 6–8.

Hartmann, D. (1996) 'The Politics of Race and Sport: Resistance and Domination in the 1968 African American Olympic Protest Movement.' *Ethnic and Racial Studies* 19: 548–66.

Harvey, J. and R. Sparks (1991) 'The Politics of the Body in the Context of Modernity.' *Quest* 43, no. 2: 164–89.

Harvey, J., G. Rail, and L. Thibault (1996) 'Globalization and Sport: Sketching a Theoretical Model for Empirical Analyses.' *Journal of Sport & Social Issues* 20, no. 3: 258–77.

Haynes, R. (1999) 'There's Many a Slip "Twixt the Eye and the Lip": An Exploratory History of Football Broadcasts and Running Commentaries on BBC Radio, 1927–1939.' *International Review for the Sociology of Sport* 34, no. 2: 143–56.

Held, D. (1989) 'The Decline of the Nation State.' *New Times: The Changing Face of Politics in the 1990s*. Ed. S. Hall and S. Jacques. London: Lawrence & Wishart. 191–204.

Herman, E.S. and R.W. McChesney (1997) *The Global Media: The New Missionaries of Global Capitalism*. London: Cassell.

Herod, A. (1997) 'Labor as an Agent of Globalization and as a Global Agent.' *Globalization: Reasserting the Power of the Local*. Ed. K.R. Cox. New York: Guilford Press. 167–200.

Hill, D. (1992) 'The White Nigger.' *The Faber Book of Soccer*. Ed. I. Hamilton. London: Faber & Faber. 270–78.

Hils, M. (1997) 'Kickup in Germany: Plan to Air Some Soccer Games on PPV Under Fire.' *Variety* 3–9 November: 31.

Hindley, B. (1999) 'A Bogey and its Myths.' *Times Literary Supplement* 22 January: 28.

Hirst, P. (1997) 'The Global Economy – Myths and Realities.' *International Affairs* 73, no. 3: 409–25.

Hirst, P. and G. Thompson (1996) *Globalization in Question: The International Economy and the Possibilities of Governance*. Cambridge: Polity.

Hoberman, J. (1992) *Mortal Engines: The Science of Performance and the Dehumanization of Sport*. New York: Free Press.

Hoberman, J. (1997) *Darwin's Athletes: How Sport has Damaged Black America and Preserved the Myth of Race*. Boston: Houghton Mifflin.

Hobsbawm, E. (1998) 'The Nation and Globalization.' *Constellations* 5, no. 1: 1–9.

Horne, J., A. Tomlinson, and G. Whannel (1999) *Understanding Sport: An Introduction to the Sociological and Cultural Analysis of Sport*. London: E.F. & N. Spon.

Houlihan, B. (1994) *Sport and International Politics*. New York: Harvester Wheatsheaf.

Houlihan, B. (1997) *Sport, Policy and Politics: A Comparative Analysis*. London: Routledge.

Houston, W. (1998) 'A Game in Crisis!' *Globe and Mail* 4 April: 1.

Hovden, J. (2000) 'Gender and Leadership Processes in Norwegian Sporting Organizations.' *International Review for the Sociology of Sport* 35: 75–82.

Huggins, T. and C. Balmer (1997) 'England Tough it out for a Finals Place.' *Sydney Morning Herald* 13 October: 28.

Hughson, J. (1997) 'The Bad Blue Boys and the "Magical Recovery" of John Clarke.' *Entering the Field: New Perspectives on World Football*. Ed. G. Armstrong and R. Giulianotti. Oxford: Berg. 239–59.

Hutchinson, J. (1999) 'Re-Interpreting Cultural Nationalism.' *Australian Journal of Politics and History* 45, no. 3: 392–407.

Ibsen, B. (1999) Review. *International Review for the Sociology of Sport* 34, no. 1: 82–84.

Ingham, A. and R. Beamish (1993) 'The Industrialization of the United States and the "Bourgeoisification" of American Sport.' *The Sports Process: A Comparative and Developmental Approach*. Ed. E. Dunning, J. Maguire, and R. Pearton. Champaign, IL: Human Kinetics. 169–206.

International Working Group on Women and Sport (1998) *Women & Sport: From Brighton to Windhoek, Facing the Challenge*. London: United Kingdom Sports Council.

IOC (n. d.) <http://www.olympic.org>

ISL Marketing AG (n. d.) <www.islword.com>

Jackson, S. (1994) 'Gretzky, Crisis and Canadian Identity in 1988: Rearticulating the Americanization of Culture Debate.' *Sociology of Sport Journal* 11, no. 4: 428–26.

Jackson, S.J. and D.L. Andrews (1999) 'Between and Beyond the Global and the Local: American Popular Sporting Culture in New Zealand.' *International Review for the Sociology of Sport* 34, no. 1: 31–42.

Jaher, F.L. (1985) 'White America Views Jack Johnson, Joe Louis, and Muhammad Ali.' *Sport in America: New Historical Perspectives*. Ed. D. Spivey, Wesport: Greenwood. 145–92.

Jakubowicz, A. (1989) 'Speaking in Tongues: Multicultural Media and the Constitution of the Socially Homogeneous Australian.' *Australian Communications and the Public Sphere: Essays in Memory of Bill Bonney*. Ed. H. Wilson. Melbourne: Macmillan. 105–27.

James, C.L.R. (1963) *Beyond a Boundary*. London: Stanley Paul.

Jameson, F. (1996) 'Five Theses on Actually Existing Marxism.' *Monthly Review* 47, no. 11: 1–10.

Jarvie, G. and I.A. Reid (1999) 'Scottish Sport, Nationalist Politics and Culture.' *Culture, Sport, Society* 2, no. 2: 22–43.

Jarvis, R.M. and P. Coleman (1999) *Sports Law: Cases and Materials*. St Paul: West Group.

Jefferson Lenskyj, H. (1998) 'Inside Sport: or "On the Margins?" Australian Women and the Sport Media.' *International Review for the Sociology of Sport* 33, no. 1: 19–32.

Jefferson Lenskyj, H. (1999) 'Gay Games or Gay Olympics?' Unpublished paper, Department of Adult Education, University of Toronto.

Jenkinson, M. (1985) 'Social Impact.' *Australian Sport: A Profile*. Ed. Department of Sport, Recreation and Tourism and Australian Sports Commission. Canberra: Australian Government Publishing Service. 20–28.

Jhally, S. (1989) 'Cultural Studies and the Sports/Media Complex.' *Media, Sports, and Society*. Ed. L.A. Wenner. Newbury Park: Sage. 70–96.

Jiobu, R.M. (1988) 'Racial Inequality in a Public Arena: The Case of Baseball.' *Social Forces* 67, no. 2: 524–34.

Joseph, M. (1995) 'Diaspora, New Hybrid Identities, and the Performance of Citizenship.' *Women and Performance* 7, nos 2–8, no. 1: 3–13.

Kamasz, S. (1989) '"Australianising" the NSL is Imperative.' *Weekend Australian* 1–2 April: 42.

Kang, J-M. (1988) 'Sports, Media and Cultural Dependency.' *Journal of Contemporary Asia* 18, no. 4: 430–43.

Kaplan, R.D. (1999) 'Could This Be the New World?' *New York Times* 27 December: A23.

Karpin, D. (1995) *Enterprising Nation: Renewing Australia's Managers to Meet the Challenges of the Asian-Pacific Century*. Canberra: Australian Government Publishing Service.

Kenway, J. (1995) 'Masculinities in Schools: Under Siege, on the Defensive and Under Reconstruction?' *Discourse: Studies in the Cultural Politics of Education* 16, no. 1: 59–79.

Keynes, J.M. (1957) *The General Theory of Employment Interest and Money*. London: Macmillan; New York: St Martin's Press.

Kidd, B. (1991) 'How Do We Find Our Own Voices in the "New World Order"? A Commentary on Americanization.' *Sociology of Sport Journal* 8, no. 2: 178–84.

Kidman, M. and E. Sexton (1997) 'League's Losers.' *Sydney Morning Herald* 6 September: 89, 93.

Kikulius, L., T. Slack, and B. Hinings (1992) 'Institutionally Specific Design Archetypes: A Framework for Understanding Change in National Sport Organizations.' *International Review for the Sociology of Sport* 27: 343–69.

King, A. (1998) *The End of the Terraces: The Transformation of English Football in the 1990s*. London: Leicester University Press.

Kirk, D. (1998) *Schooling Bodies: School Practice and Public Discourse*. London: Leicester University Press.

Klausen, A.M. (1999a) 'Introduction.' *Olympic Games as Performance and Public Event: The Case of the XVII Winter Olympic Games in Norway*. Ed. A.M. Klausen. New York: Berghahn. 1–8.

Klausen, A.M. (1999b) 'Norwegian Culture and Olympism: Confrontations and Adaptations.' *Olympic Games as Performance and Public Event: The Case of the XVII Winter Olympic Games in Norway*. Ed. A.M. Klausen. New York: Berghahn. 27–48.

Klein, A. (1991) *Sugarball: The American Game, the Dominican Dream*. New Haven: Yale University Press.

Klein, B.S. (1999) 'Cultural Links: An International Political Economy of Golf Course Landscapes.' *SportCult*. Ed. R. Martin and T. Miller. Minneapolis: University of Minnesota Press. 211–26.

Kligman, G. (1995) 'Political Demography: The Banning of Abortion in Ceaucescu's Romania.' *Conceiving the New World Order: The Global Politics of Reproduction*. Ed. F.D. Ginsburg and R. Rapp. Berkeley: University of California Press. 234–55.

Knowles, R.P. (1995) 'Post- "Grapes." Nuts and Flakes: "Coach's Corner" as Post-Colonial Performance.' *Modern Drama* 38: 123–30.

Kobe, D. (1999) 'Soccer in Australia – What's Going Wrong?' *Cyber Journal of Sport Marketing* 3.

Kohn, H. (1945) *The Idea of Nationalism: A Study in its Origins and Background*. New York: Macmillan.

Kozul-Wright, R. and R. Rowthorn (1998) 'Spoilt for Choice? Transnational Corporations and the Geography of International Production.' *Oxford Review of Economic Policy* 14, no. 2: 74–92.

Kranhold, Kathryn (2000) 'Olympic Campaign May Refocus Attention on Games After Ordeal.' *Wall Street Journal* 19 January: B7.

Kroker, A., M. Kroker, and D. Cook (1989) *Panic Encyclopedia: The Definitive Guide to the Postmodern Scene*. London: Macmillan.

Kuper, S. (1998) *Football Against the Enemy*. London: Phoenix.

LaFeber, W. (1999) *Michael Jordan and the New Global Capitalism*. New York: W.W. Norton.

Lafrance, M. (1998) 'Colonizing the Feminine: Nike's Intersections of Postfeminism and Hyperconsumption.' *Sport and Postmodern Times*. Ed. G. Rail. Albany: State University of New York Press. 117–39.

Lang, T. and C. Hines (1993) *The New Protectionism: Protecting the Future against Free Trade*. New York: New Press.

Lapchick, R.E. and J.R. Benedict (1993) '1993 Racial Report Card.' *CSSS Digest* 5, no. 1: 1, 4–8, 12–13.

Larsen, P.T. and P. McCann (1998) 'Football Bid: "Murdoch Utd" Plot Hatched in Italy.' *Independent* 9 September: 3.

Lasch, C. (1979) *The Culture of Narcissism: American Life in an Age of Diminishing Expectations*. New York: Warner.

Lash, S. and J. Urry (1994) *Economies of Signs and Space*. London: Sage.

Latour, B. (1993) *We Have Never Been Modern*. Trans. C. Porter. Cambridge, Mass.: Harvard University Press.

Lawrence, G. and D. Rowe (eds) (1986) *Power Play: Essays in the Sociology of Australian Sport*. Sydney: Hale & Iremonger.

Lawton, J. (1998) 'This Cloud over the Theatre of Dreams.' *Daily Express* 7 September: 10.

Layden, T. (1999) 'Coming out Party.' *Sports Illustrated* 8 February: 58.

Leand, A. (1999) 'French Teen Bursts onto Scene: Mauresmo Credits her Girlfriend for Success.' *USA Today* 29 January: 3C.

Lehmann, J. (1999) 'Monument to Excess.' *Weekend Australian* 30–31 January: 19.

Lehmann, J. and R. Guinness (1999) 'Coles Quits $140,000 Games Job.' *Weekend Australian* 13–14 March: 1.

Lenskyj, H. (1991) 'Combating Homophobia in Sport and Physical Education.' *Sociology of Sport Journal* 8: 61–69.

Lenskyj, H. (1995) 'Sport and the Threat to Gender Boundaries.' *Sporting Traditions* 12, no. 1: 47–60.

Lescure, P. (1998) Letter. *Variety* 19–25 January: A3.

Leseth, A. (1997) 'The Use of *Juju* in Football: Sport and Witchcraft in Tanzania.' *Entering the Field: New Perspectives on World Football*. Ed. G. Armstrong and R. Giulianotti. Oxford: Berg. 159–74.

Levinson, M. (1999) 'Who's in Charge Here?' *Dissent* 46, no. 4: 21–23.

Longman, J. (1999a) '"Booters with Hooters" are Showing Women can be Athletic and Feminine.' *National Post* 8 July: B19.

Longman, J. (1999b) 'Pride in their Play, and in their Bodies.' *New York Times* 8 July: C21, C23.

Longman, J. (1999d) 'IOC Ethics Committee Draws Many Questions.' *New York Times* 11 December: D6.

Longman, J. (1999e) 'IOC Displays Unity with its Reform Rules.' *New York Times* 12 December: 12.

Lopes, J.S.L. (1997) 'Successes and Contradictions of "Multiracial" Brazilian Football.' *Entering the Field: New Perspectives on World Football*. Ed. G. Armstrong and R. Giulianotti. Oxford: Berg. 53–86.

Lusetich, R. (1999a) 'Games Elite Faces Purge over Bribes.' *Australian* 11 January: 1.

Lusetich, R. (1999b) 'Girls Take Giant Step for Womankind.' *Weekend Australian* 17–18 July: 53.

MacAloon, J.J. (1999) 'Anthropology at the Olympic Games: An Overview.' *Olympic Games as Performance and Public Event: The Case of the XVII Winter Olympic Games in Norway*. Ed. A.M. Klausen. New York: Berghahn. 9–26.

MacClancy, J. (1996) 'Sport, Identity and Ethnicity.' *Sport, Identity and Ethnicity*. Ed. J. MacClancy. Oxford: Berg. 1–20.

Macdonald, D. (1978) 'A Theory of Mass Culture.' *Culture and Mass Culture*. Ed. P. Davison, R. Meyersohn, and E. Shils. Cambridge: Chadwyck-Healy; Teaneck, NJ: Somerset House. 167–83.

Macleod, Iain (1996) 'World Forces and the Olympic Games.' *The IOC Official Olympic Companion 1996*. Ed. Caroline Searle and Bryn Vaile. London: Brassey's Sport. 23–33.

MacSkimming, R. (1996) *Cold War: The Amazing Canada–Soviet Hockey Series of 1972*. Toronto: Greystone Books.

Magdalinski, T. (1999) 'Organised Memories: The Construction of Sporting Traditions in the German Democratic Republic.' *Sport in Europe: Politics, Class, Gender*. Ed. J.A. Mangan. London: Frank Cass. 144–63.

Maguire, J. (1993a) 'Bodies, Sportscultures and Societies: A Critical Review of Some Theories in the Sociology of the Body.' *International Review for the Sociology of Sport* 28, no. 1: 33–52.

Maguire, J. (1993b) 'Globalization, Sport Development, and the Media/Sport Production Process.' *Sport Science Review* 2, no. 1: 29–47.

Maguire, J. (1994) 'Preliminary Observations on Globalization and the Migration of Sport Labor.' *Sociological Review* 42, no. 3: 452–80.

Maguire, J. (1996) 'Blade Runners: Canadian Migrants, Ice Hockey, and the Global Sports Process.' *Journal of Sport & Social Issues* 20, no. 3: 335–60.

Maguire, J. (1999) *Global Sport: Identities, Societies, Civilizations*. Cambridge: Polity.

Maguire, J. and J. Bale (1994) 'Introduction: Sports Labor Migration in the Global Arena.' *The Global Sports Arena: Athletic Talent Migration in an Interdependent World*. Ed. J. Bale and J. Maguire. London: Frank Cass: 1–21.

Maguire, J. and E. Poulton (1999) 'European Identity Politics in Euro 96: Invented Traditions and National Habitus Codes.' *International Review for the Sociology of Sport* 34, no. 1: 17–29.

Mahjoub, F. (1999) 'Power Games.' *African Soccer* 50: 20–23.

Mangan, J.A. (1999) 'Series Editor's Foreword.' *Scoring for Britain: International Football and International Politics 1900–1939*. Peter J. Beck. London: Frank Cass. xi–xii.

Marable, M. (1993) *The Crisis of Color and Democracy: Essays on Race, Class and Power*. Monroe: Common Courage Press.

Marcano, A.J. and D.P. Fidder (1999) 'The Globalization of Baseball: Major League Baseball and the Mistreatment of Latin American Baseball Talent.' *Indiana Journal of Global Legal Studies* 6: 511–77.

Marks, J. (1998) 'Sportsmanship Finds an Opening in a Wall of Mistrust.' *Los Angeles Times* 27 February: A11.

Marks, J. (1999) 'The French National Team and National Identity: "Cette France d'un 'bleu métis'".' *France and the 1998 World Cup: The National Impact of a World Sporting Event.* Ed. H. Dauncey and G. Hare. London: Frank Cass. 41–57.

Mason, A. (1980) *Association Football and English Society 1863–1915.* Brighton: Harvester.

Mason, T. (1986) 'Some Englishmen and Scotsmen Abroad: The Spread of World Football.' *Off the Ball: The Football World Cup.* Ed. A. Tomlinson and G. Whannel. London: Pluto. 67–82.

Matthews, V. with N. Amdur (1974) *My Race Be Won.* New York: Charterhouse.

McAllister, M.P. (1997) 'Sponsorship, Globalization, and the Summer Olympics.' Paper delivered to the International Communication Association, Montréal.

McDonald, I. (1999) 'Between Saleem and Shiva: The Politics of Cricket Nationalism in "Globalizing" India.' *Sport in Divided Societies.* Ed. J. Sugden and A. Bairner. Aachen: Meyer & Meyer. 213–34.

McDonald, M. (2000) 'The Marketing of the Women's National Basketball Association and the Making of Postfeminism: A Feminist Cultural Studies Perspective.' *International Review for the Sociology of Sport,* 35: 35–47.

McGregor, A. (1998) 'A Nation's Champion.' *Australian* 26 January: 12.

McKay, J. (1991) *No Pain, No Gain? Sport and Australian Culture.* Sydney: Prentice Hall.

McKay, J. (1992) 'Sport and the Social Construction of Gender.' *Society and Gender: An Introduction to Sociology.* Ed. G. Lupton, P.M. Short, and R. Whip. Sydney: Macmillan. 245–65.

McKay, J. (1995) '"Just do it": Corporate Slogans and the Political Economy of "Enlightened Racism".' *Discourse: Studies in the Cultural Politics of Education* 16, no. 2: 191–201.

McKay, J. (1997) *Managing Gender: Affirmative Action and Organizational Power in Australian, Canadian, and New Zealand Sport.* Albany: State University of New York Press.

McKay, J. and I. Middlemiss (1995) '"Mate against Mate, State against State": A Case Study of Media Constructions of Hegemonic Masculinity in Australian Sport.' *Masculinities* 3, no. 3: 38–47.

McKay, J., G. Lawrence, T. Miller, and D. Rowe (1993) 'Globalization, Postmodernism and Australian Sport.' *Sport Science Review* 2, no. 1: 10–28.

McKay, J., T. Miller, and D. Rowe (1996) 'Americanization, Globalization and Rugby League.' *League of a Nation.* Ed. D. Headon and L. Marinos. Sydney: Australian Broadcasting Corporation. 215–21.

McMichael, P. (1996) *Development and Social Change: A Global Perspective.* Thousand Oaks: Pine Forge.

McMichael, P. (2000) 'Globalisation: Trend or Project?' *Global Political Economy: Contemporary Theories.* Ed. R. Palan. London: Routledge. 100–13.

McMurtry, R. (1993) 'Sport and the Commonwealth Heads of Government.' *The Round Table* 328: 419–26.

Messner, M. (1992) *Power at Play: Sports and the Problem of Masculinity.* Boston: Beacon Press.

Meyer, J., J. Boli, G.M. Thomas, and F.O. Ramirez (1997) 'World Society and the Nation-State.' *American Journal of Sociology* 103, no. 1: 144–81.

Michels, R. (1915) *Political Parties: A Sociological Study of the Oligarchical Tendencies of Modern Democracy.* Trans. E. and C. Paul. London: Jarrold & Sons.

Miège, B. (1989) *The Capitalization of Cultural Production.* Trans. J. Hay, N. Garnham, and UNESCO. New York: International General.

Mikosza, J. and M. Phillips (1999) 'Gender, Sport and the Body Politic: The Framing of Femininity in the *Golden Girls of Sport Calendar* and *The Atlanta Dream.*' *International Review for the Sociology of Sport* 34, no. 1: 5–16.

Miller, J.D.B. (1981) *The World of States: Connected Essays.* London: Croom Helm.

Miller, J.D.B. (1984) 'The Sovereign State and its Future.' *International Journal* 39, no. 2: 284–301.

Miller, T. (1989) 'World Series Sound and Vision.' *Meanjin* 48, no. 3: 591–96.

Miller, T. (1990) 'Mission Impossible and the New International Division of Labour.' *Metro* no. 82: 21–28.

Miller, T. (1996) 'The Crime of Monsieur Lang: GATT, the Screen and the New International Division of Cultural Labour.' *Film Policy: International, National and Regional Perspectives.* Ed. A. Moran. London: Routledge. 72–84.

Miller, T. (1998a) 'Scouting for Boys: Sport Looks at Men.' *Tourism, Leisure, Sport: Critical Perspectives.* Ed. D. Rowe and G. Lawrence. Melbourne: Cambridge University Press. 194–203.

Miller, T. (1998b) *Technologies of Truth: Cultural Citizenship and the Popular Media.* Minneapolis: University of Minnesota Press.

Miller, T. and A. McHoul (1998) *Popular Culture and Everyday Life.* London: Sage.

Mingo, J. (1997) 'Postal Imperialism.' *New York Times Magazine* 16 February: 36–37.

Ministry of Supply and Services (1991) *Beneath the Veneer: The Report of the Task Force on Barriers to Women in the Public Service.* Ottawa: Canadian Government Publishing Service.

Monnington, T. (1993) 'Politicians and Sport: Uses and Abuses.' *The Changing Politics of Sport.* Ed. L. Allison. Manchester: Manchester University Press. 125–50.

Moorhouse, H.F. (1999) 'The Economic Effects of the Traditional Transfer System in European Professional Football.' *Football Studies* 2, no. 1: 90–105.

Morgan, W.J. (1998) 'Hassiba Boulmerka and Islamic Green: International Sports, Cultural Differences, and their Postmodern Interpretation.' *Sport and Postmodern Times.* Ed. G. Rail. Albany: State University of New York Press. 345–65.

Morgenson, G. (1999) 'A Company Worth More than Spain?' *New York Times* 26 December: BU1.

Morrison, S. (1992) *The Days Canada Stood Still: Canada vs USSR 1972.* Toronto: Warwick Publishing Group.

Mossop, B. (1988) 'Best Foot Forward.' *Australia's Sport* 88: 34.

Muda, M. (1998) 'The Significance of Commonwealth Games in Malaysia's Foreign Policy.' *The Round Table* 346: 211–26.

Murray, A. (1999) 'The American Century: Is it Going or Coming?' *Wall Street Journal* 27 December: 1.

Murray, R. (1989) 'Benetton Britain.' *New Times: The Changing Face of Politics in the 1990s.* Ed. S. Hall and M. Jacques. London: Lawrence & Wishart. 54–64.

Nader, R. (1999) 'Introduction.' *The WTO: Five Years of Reasons to Resist Corporate Globalization.* L. Wallach and M. Sforza. New York: Seven Stories Press. 6–12.

Nafziger, J.A.R. (1992) 'International Sports Law: A Replay of Characteristics and Trends.' *American Journal of International Law* 86, no. 3: 489–518.

Nafziger, J.A.R. (1999) 'Sports Law in the 21st Century: Globalizing Sports Law.' *Marquette Sports Law Journal* 9: 225–38.

Nairn, T. (1993) 'Internationalism and the Second Coming.' *Daedalus* 122, no. 3: 155–70.

Nandy, A. (1989) *The Tao of Cricket: On Games of Destiny and the Destiny of Games.* New Delhi: Viking/Penguin.

Naughton, P. (1999) 'Davenport Asks: Who is this Guy?' *Reuters* 28 January.

Nauright, J. and P. White (1996) 'Nostalgia, Community, and Nation: Professional Hockey and Football in Canada.' *Avante* 2, no. 3: 24–41.

Nkwi, P.N. and B. Vidacs (1997) 'Football: Politics and Power in Cameroon.' *Entering the Field: New Perspectives on World Football.* Ed. G. Armstrong and R. Giulianotti. Oxford: Berg. 123–39.

Ohmae, K. (1995) *The End of the Nation-State: The Rise of Regional Economies.* New York: Free Press.

Orakwue, S. (1999) *Pitch Invaders: The Modern Black Football Revolution.* London: Orion.

Overbeek, H. (1990) *Global Capitalism and National Decline: The Thatcher Decade in Perspective*. London: Unwin Hyman.

Palley, T.I. (1999) 'Toward a New International Economic Order.' *Dissent* 46, no. 2: 48–52.

Patel, N. (1999) 'Letter.' *Toronto Star* 18 February.

Penner, M. (1999) 'Looking Good.' *Los Angeles Times* 8 July: D1, D8.

Peterson, V.S. (1996) 'The Politics of Identification in the Context of Globalization.' *Women's Studies International Forum* 19, nos. 1–2: 5–15.

Phillips, H. (1998) 'Golf, American Style: Driving the World's Game.' *Hemispheres* May: 99–103.

Phillips, M. (1994) 'Rugby.' *Sport in Australia: A Social History*. Ed. W. Vamplew and B. Stoddart. Cambridge: Cambridge University Press. 193–212.

Phillips, R. (2000) 'The Business Olympics: Sydney's Other Games. 'World Socialist Web Site <www.wsws.org>

Pickard, C. (1997) 'Cup Runneth over Summer's O'Seas B.O.' *Variety* 15–21 December: 9–10.

Pieterse, J.N. (1995) 'Globalization as Hybridization.' *Global Modernities*. Ed. M. Featherstone, S. Lash, and R. Robertson. London: Sage. 45–68.

Pieterse, J.N. (1997) 'Going Global: Futures of Capitalism.' *Development and Change* 28, no. 2: 367–82.

Poiner, G. and S. Wills (1991) *The Gifthorse: A Critical Look at Equal Opportunity in Australia*. Sydney: Allen & Unwin.

Price, C. (1968) 'Southern Europeans in Australia: Problems of Assimilation.' *International Migration Review* 11, no. 3: 3–26.

Pronger, B. (1990a) 'Gay Jocks: A Phenomenology of Gay Men in Athletics.' *Sport, Men and the Gender Order: Critical Feminist Perspectives*. Ed. M. Messner and D. Sabo. Champaign, IL: Human Kinetics. 141–52.

Pronger, B. (1990b) *The Arena of Masculinity: Sport, Homosexuality, and the Meaning of Sex*. New York: St. Martin's Press.

Pujik, R. (1999) 'Producing Norwegian Culture for Domestic and Foreign Gazes: The Lillehammer Olympic Opening Ceremony.' *Olympic Games as Performance and Public Event: The Case of the XVII Winter Olympic Games in Norway*. Ed. A.M. Klausen. New York: Berghahn. 97–136.

Pursell, C. (1998) 'Fields of Competition: American Pastimes Going for O'Seas Gold.' *Variety* 29 June–12 July: 27, 30.

Pusey, M. (1992) *Economic Rationalism in Canberra: A Nation-Building State Changes its Mind*. London: Cambridge University Press.

Real, M. (1989) *Super Media: A Cultural Studies Approach*. Newbury Park: Sage.

Real, M. (1996) *Exploring Media Culture: A Guide*. Thousand Oaks: Sage.

Redhead, S. (1997) *Post-Fandom and the Millennial Blues: The Transformation of Soccer Culture*. London: Routledge.

Reich, R. (1999) 'Brain Trusts.' *New York Times Book Review* 19 December: 10.

Robbins, E. (1998) 'Golf War Syndrome: How Playing 18 Holes Endangers the Earth.' 26 August: <www.utne.com/atc/15atcgolf.html>

Robertson, R. (1995) 'Globalization: Time–Space and Homogeneity–Heterogeneity.' *Global Modernities*. Ed. M. Featherstone, S. Lash, and R. Robertson. London: Sage. 25–44.

Robinson, W.I. (1996) 'Globalization: Nine Theses of our Epoch.' *Race & Class* 38, no. 2: 13–31.

Rosenberg, T. (1999) 'Beating the Yanquis at their Game.' *New York Times* 11 January: A16.

Ross, R. and K. Trachte (1990) *Global Capitalism: The New Leviathan*. Albany: State University of New York Press.

Rousseau, J-J. (1975) *The Social Contract and Discourses*. Trans. G.D.H. Cole. London: J.M. Dent & Sons.

Rowe, D. (1992a) 'Modes of Sports Writing.' *Journalism and Popular Culture*. Ed. P. Dahlgren and C. Sparks. London: Sage. 96–112.

Rowe, D. (1992b) '"That Misery of Stringers' Clichés": Sports Writing.' *Cultural Studies* 5, no. 1: 77–90.

Rowe, D. (1995a) 'Big Defence: Sport and Hegemonic Masculinity.' *Gender, Sport and Leisure: Continuities and Challenges (Topic Report 4)*. Ed. A. Tomlinson. Brighton: Chelsea School Research Centre. 123–33.

Rowe, D. (1995b) *Popular Cultures: Rock Music, Sport and the Politics of Pleasure*. London: Sage.

Rowe, D. (1996) 'The Global Love-Match: Sport and Television.' *Media, Culture & Society* 18, no. 4: 565–82.

Rowe, D. (1997) 'Rugby League in Australia: The Super League Saga.' *Journal of Sport & Social Issues* 21, no. 2: 221–26.

Rowe, D. (1999) *Sport, Culture and the Media: The Unruly Trinity*. Buckingham: Open University Press.

Rowe, D. (2000) 'No Gain, No Game? Media and Sport.' *Mass Media and Society*, 3rd edn. Ed. J. Curran and M. Gurevich. London: Edward Arnold. 346–61.

Rowe, D. and G. Lawrence (1986) 'Saluting the State: Nationalism and the Olympics.' *Power Play: Essays in the Sociology of Australian Sport*. Ed. G. Lawrence and D. Rowe. Sydney: Hale and Iremonger. 196–203.

Rowe, D. and P. Brown (1994) 'Promoting Women's Sport: Theory, Policy and Practice.' *Leisure Studies* 13: 97–110.

Rowe, D. and G. Lawrence (1998) 'Framing a Critical Sociology of Sport in the Age of Globalization.' *Tourism, Leisure, Sport: Critical Perspectives*. Ed. D. Rowe and G. Lawrence. Melbourne: Cambridge University Press. 159–69.

Rowe, D. and J. McKay (1999) 'Field of Soaps: Rupert v. Kerry as Masculine Melodrama.' *SportCult*. Ed. R. Martin and T. Miller. Minneapolis: University of Minnesota Press. 191–210.

Rowe, D. and D. Stevenson (1995) 'Negotiations and Mediations: Journalism, Professional Status and the Making of the Sports Text.' *Media Information Australia* 75: 67–79.

Rowe, D., J. McKay, and T. Miller (2000) 'Sports and Postmodern Bodies.' *Men, Masculinities, and Sport*. Ed. J. McKay, M. Messner, and D. Sabo. Thousand Oaks: Sage. 245–62.

Ruffini, P. (1999) 'SOC: Glory Changing the Face of the League.' *AAP Sports News*: 21 May.

Russell, M. (1993) 'It's Just Not Cricket.' *Sydney Morning Herald* 11 September: 4A.

Sacks, H. (1972a) 'An Initial Investigation of the Usability of Conversation for Doing Sociology.' *Studies in Social Interaction*. Ed. D. Sudnow. New York: Free Press. 31–74.

Sacks, H. (1972b) 'On the Analyzability of Stories by Children.' *Directions in Sociolinguistics*. Ed. J.J. Gumperz and D. Hymes. New York: Holt, Rinehart & Winston. 325–45.

Sacks, H. (1995) *Lectures on Conversation*. Ed. G. Jefferson. Oxford: Blackwell.

Sage, G. (1994) 'Deindustrialization and the American Sporting Goods Company.' *Sport in the Global Village*. Ed. R. Wilcox. Morgantown: Fitness Information Technology. 39–51.

Sage, G. (1999) 'Justice Do It! The Nike Transnational Advocacy Network: Organization, Collective Actions, and Outcomes.' *Sociology of Sport Journal* 16, no. 4: 206–35.

Saint-Germain, M. and J. Harvey (1998) 'Commodification, Globalization and the Canadian Sport Industry.' *Avante* 4, no. 1: 90–112.

Sandomir, R. (1999) 'When a TV Network is Your Chef.' *New York Times* 8 November: C21.

Sandomir, R. (2000) 'Canada Kills Subsidy Plan for 6 NHL Teams.' *New York Times* 22 January: D1–D2.

Santina, W. (1988) 'Move to Better Administration.' *Australian Soccer Weekly* 9, no. 342: 17.

Schaeffer, R.K. (1997) *Understanding Globalization: The Social Consequences of Political, Economic, and Environmental Change*. Lanham, MD: Rowman & Littlefield.

Schlesinger, P. (1991) *Media, State and Nation: Political Violence and Collective Identities*. London: Sage.

Shapiro, M.J. (1989) 'Representing World Politics: The Sport/War Intertext.' *International/Intertextual Relations: Postmodern Readings of World Politics*. Ed. J. Der Derian and M.J. Shapiro. Lexington: Lexington Books. 69–96.

Shapiro, M.J. (1992) R*eading the Postmodern: Political Theory as Textual Practice*. Minneapolis: University of Minnesota Press.

Shapiro, M.J. (1993) *Reading 'Adam Smith': Desire, History and Value*. Newbury Park: Sage.

Sheats, M. (1998) 'U.S. Icons Appeal to Foreign Viewers.' *Variety* 19–25 January: A2, A13.

Shils, E. (1966) 'Mass Society and its Culture.' *Reader in Public Opinion and Communication*, 2nd edn. Ed. B. Berelson and M. Janowitz. New York: Free Press; London: Collier-Macmillan. 505–28.

Shropshire, M. (1999) 'Heavy Lifting.' *Sports Illustrated* 20 September.

Siano, J. (1998) '2 Words U.S. Race Fans Don't Hear: Formula One.' *New York Times* 21 October: 32.

Silver, J. (1996) *Thin Ice: Money, Politics, and the Decline of an NHL Franchise*. Halifax, NS: Fernwood Publishing.

Singh, T. (1987) 'At Test Time War Just Would Not Be Cricket.' *Australian* 13 February: 17.

Skillen, A. (1993) 'Sport: An Historical Phenomenology.' *Philosophy* 68, no. 265: 343–68.

Slack, T. and B. Hinings (1994) 'Institutional Pressures and Isomorphic Change: An Empirical Test.' *Organization Studies* 15: 803–27.

Smith, A. (1970) *The Wealth of Nations Books I–III*. Ed. A. Skinner. Harmondsworth: Penguin.

Smith, A.D. (1996) 'LSE Centennial Lecture: The Resurgence of Nationalism? Myth and Memory in the Renewal of Nations.' *British Journal of Sociology* 47, no. 4: 575–98.

Smith, P. (1997) *Millennial Dreams: Contemporary Culture and Capital in the North*. London: Verso.

Smith, W. (1999) 'Price of Gold.' *Courier-Mail* 16 January: 21.

Solaja, K. (1999) 'A Long Long Road.' *African Soccer* 50: 26–31.

Southcott, C. (1987) 'Au-delà de la Conception politique de la nation.' *Communications* 45: 51–67.

Spillman, L. (1997) *Nation and Commemoration: Creating National Identities in the United States and Australia*. Cambridge: Cambridge University Press.

Stead, G. (1988) 'Sleeping Giant Has Finally Stirred.' *Sunday Mail* 24 July: 54.

Stevens, M. (1999a) 'Open Slather on Rats in the Ranks.' *Australian* 26 January: 4.

Stevens, M. (1999b) 'Prince of the Past Shames the Games.' *Weekend Australian* 6–7 February: 19.

Stevenson, D. (1999) 'Global Gender Games: Women, Sport and Globalisation.' Paper presented at the International Sociology of Sport Association Conference, Budapest.

Stoddart, B. (1986) *Saturday Afternoon Fever: Sport in the Australian Culture*. Sydney: Angus & Robertson.

Stoddart, B. (1988) 'Sport, Cultural Imperialism, and Colonial Response in the British Empire.' *Comparative Studies in Society and History* 30, no. 4: 649–73.

Stolcke, V. (1981) 'Women's Labours: The Naturalisation of Social Inequality and Women's Subordination.' *Of Marriage and the Market*. Ed. K. Young, C. Wolkowitz, and R. McCullagh. London: CSE Books. 39–49.

Strange, S. (1995) 'The Defective State.' *Daedalus* 124, no. 2: 55–74.

Sugden, J. and A. Tomlinson (1998a) *FIFA and the Contest for World Football: Who Rules the People's Game?* Cambridge: Polity.

Sugden, J. and A. Tomlinson (1998b) 'Power and Resistance in the Governance of World Football: Theorizing FIFA's Transnational Impact.' *Journal of Sport & Social Issues* 22, no. 3: 299–316.

Sugden, J. and A. Tomlinson (1999) *Great Balls of Fire: How Big Money is Hijacking World Football*. Edinburgh: Mainstream.

Sussman, G. and J.A. Lent (eds) (1998) *Global Productions: Labor in the Making of the 'Information Society'*. Cresskill, NJ: Hampton Press.

Sylvester, R. (1999) 'Start Playing to Win, Says Blair.' *Independent on Sunday* 20 June: 6.

Synnott, A. (1993) *The Body Social: Symbolism, Self and Society*. London: Routledge.

Tagliabue, J. (1997) 'Europe Enters the Big Leagues: Playing Catch-Up to the U.S., Commerce Takes the Field.' *New York Times* 10 September: D1, D4.

Talbot, M. (1998) 'Opportunities and Barriers for Commonwealth Women in Sport: Challenges for Sports Sciences and Sports Organisations.' Paper presented at Commonwealth Scientific Congress, University of Malaysia, Kuala Lumpur.

Taylor, G. (2000) 'The Players' Perspective.' *Football in the Digital Age: Whose Game is it Anyway?* Ed. S. Hamil, J. Michie, C. Oughton, and S. Warby. Edinburgh: Mainstream. 47–54.

Taylor, J. (1988) 'Unity.' *Australian Soccer Weekly* 9, no. 346: 22.

Teeple, G. (1995) *Globalization and the Decline of Social Reform*. Englewood Cliffs, NJ: Humanities Press.

Tew, S. (1994) 'Leadership Issues in Sport.' *Sport Management in New Zealand: An Introduction*. Ed. L. Trenberth and C. Collins. Palmerston North: Dunmore Press. 177–91.

Theberge, N. (1997) '"It's Part of the Game": Physicality and the Production of Gender in Women's Hockey.' *Gender & Society* 11, no. 1: 69–87.

Thomas, P. (1997) *Change of Hart*. Auckland: Hodder Moa Beckett.

Thompson, P. and C. Smith (1999) 'Beyond the Capitalist Labor Process: Workplace Change, the State and Globalisation.' *Critical Sociology* 24, no. 3: 193–215.

Thornton, M. (1994) 'The Seductive Allure of EEO.' *Australian Women: Contemporary Feminist Thought*. Ed. N. Grieve and A. Burns. Melbourne: Oxford University Press. 215–24.

Tomlinson, A. (1986) 'Going Global: The FIFA Story.' *Off the Ball: The Football World Cup*. Ed. A. Tomlinson and G. Whannel. London: Pluto. 83–98.

Tomlinson, J. (1999) *Globalization and Culture*. Cambridge: Polity.

Tourism New South Wales Bulletin (2000) <HTTP://www.visitnsw.com.AU/News/TNSW_NB_Home.ASP>

Townsend, B. (1997) 'World Events Will Change Course of Golf, Finchem Says.' *Dallas Morning News* 30 October: 5B.

Tuastad, D. (1997) 'The Political Role of Football for Palestinians in Jordan.' *Entering the Field: New Perspectives on World Football*. Ed. G. Armstrong and R. Giulianotti. Oxford: Berg. 105–21.

Verdier, M. (1996) 'The Olympic Games and the Media.' *The IOC Official Olympic Companion 1996*. Ed. C. Searle and B. Vaile. London: Brassey's Sport. 34–37.

Vertinsky, P. (1998) '"Run, Jane, Run": Central Tensions in the Current Debate about Enhancing Women's Health through Exercise.' *Women & Health* 27, no. 4: 81–111.

Villarosa, L. (1994) 'Gay Games IV.' *Gay Games IV Official Souvenir Program*. 17–19.

Vinocur, J. (1999) 'Just a Soccer Star, After All.' *New York Times Magazine* 14 March: 32–35.

Volkerling, M. (1994) 'Death or Transfiguration: The Future for Cultural Policy in New Zealand.' *Culture and Policy* 6, no. 1: 7–28.

Waddingham, S. and G. Stead (1993) 'The Air to an Aussie Throne.' *Sunday Mail* 5 September: 82–83.

Wagg, S. (1984) *The Football World: A Contemporary Social History*. Brighton: Harvester.

Waters, M. (1995) *Globalization*. London: Routledge.

Weinbach, J.B. (1999) 'Mastering the Art of the (Golf) Deal.' *Wall Street Journal* 28 December: B1, B6.

Weir, T. (1999) 'Revelation Can Often Take a Toll. Mauresmo Faces Scrutiny on, off the Court.' *USA Today* 4 February: 3C.

Welch, L.S. and R. Luostarinen (1988) 'Internationalization: Evolution of a Concept.' *Journal of General Management* 14, no. 2: 34–55.

Wenner, L.A. (1994) 'The Dream Team, Communicative Dirt, and the Marketing of Synergy: USA Basketball and Cross-Merchandising in Television Commercials.' *Journal of Sport & Social Issues* 18, no. 1: 27–47.

Wenner, L.A. (1998) 'In Search of the Sports Bar: Masculinity, Alcohol, Sports, and the Mediation of Public Space.' *Sport and Postmodern Times*. Ed. G. Rail. Albany: State University of New York Press. 302–32.

Whannel, G. (1992) *Fields in Vision: Television Sport and Cultural Transformation*. London: Routledge.

White, A. (1998) 'Free TV Thrives Down Under with Sports Fare.' *Variety* 29 June–12 July: 32.

Whitnell, I. (1999) 'International Players Impact the NBA.' <www.nba.com>

Whitson, D. (1998) 'Circuits of Promotion: Media, Marketing and the Globalization of Sport.' *MediaSport: Cultural Sensibilities and Sport in the Media Age*. Ed. L.A. Wenner. New York: Routledge. 57–72.

Whitson, D. and R. Gruneau (1997) 'The (Real) Integrated Circus: Political Economy, Popular Culture, and Major League Sport.' *Understanding Canada: Building on the New Canadian Political Economy*. Ed. W. Clement. Montréal: McGill–Queen's University Press. 359–85.

Whitson, D. and D. Macintosh (1990) 'Equity vs. High Performance in Canadian Amateur Sport.' *CAHPER Journal* May/June: 27–30.

Whitson, D. and D. Macintosh (1996) 'The Global Circus: International Sport, Tourism, and the Marketing of Cities.' *Journal of Sport & Social Issues* 20, no. 3: 278–95.

Wieneke, C. (1992) 'Does Equal Employment Opportunity Serve the Women's Movement? A Case Study from Australian Higher Education.' *Working Out: New Directions for Women's Studies*. Ed. H. Hinds, A. Phoenis, and J. Stacey. London: Falmer Press. 131–41.

Williams, J. (1999) 'Ups.' *When Saturday Comes* 155: 24.

Williams, M.L. (1998) 'Ad Deals Strike a Cultural Match.' *Variety* 19–25 January: A8.

Williams, M. (1999) 'Soccer Kicky for Congloms.' *Variety* 20–26 September: 1, 104.

Wilson, B. (1997) '"Good Blacks" and "Bad Blacks": Media Constructions of African-American Athletes in Canadian Basketball.' *International Review for the Sociology of Sport* 32, no. 2: 177–89.

Wilson, H. (1998) 'Television's *Tour de Force*: The Nation Watches the Olympic Games.' *Tourism, Leisure, Sport: Critical Perspectives*. Ed. D. Rowe and G. Lawrence. Melbourne: Cambridge University Press. 135–45.

Winegardner, M. (1999) 'Los Naturales.' *New York Times Magazine* 3 October: 44–45.

Wise, M. (1999) 'Empty Seats are a Concern for the NBA.' *New York Times* 19 December: 7.

Wiseman, J. (1998) *Global Nation? Australia and the Politics of Globalization*. Cambridge: Cambridge University Press.

Yeates, H. (1995) 'The League of Men: Masculinity, the Media, and Rugby League Football.' *Media Information Australia* 75: 35–45.

Yeatman, A. (1990) *Bureaucrats, Technocrats, Femocrats: Essays on the Contemporary Australian State*. Sydney: Allen & Unwin.

Young, J. (1999) 'Mauresmo Creates a PR Problem.' *Washington Times* 5 February: B6.

Yúdice, G. (1995) 'Civil Society, Consumption, and Governmentality in an Age of Global Restructuring: An Introduction.' *Social Text* 13, no. 4: 1–25.

Zecchinelli, C. (1998) 'Murdoch Streams into Italy.' *Variety* 28 December: 1, 12.

Zengerle, J. (1999) 'Let's Just Call the Whole Thing Off.' *Weekend Australian* 6–7 February: 19.

Index